FINANCE AND THE ECONOMICS OF UNCERTAINTY

FINANCE AND THE ECONOMICS OF UNCERTAINTY

Gabrielle Demange and Guy Laroque

Blackwell
Publishing

BLACKWELL PUBLISHING
350 Main Street, Malden, MA 02148-5020, USA
9600 Garsington Road, Oxford OX4 2DQ, UK
550 Swanston Street, Carlton, Victoria 3053, Australia

First published 2006 by Blackwell Publishing Ltd

1 2006

Library of Congress Cataloging-in-Publication Data

Demange, Gabrielle.
  [Finance et economie de l'incertain. English]
  Finance and the economics of uncertainty / Gabrielle Demange and Guy Laroque; translated
  by Paul Klassen.
      p. cm.
  Includes index.
  ISBN-13: 978-1-4051-2138-5 (hardcover)
  ISBN-10: 1-4051-2138-6 (hardcover)
  ISBN-13: 978-1-4051-2139-2 (pbk.)
  ISBN-10: 1-4051-2139-4 (pbk.)
    1. Uncertainty. 2. Finance—Mathematical models. I. Laroque, Guy. II. Title.

HB615.D4613 2006
338.5—dc22

                                                                                    2005021158

A catalogue record for this title is available from the British Library.

Set in 10/12.5 pt Dante
by Newgen Imaging Systems (P) Ltd, Chennai, India

For further information on
Blackwell Publishing, visit our website:
www.blackwellpublishing.com

Contents

Contents

List of main symbols

$e \in \mathcal{E} = \{1, \ldots, E\}$	States of nature
$\pi(e)$	Probability of state e
$q(e)$	State price or price of the Arrow–Debreu security corresponding to state e
$k = 1, \ldots, K$	Index of risky securities
$k = *$	Index of risky-free securities
$z = (z_k)$	Portfolio
p_k	Price of security k
$p = (p_k)$	Column vector of security prices
$p'z = \Sigma_k p_k z_k = z'p$	Value of portfolio z
$a_k(e)$	Income (payoff) served by one unit of security k in state e
$\tilde{a}_k = (a_k(e)) \in \mathbb{R}^E$	Row vector of contingent income accruing to the owner of one unit of security k
$\tilde{a} = (a_k(e))$	$K \times E$ matrix of securities payoffs
$\tilde{c}_z = z'\tilde{a}$	Contingent incomes associated with z
r	Riskless rate of return (interest rate)
$\tilde{R}_k = \tilde{a}_k / p_k$	Gross return of security k
$\tilde{r}_k = \tilde{R}_k - 1$	Net return of security k
$d_k(e)$	Dividend per unit of security k in state e
$x_k = p_k z_k / (\Sigma_h p_h z_h)$	Share of security k in portfolio z
$x = (x_k)$	Portfolio composition
$i = 1, \ldots, I$	Index of investor
c	Income or consumption
$c^i, z^i \ldots$	Investor i's decision (superscript)
z^m	Market portfolio
u, v	Von Neumann Morgenstern utility indices

δ	Psychological discount factor
j such that $\delta = 1/(1+j)$	Psychological discount rate
ω_0	Nonfinancial income at date 0
$z(0)$	Initial portfolio at date 0
$\tilde{\omega}_1$	Random nonfinancial income at date 1

Introduction

A large number of economic decisions have implications on the future and are made under uncertainty. This is the case, for instance, of individual saving, insurance and portfolio choices, and investment decisions of firms. A variety of institutional arrangements and financial tools facilitate these decisions and allow risk taking and risk sharing: insurance companies, stock exchanges, futures and derivatives assets, to name a few. Research in finance and the economics of uncertainty aims to understand the emergence of these tools, their functioning and adequacy to allocate risks.

Uncertainty is ubiquitous. An investment requires a certain time lag before it yields an income, which in turn depends on random events that impact upon prices of raw inputs, production processes, and competition. The future financial resources and needs of households vary owing to illness, family composition, or unemployment. At the macroeconomic level, uncertainty is also pervasive making forecasts on future aggregate variables prone to errors.

In order to cope with resources and needs that fluctuate over time, economic agents, whether households or firms, save and borrow for *intertemporal income smoothing*. A more uncertain future may induce households to save more for what is called a *precautionary* motive. It may also lead to the creation of institutions to allow risk sharing between economic agents. Futures markets, for instance, simplify the management of risks stemming from changes in the supply and the price of commodities. Mutual corporations and insurance companies specialize in covering individual risks, such as car accidents, house fires, and the like. Stock markets enable entrepreneurs to finance their activities by going public. Stockholders invest by buying a stake in the company (*stocks*) and share future profits or losses, which often entail too much risk for a small number of individuals to assume. Thus, the public becomes involved while benefiting from the expertise and economies of scale associated with an activity that can be conducted more effectively by professionals than by amateurs. More generally, stock markets allow risky participations in productive activities to be *diversified* through appropriate portfolio choices. Finally, derivative financial instruments (options, swaps, etc.) have recently experienced a prodigious expansion, linked to *hedging* requirements of the investors vis-à-vis movements in interest rates and stock market prices.

How do these institutions work? Are they well designed? What is the role of financial markets? These questions have given rise to a very large body of work, especially in the past 30 years, in both finance and economics. Initially, each discipline worked separately, developing its own models and approach, to treat uncertainty.

Finance is marked by two pioneering works: the Black and Scholes's method for establishing the value of an option by *arbitrage*, and the equilibrium relationships of Sharpe and Lintner's *capital asset pricing model* (CAPM), which relate the expected returns of financial securities to simple statistical characteristics. Professionals soon recognized the practical values of these contributions, which facilitated the proliferation of derivatives and the development of quantitative portfolio management techniques.

Economics took the path of extending the general equilibrium theory to an uncertainty framework, building on the decision models under risk proposed by von Neumann and Morgenstern. As the works of Arrow and Debreu, among others, made clear, the usual welfare properties of equilibrium cannot be taken for granted. The absence of markets, more precisely their *incompleteness*, was, and remains, the focus of a great deal of attention. Why are some markets not viable? What implications does that have?

In the 1980s, whereas the links between the two bodies of works were better understood, it became clear that a crucial piece was missing. Indeed, both approaches assumed all stakeholders to have access to identical information. Everyone was supposed to evaluate future prospects in the same way, to use the same model with the same probabilities of the evolution of the economy, the dividend process, or the bankruptcy of the firms. This is known as the *symmetric information* framework. Since then research in both economics and finance has emphasized the differences in the information available to economic agents, how news is disseminated, and the role this plays in price setting, in risk undertaking, and in financial contracting. In particular, the concept of *rational expectations*, introduced by Muth, made possible the study of the transmission of information through prices.

This book has two main goals. The first is to present the fundamental principles of risk allocation in a unified framework, assuming symmetric information. Models employed in this book are as simple as possible so as to underscore the relationships between the techniques currently used in finance and the economic analysis of risk. The second goal is to look into information dissemination and thus identify some key limits of the basic models. Are financial markets, as some maintain, the ideal locations for the exchange of information? Should insiders' use of privileged information be controlled? Is the release of information always a good thing?

The book is divided into three parts.

After a brief description of the most common financial instruments, Part 1 presents the notion of arbitrage and the derived techniques of valuation by duplication. Chapter 1 gives a basic introduction to stocks, bonds, interest rates, and the spot rate curve and describes some derivatives (options and futures). It explains how markets operate with emphasis on futures markets for commodities and financial instruments. Derivative securities have proliferated in the past 20 years. They are built on preexisting assets using formulas that are often quite complex. It is important to understand how they are most often priced and the assumptions that underlie their valuation. This is the goal of Chapter 2, which deals with the fundamental principle of *absence of opportunities for arbitrage* and valuation by *duplication*. Duplication of a derivative is possible when its risky payoff can be reproduced with financial instruments available on the markets. It turns out that this very simple idea yields surprisingly strong conclusions that are abundantly (and sometimes abusively?) used in financial practice.

Part 2, the heart of the book, deals with exchanges of risks. The basic model is that of an economy in which future income, possibly random, is to be divided between the economic agents (also called investors). How do markets for financial assets perform this division? Is the resulting allocation optimal? Can market participants benefit from insider information?

To answer these questions, a first step is to describe how individual investors behave in an uncertain environment. Some basic concepts such as attitudes toward risk, how expectations are formed, and the value of information are introduced in Chapter 3. The guiding principles of portfolio choice (hedging and speculation) and risk diversification are derived in Chapter 4.

Once the individual's behavior is set, market functioning at the aggregate level can be studied. The traditional economic approach to optimality and equilibrium under symmetric information is the subject of Chapters 5 and 6. The optimality of risk-sharing contracts between a group of individuals quite naturally leads to separate individual idiosyncratic risks from macroeconomic risks. Optimality implies spreading individual risks providing the rationale for their *mutualization*. Macroeconomic risks, on the other hand, are unavoidable. Allocating them efficiently among economic agents requires taking into account their individual attitudes toward risk. The incomes of those who are most risk averse will scarcely be affected by the vagaries of the macroeconomy, while the less risk averse will accept wide fluctuations, perhaps compensated by a higher average income than the former.

A natural question is whether the existing financial markets lead to an optimal allocation. The answer is positive if markets are complete. This is the case when there is a sufficiently large number of derivatives, especially on market indexes. In terms of positive analysis, we examine how – complete or incomplete – asset markets function and allocate risks in the mean–variance CAPM framework. Introducing risky nonfinancial incomes allows us to bridge the most widely used model in finance with the standard equilibrium approach in economics.

Whereas financial markets play an important role for trading goods and allocating risks over time, the casual observation of the day-to-day movements of the markets leads to emphasize their sensitivity to the arrival of new information. News often motivates transactions and causes market prices to move. Chapter 7 addresses this issue. A new piece of information modifies the perceived probability of occurrence of the future events. It may be available to all participants (*public* information), or only to a selected few insiders (*private* information). The analysis is conducted in a framework characterized by *rational expectations* – a concept that is illustrated with several examples (including Muth's celebrated case) – in which investments made today change the distribution of prices tomorrow. Insurance dissipates as events become public knowledge. Allowing insiders to trade a stock on which they have access to relevant information in advance of the general public may create adverse selection effects: non informed investors who are aware of the presence of insiders may feel duped and may withdraw from the market. Finally, Chapter 8 is devoted to intertemporal dynamics and discusses the *equity premium puzzle*, as well as speculative bubbles.

The firm and how it is financed are the subject of the last part of the book (Chapters 9 and 10). The issues addressed here are at the frontier between management, corporate finance, and economics. The interaction between decision making and the financial structure of the firm is emphasized. Building on a simplified representation of balance sheets, the famous Modigliani and Miller theorem is presented. Most often the liability of the stockholders is limited to their original outlay. Several issues are investigated in this context. The risk of bankruptcy, the relationship between the values of the various securities issued by the firm, and the potential sources of conflict between the various stakeholders in the event of bankruptcy are investigated. The functioning of the credit market is also affected by limited liability, which may induce borrowers (entrepreneurs) to choose investments that are increasingly risky as the nominal interest rate rises. We conclude with a look at the issue of asymmetric information between an entrepreneur and her financial backers, whether stockholders or banks, and present a rationale for prohibiting insider trading.

This book is based on lectures given at the École polytechnique and at the DEA Analyse et politique économiques of the École des hautes études en Sciences Sociales. We wish to thank our students and our fellow staff members, some of whom occasionally moderated exercise sessions, for their remarks and suggestions. We are particularly indebted to Isabelle Braun Lemaire, Bruno Jullien, and Bernard Salanié.

Valuation by Arbitrage

Financial instruments: an introduction / 1

Price fluctuations are a major source of risks. A farmer who sows his field does not know what price he will receive for his crop. An exporter must deal with exchange rate fluctuations. In order to spread better the risks associated with these price movements, futures markets were established to fix the terms of trades to be conducted at predetermined future dates.

Similarly, the prices of *financial assets*, in particular, stocks and bonds, are subject to strong fluctuations. Entrepreneurs and governments require capital to finance risky activities. When these activities are clearly identified (e.g., by the enactment of a law), and when the identity and stability of a borrower is established beyond doubt, securities representing loans such as stocks and bonds can be traded on markets, called financial markets. The prices of these securities fluctuate in response to numerous factors: The business cycle, earnings reports, and so on. Markets for futures and *derivatives* came into existence to make better management of the risks associated with price movements possible.

The purpose of this chapter is to describe the main characteristics of common financial instruments and of the markets on which they are traded, and to present some simple arbitrage mechanisms. We begin by describing assets usually referred to as *primary* assets: Fixed-income securities – monetary securities and bonds – and stocks. Interest rates are defined and linked to the prices of bonds. We introduce zero-coupon bonds and explain why the *spot curve* provides a useful tool for valuing fixed-income securities. The second part presents the derivatives markets, the instruments traded on them (futures and options), and the *forward rate curve*.

1 Money, Bond, and Stock Markets

Borrowers, usually firms or governments, issue IOUs in the form of stocks, bonds, or other certificates to lenders, *in fine* mostly households. Financial markets allow lenders to construct their portfolios in a flexible manner and to diversify their assets: They play a key role by creating *liquidity*. This allows lenders to *sell* unsecured claims on the market before maturity, which would be impossible or at least very expensive otherwise.

1.1 Money Markets

Money markets are for borrowing and lending money for short periods of time, less than 2 years. Customarily, short-term debts are priced in terms of an annual interest rate on these markets. The rate is measured in percentages, for example, 4.07 percent, or in basis points, which are one hundredth of a percent, for example, 407 basis points. Central banks, commercial banks, financial institutions, and large corporations are active on money markets. Rates vary with the duration of the operation. For example, the federal funds rate (overnight) and the 3-month treasury bills are differentiated. At maturity, the borrower reimburses the loan plus interest at the agreed upon rate, which is computed according to conventions that account for the duration of the loan.

1.2 Bonds

A bond is an IOU agreed to by the issuer, who commits to making payments to the bondholder at various future dates, in general, over a finite time horizon. When issued, the life span of a bond exceeds 2 years. The date at which the final payment is made is called the *maturity date* or in short the maturity.[1] Payments may be of two types: Recurring installments, which are called *coupons* and are usually disbursed at regular intervals, and a final payment, called the *face value, nominal value*, or *principal*, which is frequently approximately equal to the initial loan. The bond is issued *at par* when its issue price is equal to its face value, which is achieved by adjusting the coupons.

---

1 Sometimes, the maturity of a bond also refers to its remaining length of life.

Bonds can have complicated payoff structures. For example, coupons may be linked to the market interest rate (variable rate bond), the date of the final payment may be left up to the debtor with provision for a penalty to compensate for expected depreciation, and the like. To keep the following discussion as tractable as possible, we limit it to a particularly simple category of bonds, *fixed-income bonds*: These have proceeds that are not, a priori, stochastic. *On the issue date, the amounts and dates of the payments are fixed, whatever the future circumstances.*

Thus, the only remaining uncertainty is that the debtor may fail to abide by the contract, or may default. The associated risk is called *default risk* or *counterparty risk* because it depends upon the issuer.[2] This risk can rarely be neglected in the case of corporate bonds, bonds that are issued by firms. It is also considerable in the case of some countries. In the rest of this chapter, we consider bonds for which the risk of default can be considered nil, such as those issued by the governments of the wealthiest nations.

On any given day, many bonds issued on different dates can be traded on the market. In practice, comparisons between bonds are often based on the notion of yield to maturity (in France, all new bond issues contain their yield to maturity in their product description).

Usually, the unit of time is the year. The following definition deals with a security that pays at the same date every year (see Remark 1.1 to take into account fractions of years).

Definition 1.1 *Given a bond with a price p at date 0 that yields a series of positive payments, $a(t), t = 1, \ldots, T$, its yield to maturity or actuarial rate denotes the unique rate r for which the current value of these payments is equal to p*

$$p = \sum_{t=1}^{T} \frac{a(t)}{(1 + r)^t}. \qquad (1.1)$$

∎

Consider, for example, a bond indexed by 1, with a face value of $100, a maturity of 10 years ($T = 10$), and paying an annual coupon equal to 5 percent of the face value. We say that the *coupon rate* is 5 percent. Formally, if we set $i = 0.05$, we have

$$a_1(t) = 100i, \ \text{for } t = 1, \ldots, T - 1, \quad \text{and} \quad a_1(T) = 100(1 + i).$$

---

2 Obviously, the reality is somewhat more complicated, since repayment of some debts is prioritized in the event that a firm declares bankruptcy.

Assume that this bond is issued at par. Its issue price is equal to its face value, or $100. A simple calculation reveals that $r = i$.[3] At later dates, as market conditions evolve, the bond price will change and with it the yield to maturity.

To illustrate this point, let us examine time $t = 1$. Consider a new bond that is issued on that date, indexed by 2, maturing in 9 years, whose principal is $100, and with a coupon rate of i'. After payment of the date 1 coupon on bond 1, the income streams yielded by the two bonds are

$100i$ at $t = 2, \ldots, T - 1$ and $100(1 + i)$ at T for bond 1

$100i'$ at $t = 2, \ldots, T - 1$ and $100(1 + i')$ at T for bond 2.

Assume that, as is often the case in practice, i' is chosen such that bond 2 is issued at par. Typically, conditions change and i' differs from i. To clarify this concept, let us set $i' < i$. In this case, the second bond yields less than the first at all times from 2 to T. Consequently, the price of bond 1 must exceed that of bond 2. Otherwise, all the investors would buy the first bond and sell the second and make a profit at all dates. This is called an opportunity for arbitrage. Thus, at time 1, the price of bond 1 rises above $100, which is the price of bond 2, issued at par. The price of bond 1 *increases* as i' decreases. Also its actuarial rate *falls*, remaining above i', as we can easily verify. Similarly, the price of bond 1 decreases as i' increases.

Remark 1.1 In practice, assets are not constrained to serve coupons or dividends at exact yearly intervals. This is easily accommodated by considering continuous time. For instance, in the definition of the yield to maturity, in Eqn (1.1), for a bond that distributes coupons every semester up to time T, the index of time takes values $t = \tau/2, \tau = 1, 2, \ldots, 2T$. ∎

---

3 If $p = 100$, the actuarial rate is defined by

$$1 = i \left[\sum_{t=1}^{T} \frac{1}{(1 + r)^t} \right] + \frac{1}{(1 + r)^T}.$$

The part in square brackets, computed as the sum of the first terms of a geometrical series for $1/(1+r)$, is equal to $(1 - 1/(1 + r)^T)/r$. This gives $r = i$.

1.3   The Spot Curve

As we have just seen, the actuarial rate of a bond adjusts to the market evolution. Its movement also depends on the specific repayment structure of the bond – the payments schedule and amounts – which, unlike in the preceding example, varies greatly from one bond to the other. Thus, it is convenient to introduce standardized assets, zero coupons, and their implicit actuarial rates. The derived spot curve allows the variations in bond prices to be determined as a function of their maturity and the repayment structure. In fact, experts in the field are phasing out the use of the concept of an actuarial rate and are switching to a valuation that is based on the spot curve when setting the price of a bond.

Zero Coupons

Consider a family of bonds, called *zero-coupon bonds*, that yield no payment prior to reaching maturity and pay one dollar then. Their face value is thus equal to one dollar, and they only vary in terms of the maturity. Denote $q(t)$ as today's price of one zero-coupon unit maturing in t years. If zero coupons exist, knowledge of their prices allows the valuation, by arbitrage, of any risk-free asset. Let $a(t)$ represent the payments to which possession of one unit of some asset confers a claim in the future. A portfolio consisting of $a(t)$ zero-coupon units maturing at t, $t = 1, \ldots$, yields exactly the same income as one unit of the asset in question: We say that it *replicates* it. Thus, the price of the asset, p, must equal the value of the portfolio, so as to eliminate opportunities for arbitrage,[4] which gives

$$p = \sum_t q(t)a(t). \tag{1.2}$$

This expression makes clear the relevance of zero coupons: If we knew their price at all possible payment dates, we could assign a value to all fixed-income securities, and detect whether some assets are incorrectly priced. The zero-coupon prices correspond to different maturities. Interest rates, called *zero-coupon rates*, are associated with the prices of zero coupons.

4 For example, p cannot be strictly greater than $\sum_t q(t)a(t)$ when there are individuals who possess a strictly positive amount of the asset. Otherwise, it would be in the interest of these investors to sell the asset and to obtain the same income flow by buying the replicating portfolio made of zero coupons. Section 2 more precisely formalizes the conditions under which the formula obtains.

Definition 1.2 *Let $q(\tau)$ be today's price for a risk-free zero coupon maturing at τ. The interest rate, $r(\tau)$, for operations maturing at τ is given by*

$$\frac{1}{(1+r(\tau))^{\tau}} = q(\tau).$$

The spot rate curve, or spot curve, is the curve giving $r(\tau)$ as a function of τ. ∎

Since the unit of time is a year, $r(\tau)$ represents the constant annual interest rate until maturity, such that investing $q(\tau)$ today, and reinvesting the interest earned each year at the same rate, will yield one dollar at maturity.

The spot curve is thus the preferred instrument for pricing fixed-income securities. There is however a problem: Zero-coupon bonds are virtually nonexistent for maturities greater than 1 year (though they have recently begun appearing more frequently, especially in the United States). Thus, it is necessary to *recover* the spot curve from the securities that are traded on markets.

Recovering the Spot Curve

Consider a sample of fixed-income securities, indexed by $k = 1, \dots, K$, having solid counterparts and yielding income at assorted dates. Assuming that there are no arbitrage opportunities for any of these securities, we have

$$p_k = \sum_t q(t) a_k(t).$$

The prices p_k as well as the values $a_k(t)$, which are part of the definition of the assets, are observed. The spot curve is constructed by determining the values for $q(t)$. This is done by using least squares, or sometimes by postulating that the curve belongs to a family of distributions depending on a small number of well-chosen parameters. Figure 1.1 show examples of such a curve on US Treasury bonds for a choice of dates since 1990.[5] If it were possible to buy and sell some combination of assets so as to recompose zero coupons, then according to the duplication principle explained in footnote 4, everything would transpire as if they actually existed. Differences with the adjusted theoretical values, gaps

5 The web site of the US Treasury provides historical estimates of these curves, as well as a description of the methodology used in their construction, at http://www.treasury.gov/offices/domestic-finance/debt-management/interestrate/yield-hist.html. We have added to the curves an intercept equal to the daily federal reserve rate found at http://www.federalreserve.gov/releases/h15/data/d/fedfund.txt.

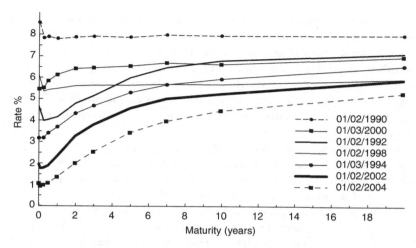

Figure 1.1   Selected US spot rate curves of the past 15 years.

representing the distance $p_k - \sum_t \hat{q}(t) a_k(t)$ in which $\hat{q}(t)$ is estimated, may indicate failures of arbitrage and must be analyzed carefully. Prohibitions on short sales of government bonds and peculiarities related to tax law may be responsible. The security in question may also feature a risk that was overlooked.

1.4   Stocks

Stocks are stakes in a company that confer the right to a fraction of the revenue stream created by its activities, which are distributed in the form of dividends. The firm's initial owners who contribute to the creation or expansion of its activities by providing funds or intangible contributions receive securities indicative of their property rights. By bringing their company to the stock market, the incumbent owners can raise capital useful for developing their activities and share the risk with new investors. They can also divest themselves of the firm by reselling their shares at any time.

Along with shipping companies, the first stock exchanges appeared in Italy and the Hanseatic League during the heyday of the great explorations, soon after lawyers had invented the concept of an incorporated company. Chartering a ship to sail to the East Indies was a monumental undertaking, requiring a great outlay of capital and, obviously, involving grave risks: Substantial earnings in the event of success, but a total write-off if the ship sank. The corporation thus allowed these risks to be shared. With the stock exchange, the entire outlay did not need to be locked up for the full duration of the expedition. The initial backers could re-sell their shares before the business was completed, for example, to deal with unexpected personal or political reversals of fortune. The guarantees provided by the organization of the market attracted small investors and allowed for a division into smaller shares, permitting a diversification of risk between several ships, for example.

Stockholders are entitled to the wealth generated by the firm and participate in setting its broad strategic orientation. Most often, stockholders bear a *limited* liability, meaning that losses incurred by the firm do not entail any personal liability on their behalf exceeding the initial contribution.

Chapters 6 and 9 give data on corporate debt and equity financing, along with information on the orders of magnitude of transactions on the stock exchange. In fact, only the shares of large firms are traded on stock exchanges. As to bonds, only large firms issue them – the others incur debt exclusively through financial intermediaries. The impact that the risk of default on debt repayment has on the financing of firms will be addressed in Chapter 10.

2 Derivatives Markets

By definition, futures (and, more generally, derivatives) are a function of preexisting, primary assets, the underlying assets. Derivatives, such as options, were set up by financial intermediaries to satisfy the needs of their clients. In practice, a distinction is made between the two types of operators on derivatives markets: End users and financial intermediaries. End users, such as firms, households, governments, and municipalities, invest or lend money through instruments corresponding to their own financing needs: Pooled investment funds, options, forward and futures contracts, and the like. Financial intermediaries, especially banks and insurance companies, play a key role by designing derivatives that correspond to the needs of their clients, the end users.

We shall describe a very limited number of derivatives that are standardized and traded on organized exchanges. There is also a huge informal over-the-counter (OTC) market, in which traders negotiate transactions over electronic communications networks. Contracts are more flexible and are not managed by a clearinghouse.

2.1 Futures Markets for Commodities and Currencies

How They Work

On a spot market, sellers offer fixed amounts of some commodity or asset, say wheat, for sale available immediately at a specified location. The market links the buyers and the sellers, establishes the price at which supply equals demand, possibly through an auction mechanism, and provides that the exchange occurs immediately.

Futures and forward markets seek to replicate the functioning of spot markets at some future date, the *term*. These markets set the price and location for delivery at term: For example, 1 ton of wheat of a specified quality delivered to a predetermined location next July 30. The exchange – delivery and payment – occurs at a later date but the price is set today. This type of transaction is useful under many circumstances in which prices fluctuate. Thus, an agricultural firm that will be selling its wheat harvest next July 30 runs a risk that is not only related to the quantity of the crop, but also to the fact that prices may be very different from their current value because of various sociopolitical events that may be difficult to anticipate. Denote a (random) crop by[6] $\tilde{x}$. By selling an amount that is close to the expected crop on the futures market, $E[\tilde{x}]$, the firm reduces its risk and ensures an income $p_0^t E[\tilde{x}]$, where p_0^t is the futures price (delivery at date t) on today's market (the date 0 indicated by the subscript). Notice that there remains a residual risk associated with the difference between the actual crop $\tilde{x}$ and its expectation. The overall income received on July 30 will be $p_0^t E[\tilde{x}] + \tilde{p}_t^t (\tilde{x} - E[\tilde{x}])$, where $\tilde{p}_t^t$ is the spot price for wheat on July 30 (the superscript and the subscript are equal). If the realized crop x is greater than $E[\tilde{x}]$, the crop exceeds expectations, and the surplus is sold on the spot market. Conversely, if x is less than $E[\tilde{x}]$, the farmer must buy $E[\tilde{x}] - x$ on the spot market to fulfill his commitment on the futures market.

Similarly, an exporter into the French market who will be ensured a revenue of x euros in 3 months, and who is only interested in her income in dollars, can eliminate this risk by selling x euros for dollars on the 3-month forward market. If the forward exchange rate, as set on today's market, is p_0^t, she will receive $p_0^t x$ dollars at term. Without transacting on forward markets, she would have received $\tilde{p}_t^t x$, where $\tilde{p}_t^t$ is the spot-market exchange rate after 3 months. Thus, selling x euros forward eliminates the risk associated with uncertainty on the

---

6 Throughout the book, we denote a random variable by $\tilde{x}$ and its realization by x.

value of $\tilde{p}_t^t$. No losses will be sustained if $\tilde{p}_t^t$ turns out to be less than p_0^t, but any potential profits will also be forfeited in the opposite case.

Forward markets require more precautions for their good functioning than do spot markets. In a forward transaction, the buyer undertakes to buy, and the seller to sell, a good at a future date. All of the features of the transaction, that is, price, quantity, and term, are fixed today, but the actual physical exchange, that is, delivery and payment, takes place at term. While the fact that the buyer actually has the funds, and the seller the goods, is immediately verified in the case of a spot market, this is inherently impossible for futures contracts. The crop is yet to be grown, or the exporter's debtor may default. In order to make it materially impossible to renege on the transaction, the institution organizing the market will often require down payment of an initial margin from both parties. This deposit, sometimes proportional to the amount of the transaction, is intended to cover foreseeable variations in the price with respect to the futures price, $\tilde{p}_t^t - p_0^t$. There is a distinction between *forward* and *futures* markets.

In the former, the initial margin represents the only movement of funds before maturity. At term, a contract purchased yields a unit of the underlying product (e.g., a ton of wheat) at the forward price, which can be immediately resold on the spot market. Its value is thus equal to the difference between the product spot and forward prices, or $p_t^t - p_0^t$, which may be positive or negative. Frequently, there is no obligation to deliver the product, and the balance of the contract can be settled with cash. The seller pays the buyer the value of the contract purchased, $p_t^t - p_0^t$, provided this amount is positive or, conversely, receives $p_0^t - p_t^t$ if it is negative.

As to *futures* contracts, there are daily *margin calls* reflecting day-to-day fluctuations in the contract's value. If the futures price increases from p_τ^t to $p_{\tau+1}^t$ between dates τ and $\tau + 1$, sellers pay $(p_{\tau+1}^t - p_\tau^t)$ per unit sold to buyers (the institution that manages the market transfers the money from the seller's to the buyer's account). Abstracting from the fact that these transfers occur over the entire life span of the contract instead of at maturity, the (algebraic) sum of margin calls paid by the seller is thus equal to $p_t^t - p_0^t$, or identical to the final payment of the futures contract. In this book, we abstract from the distinction between "futures" and forward markets and the two terms are used interchangeably.

How is the price of futures determined? One particularity of the futures market is that the number of contracts purchased is equal to the number sold (or, alternatively, the algebraic sum of the positions of all the participants is identically equal to zero). There is no reason why the hedging needs of the final buyers should always equal those of the final sellers. Futures markets work because of the presence of intermediaries who absorb the residual supply or demand (we say that they insure the counterpart), and they can, in exchange, require compensation for the costs or risks they incur. We establish here some relationships between prices on futures markets, on spot markets, and the transfer costs between the present and the term. These relationships are called arbitrage relationships. If they do not hold, then there are arbitrage opportunities: A sure profit can be made in the future with no commitment of funds.

Arbitrage Relationships

As a first example, let us look at the simplest case, that of currency forward markets. Let p_0^t be the 3-month dollar–euro exchange rate on the forward market, that is, the price in dollars of one euro, and p_0^0 the current dollar–euro exchange rate on the spot market. Assume that it is possible to lend or borrow dollars for 3 months without limitation and at the interest cost[7] $c_\$$, euros at cost $c_\mathord{\in}$, and that short-term credit and investment operations present no risk. If the relationship

$$\frac{p_0^0}{p_0^t} = \frac{1 + c_\$}{1 + c_\mathord{\in}},\qquad(1.3)$$

does not hold, we show that an operator can make a certain profit at t with no investment today. Consider the following operations:

1 buy a euro on the forward market;
2 borrow $1/(1 + c_\mathord{\in})$ euros today, which by definition of the interest rate is associated with a reimbursement of one euro at t;
3 sell the $1/(1 + c_\mathord{\in})$ euros on the foreign exchange spot market for dollars, which are in turn invested for 3 months to yield $p_t^t(1 + c_\$)/(1 + c_\mathord{\in})$ dollars at time t.

The two first operations are designed so that, at maturity t, the amount of euros borrowed can be repaid from the proceeds of the forward purchase. The third ensures that no commitment of funds is required. It remains to compute the balance of the operation in dollars at 0 resulting from the investment of dollars

---

7 If the annualized rate is r, the interest cost for one quarter is, depending on convention, $r/4$ or $[(1 + r)^{1/4} - 1]$. To simplify the notation, we denote by $c_\mathord{\in}$ and $c_\$$ the interest cost to be paid in 3 months, respectively, for borrowing one € and one $.

and the forward purchase of one euro. This yields an amount in dollars equal to

$$p_0^0(1 + c_\$)/(1 + c_€) - p_0^t.$$

If this quantity is strictly positive, the operation guarantees a sure income: This is called an *arbitrage opportunity*. When such an opportunity exists, arbitrageurs take advantage of it by proceeding with the operation, and do it so effectively that the purchase of euros on the forward market and their sale on the spot market create a pressure on prices, which subsequently adjusts until the opportunity has been dissipated.

If p_0^t were less than $p_0^0(1+c_\$)/(1+c_€)$, the operation could be performed in the opposite direction: Buy dollars on the forward market and sell the corresponding amount on the spot market, financed by a loan denominated in euros. This would also yield a sure profit. Arbitrage thus implies that the equality (1.3) holds.

Arbitrage operations involve simultaneous trades on the currency forward market and the spot market. In practice, neither individuals nor firms conduct these arbitrage operations.[8] They are performed by specialized financial intermediaries, who respond to the hedging requirements of importers and exporters.

Arbitrage relationships on the commodities market are looser. Indeed, if we wish to repeat the previous exercise, but with wheat instead of dollars, we see that it is not always possible to borrow wheat. Moreover, buying wheat implies having to store it, which entails costs incurred between the present and the term. Assume, to begin, that the total cost of storage is fully known and certain, and that supply on the spot market is sufficient for it to be perfectly competitive. Let $c(0, t)$ be the total per-unit storage cost of 1 ton of wheat between the dates 0 and t, and let this be payable at time 0. This yields the following inequality:

$$p_0^t \leq [p_0^0 + c(0, t)](1 + r)^t,$$

where r is the interest rate on a risk-free loan between 0 and t. If this inequality does not hold, then the following *risk-free* arbitrage operation will be profitable. Purchase 1 ton of wheat (cost: p_0^0), store it until maturity (cost: $c(0, t)$), and simultaneously sell a ton of wheat on the futures market (receipt: p_0^t at the 3-month maturity), which then only needs to be delivered to the silo at time t.

8 Lending rates (paid by borrowers) are higher than borrowing rates (paid to individuals who invest their assets), and arbitrage only provides a range of values to link spot market and futures market exchange rates.

The opposite relationship cannot be obtained by arbitrage. Nonetheless, if there are investors who intend to store the wheat *with certainty* beyond time t, the inequality must obtain in both directions. Otherwise, anyone with stocks would be better off selling them on the spot market and buying the same quantity back on the futures market. This leads to the following relationship: $p_0^t = [p_0^0 + c(0, t)](1 + r)^t$.

In the colorful language of futures markets, when the difference $p_0^t - p_0^0$ is positive, which is usually the case, it is called *contango*. Contango includes all costs for storage: Interest, compensation to the storage facility, depreciation, and the like. In contrast to the assumption made above, there are generally risks associated with storage (fire, etc.) that may, or may not, be assumed by arbitrageurs, and *contango* may reflect this risk. During times of trouble, we may observe inversions, that is, the futures price below the spot-market price: This is called *backward-ation*.[9] Following the same reasoning, this occurs when the spot market is highly stretched during the period after a bad crop and before the new crop is harvested. Stocks are exhausted, spot-market prices are (very) high, and an abundant crop is expected to drive down prices. The futures price thus directly translates the market's expectation regarding the size of the coming crop, which is not directly linked to conditions on the spot market.

2.2 Futures Markets for Financial Instruments

The evolution of the spot curve is stochastic, as are the goods prices from the previous section, giving rise to a *rate risk*. To illustrate, this risk is borne by a bank that extends a 15-year loan to a client at a fixed rate, and then partially refinances over a shorter term. The refinancing cost depends upon the movement of the rate. The rate risk mostly affects actors on financial markets. The owner of a fixed-income bond from a top grade[10] fully knows the revenue stream the bond will yield until maturity. However, the price of the bond will change over time. This is reflected in the financial balances of the owner and the issuer, when the bond is evaluated *marked to market*, that is at market price.

9 Backwardation refers to a commission paid by the seller to delay delivery of the promised quantity. *Contango* is a commission paid by the buyer to delay payment and delivery.
10 As alluded to before, for an identical maturity, the lending rate varies with the borrower, more precisely with its risk of default. Banks and firms that seek external funding by issuing bonds are ranked according to this risk. A top-grade issuer is one that is considered as having no default risk.

To manage these risks, futures markets have been created on the model of commodities futures markets. These markets are complemented by derivatives markets (which are defined in the following section). In the United States, the Chicago Board of Trade has been a leader in futures trading. Futures trading is regulated by the Commodity Futures Trading Commission (CFTC), an independent agency of the US government. The National Futures Association (NFA) also plays a regulatory role under the supervision of the CFTC.

The price of the "good" purchased forward, whether commodities or financial instruments, must be observed at maturity without contestation by the two contractors. For forwards on short-term loans for instance, in which a contract bears on an interest rate, the contract specifies which rate is used (since rates may differ according to the issuer). The London Interbank Offered Rate (LIBOR) is a most widely used benchmark for short-term interest rates. It serves as an underlying rate of many derivatives transactions, both OTC and exchange traded. Also, since the introduction of the euro in 1999, European banks agreed on a new interbank reference rate within the Economic and Monetary Union: *Euribor*. It is the rate at which euro interbank term deposits are offered by one prime bank to another prime bank (prime banks are first-class credit standing banking institutions).

Let us describe a simple example. On June 1, the purchaser of a 3-month LIBOR futures contract on $1 million (called notional principal) maturing (or settled) the following July 1, is guaranteed on June 1 a fixed interest rate – the forward rate – for a 3-month loan of 1 million dollars, which can be underwritten on the interbank market on July 1.[11] This is a *forward* market: No money changes hands before the settlement date (the maturity of the contract). At maturity on July 1, the contract is settled financially: The purchaser receives the difference between the interest charge corresponding to the current 3-month LIBOR rate and the previously agreed upon rate, when the latter is lower, and pays the differential to the seller when it is greater.

This type of operation allows a large firm – a bank or an insurance company – that knows it will need to contract a 3-month loan of 1 million dollars next July 1 to protect itself against fluctuations in the rate that may occur in the interim.

More generally, there are futures markets for long-term rates, for market indices, swaps on interest rates that combine several forward contracts, and the

---

11 Such a contract is often called a forward rate agreement (FRA). The settlement dates of the futures contracts, from 1 to 12 months, correspond to the subscription dates of the 3-month LIBOR loan. There are as many rates posted on the market as there are settlement dates.

like. Some of these markets are related through arbitrage relationships as we now show.

What price (or what rate) is established on the futures market? Arbitrage creates a link between the spot curve we saw in the previous section and the futures markets, assuming that zero-coupon bonds exist or can be recomposed and short-selling is possible. Indeed, to determine the forward price of a zero coupon of life span m to be bought at t, one can proceed with the following operation today (in our example t corresponds to July 1, $t + m$ to September 30, and m represents a quarter):

– sell $q(t)/q(t + m)$ zero coupons, maturing at $t + m$;
– buy a zero coupon maturing at t.

By construction, this operation, called *cash and carry*, does not cost anything today: The purchase costs $q(t)$ dollars and the sale yield the same amount. At t, it will yield 1 dollar and at $t + m$ it will cost $q(t)/q(t + m)$ dollars.

Thus, the operation is identical to a forward loan of 1 dollar at t for m periods (3-month loan of 1 dollar taken on July 1) with a final repayment of $q(t)/q(t + m)$, that is, with interest cost $q(t)/q(t + m) - 1$.

Because of arbitrage, it follows that the forward price $q^t(m)$ of a zero coupon bought at t, maturing at $t + m$ is $q(t + m)/q(t)$ dollars.

In addition to spot rates, forward rates for operations of maturity t can be defined. They are often denoted by f. We start with 1-year operations, for which the interest cost is $q(t)/q(t + 1) - 1$.

Definition 1.3 *Let $q(\tau)$ be today's price for a zero coupon maturing at τ for $\tau = 0, \dots$. The 1-year forward interest rate for a contract maturing at time t, $f^t(1)$, is defined by*

$$1 + f^t(1) = \frac{1}{q^t(1)} = \frac{q(t)}{q(t + 1)}.$$
∎

The forward rate $f^t(1)$ is the prevailing rate fixed at time 0 for loan operations starting at time t for a period of 1 year.[12] Note that all the values (prices and forward rates) just defined are relative to the current date at which the asset prices

12 A second index to designate the reference date, here 0, would eliminate any possible confusion (f^t_0 would designate the forward rate on markets opened at date 0 for maturity t), but we have omitted it to simplify the notation.

are observed. The price of zero coupons maturing after t full years is linked to the 1-year forward rates by the discounting formula:

$$q(t) = \prod_{\tau=0}^{t-1} \frac{1}{1+f^\tau(1)}.$$

Typically, the forward rates evolve over time. Also, whereas $f^t(1)$ is the forward rate at time 0 for 1-year loan operations at time t, the 1-year rate observed at time t will typically differ from this forward rate: The relationship between these two rates will be studied in Chapter 8.

Similarly, the forward interest rate, $f^t(m)$, for zero-coupon loans of life span m to be executed at time t is defined by

$$\frac{1}{[1+f^t(m)]^m} = \frac{q(t+m)}{q(t)}. \tag{1.4}$$

Finally, the instantaneous forward rate curve is frequently constructed in parallel to the spot curve. With the "instantaneous forward rate" at time t, we mean a rate $f_{i,t}$ that yields a forward investment of 1 dollar in t periods for an infinitesimal duration. Using the above expression, this gives rise to Definition 1.4.

Definition 1.4 *The "instantaneous forward rate" with maturity t is defined as*

$$f_{i,t} = \lim_{dt \to 0} \frac{1}{dt} \left[\frac{q(t)}{q(t+dt)} - 1 \right]. \qquad \blacksquare$$

By construction, the forward rate curve is approximately equal to the derivative of the spot curve.[13] A curve of the instantaneous forward rate is depicted together with an associated (bold) spot curve in Figure 1.2. Since the overnight rate is directly controlled by monetary authorities, the forward rate curve is often considered to be an indicator of the market's expectations vis-à-vis the central bank's policies.

---

13 Indeed, if the price function is continuously differentiable, we have

$$f_{i,t} = -\frac{q'(t)}{q(t)}, \quad q(t) = \exp\left(-\int_0^t f_{i,u} du\right)$$

$$\log(1+r(t)) = \frac{1}{t} \int_0^t f_{i,u} du.$$

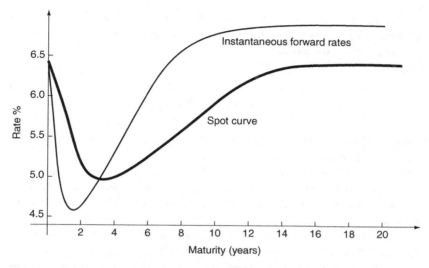

Figure 1.2 An example of spot and forward curves: French Franc December 31, 1993.

2.3 Options

There are two broad categories of options: *Call options* and *put options*, which allow the purchase or sale of a security (the *underlying* security) at a future date. The specific characteristics of an option determine when, and at what price, this right may be exercised. *European* options can only be exercised at a given date, while *American* options can be exercised by their owners at any time prior to maturity. We shall focus on the former.

Definition 1.5 *European option – a call (put) option on a security gives the right, but not the obligation, to buy (sell) one unit of the security at a previously specified price and date. The price is called the strike price or the exercise price, and the date is the maturity or expiration date.* ∎

In what follows, the price of a call option is denoted by C, and the price of a put by P. An option can be used for hedging and, like any other security, for speculation.

Thus, a 3-month call option of 1 euro against dollar with a strike price of $\$K$ makes it possible to guarantee against an increase of the euro in 3 months. If the euro exchange rate exceeds $\$K$ in 3 months, the holder of the option will exercise it, earning the difference between the going rate and K. If the euro exchange rate is below K, she has no interest in exercising the option.

More generally, the payoff to the holder of a call option at the expiration date is equal to

$$\max(S - K, 0),$$

where S is the security price at the expiration date, and K the strike price.

In what follows, we denote $a^+ = \max(a, 0)$.

As a result of the arbitrage activities of financial intermediaries, the prices of various derivatives and of the underlying asset are interrelated.[14] In particular, a fundamental arbitrage relationship holds between the prices of put and call options.

Put–call parity: Consider, at $t = 0$, a call and a put option with the same strike price, K, the same maturity, on the same stock. The risk-free interest rate is r per unit of time. Let us denote the spot-market price of the stock, the price of the call, and the price of the put at time $t = 0$ as S_0, C, and P, respectively.

The payoffs of the call and put options at time T are, respectively, equal to $(S - K)^+$ and $(K - S)^+$, if S is the price of the stock at $t = T$ (unknown at time $t = 0$).

Now, *whatever this price*, we have

$$(S - K)^+ - (K - S)^+ = S - K.$$

The term on the left-hand side is the payoff at T obtained by buying a unit of the call option and selling a unit of the put option at $t = 0$.

The term on the right-hand side is the payoff one gets when buying a portfolio comprising a stock and a loan of $K(1 + r)^{-T}$ at $t = 0$. Since the final payoffs of these two strategies are identical for any future price of the stock, the condition of the absence of arbitrage opportunities forces their costs today to be identical, whence the *parity relationship*

$$C - P = S_0 - K(1 + r)^{-T}.$$

14 These relations do not determine the price levels. How the prices themselves are determined by markets forces is a quite complex issue, which will be touched upon later in this book.

BIBLIOGRAPHICAL NOTE

The purpose of this short chapter was merely to introduce the vocabulary and operating principles of financial markets and futures and forward markets. For a more thorough understanding of these concepts, the reader may refer to Duffie (1989), who provides a more detailed presentation. The first part of the Allen and Gale (1994) book provides a brief overview of the historical development of financial innovation.

Allen, F. and D. Gale (1994). *Financial innovation and risk sharing*, MIT Press, Cambridge.
Duffie, D. (1989). *Futures markets*, Prentice Hall, Englewood Cliffs, NJ.

Exercises

1.1 *Relationships between options prices*

1. We consider three European call options on the same asset and with the same time to expiration, whose strike prices are $K_1, K_2, K_3 = \lambda K_1 + (1 - \lambda)K_2$ with $\lambda \in [0, 1]$, respectively.

   At some point in time before maturity, let us denote by $C(K_i)$ the price of the option with a strike price of K_i at that time. Show that the absence of opportunities for arbitrage implies:

   $$C(K_3) \leq \lambda C(K_1) + (1 - \lambda)C(K_2).$$

2. Consider two assets, 1 and 2, and let three European call options, having the same time to expiration written on (respectively):
   (a) asset 1 with strike price K_1,
   (b) asset 2 with strike price K_2,
   (c) a portfolio comprising one unit of each of assets 1 and 2 with the strike price $K_1 + K_2$.

If we denote the prices of these options at a given date C_1, C_2, and C_{12}, respectively, show that the absence of opportunities for arbitrage implies that

$$C_{12} \leq C_1 + C_2.$$

Explain your results.

Arbitrage $\quad$ 2

Financial futures, and derivatives in general, are built on preexisting *underlying* securities. By simultaneously conducting operations on several markets, specialized intermediaries intervene whenever an *opportunity for arbitrage* arises that ensures a profit in all contingencies. With the increasing sophistication of derivatives, the ancient art of arbitrage can become very complicated today. These interventions ensure some price consistency across markets. In particular, they induce relationships between the prices of securities and derivatives that lead to the procedures of *valuation by arbitrage* that are systematically used by financial institutions.

The goal of this chapter is to formalize and analyze the notion of arbitrage. The underlying assumptions and the limits of the arbitrage-based valuation procedures that are used by financial institutions are made explicit.

Uncertainty is described in terms of *states of nature* that determine future payoffs. An *opportunity for arbitrage* consists of transactions in which no money can be lost and some can be earned in certain states of nature. In the absence of friction, such opportunities should not last, which motivates the study of markets without arbitrage opportunities. The absence of arbitrage opportunities dictates some relationships between the prices of securities and their payoffs that are easily expressed in terms of *state prices*. These relationships also allow the *valuation* of some securities on the basis of the prices of other securities. This procedure, however, is only valid under certain conditions. In particular, a natural and key distinction is made between *complete* markets, for which the valuation procedure is always valid, and markets that are *incomplete*.

Section 1 studies a static framework. In Section 2, the analysis is extended to the dynamic framework that underlies the most commonly used valuation methods, at the cost of strong assumptions on expectations. We emphasize that arbitrage relationships only allow to get the prices of some derivatives from others, but never determine the prices of the whole set of securities: Such a determination typically requires a complete economic model, similar to that discussed in Chapters 5 and 6.

1 Static Arbitrage

1.1 States of Nature

Consider an economy at time 0, with a future that may be uncertain. In this section, the future is reduced to a single point in time, $t = 1$. Uncertainty is modeled by a set of *states of nature* that represents all possibilities at time 1. A state of nature e provides a description of the economic environment: It includes all relevant information, such as agents' tastes, their resources, firms' profits, dividends paid by each asset, and so on. We assume here that the number of states is finite, with $\mathcal{E}$ denoting the set of states and E representing the number of states in $\mathcal{E}$.

The appropriate set of states depends on the problem under investigation and may be more or less complex. The only constraint is that the characteristics of the economy can be expressed as a deterministic function of the state. For example, to price a European call option, the state may be summarized by the price of the underlying security, S (assumed to take a finite number of values), because the payoff accruing to the holder of this option is a function of that price, $\max(S - K, 0)$.

The set of states of nature is analogous to the fundamental space of probability theory. However, notice that throughout this chapter we never say that some states are more or less probable than the others. No probability distribution is specified over the state space. Indeed, an opportunity for arbitrage arises when operations can be conducted that yield profits in some states of nature without generating losses in any other state. The existence, or absence, of any such opportunity depends exclusively on the set of possible states and not on any probability distribution on these states.

1.2 Securities

Consider a market, opened at time 0, on which are traded $k = 1, \ldots, K$ securities. A unit of security k is defined by a payoff (coupons, dividends, resale price at some future date) in dollars, which the owner receives in the various states of nature: $a_k(e)$ represents the payoff contingent on the occurrence of state e, e in $\mathcal{E}$. The vector of payoffs to security k is the row vector $\tilde{a}_k$ of dimension E, made of $a_k(e)$ for e running in $\mathcal{E}$.

The matrix of the securities payoffs is denoted $\tilde{a}$, its elements by $a_k(e)$ and its dimension by $(K \times E)$. The price of security k today is designated p_k, and the vector of the prices p is a column vector in $\mathbb{R}^K$.

The set of all states, the contingent payoffs, and the prices of the securities are the data characterizing the markets. They are summarized by $(\mathcal{E}, \tilde{a}, p)$.

A portfolio specifies the (positive) holdings, or long positions, as well as the debts (negative), or short positions in the various securities. It is represented by a column vector, $z = (z_k)_{k=1,\dots,K}$, the kth element of which, z_k, indicates the number of units of security k in the portfolio when it is positive. If it is negative, the portfolio is *short* on security k which commits its owner to paying $|z_k|a_k(e)$ at time $t = 1$ in the event that state e materializes.

The *value* of the portfolio is equal to

$$\sum_{k=1}^{K} p_k z_k = p'z.$$

The portfolio yields in state e the payoff (also called revenue or income):

$$c_z(e) = \sum_{k=1}^{K} a_k(e) z_k.$$

The vector of contingent payoffs associated with z, a row vector in $\mathbb{R}^E$, is simply written as

$$\tilde{c}_z = z'\tilde{a}.$$

We shall use this convention throughout this book: *Securities prices and portfolios are represented by column vectors while contingent payoffs by row vectors.*

This representation encompasses financial instruments that obligate their owners to pay out in some states of nature, such as bets on elections. Formally, some of the payoffs $a_k(e)$ may be negative.

Consider, for example, a forward market on a commodity, say wheat, opened at time 0 and maturing at time 1. Recall that at maturity the payoff of the forward contract is the difference between the price of wheat on the spot market, and the forward price, f, determined at time 0.

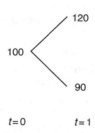

100 < 120 / 90

$t = 0$ $\qquad$ $t = 1$

Figure 2.1 Two-state model.

Let $w(e)$ denote the spot price of wheat at time 1 where e is the state that materializes. If we abstract from guarantee deposits, no payments are made when the contract is signed. At maturity, the buyer of a contract gets the (positive or negative) payoff $w(e) - f$, if e materializes. Thus, in terms of our conventions, a forward contract corresponds to a financial instrument k, the price of which *today* is nil, $p_k = 0$, and which yields the contingent payoff, $a_k(e) = w(e) - f$, tomorrow. Typically, there are states in which the spot price exceeds the futures price and vice versa.

Example 2.1 There are two states of nature and two securities: A risk-free security with rate r, and a stock whose price[1] S at $t = 0$ can move to $(1 + h)S$ in one state and $(1 + b)S$ in the other. The model is written as

$$\mathcal{E} = \{h, b\}, \quad p = \begin{bmatrix} 1 \\ S \end{bmatrix}, \quad \tilde{a} = \begin{bmatrix} 1 + r & 1 + r \\ (1 + h)S & (1 + b)S \end{bmatrix}.$$

The payoff of portfolio z is

$$[z_1(1 + r) + z_2(1 + h)S, z_1(1 + r) + z_2(1 + b)S].$$

Figure 2.1 represents the case of a stock that increases by 20 percent or decreases by 10 percent.

---

1 This model will be used and developed to price an option on the stock. Thus we use the standard notation of option models: S denotes the price of the underlying security.

1.3 Absence of Arbitrage Opportunities and Valuation

Pure arbitrage theory is set in a perfectly competitive market for financial assets. At a given market price p, a stakeholder can buy or sell any quantity of assets. Moreover, there are no limits on allowable short positions. Thus, the theory does not account for possible transaction costs, prohibitions on short sales, or limitations on buying or selling.[2]

An opportunity for arbitrage is a possibility to realize nonnegative profits in all states of nature, today or in the future, with a strictly positive profit in at least one state.[3] In the absence of constraints on transactions, this leads to the following definition:

Definition 2.1 Arbitrage opportunity *An opportunity for arbitrage in markets* $(\mathcal{E}, \tilde{a}, p)$ *is a portfolio z such that*

$$\sum_{1}^{K} z_k a_k(e) \geq 0 \quad \forall\, e \text{ and } z'p \leq 0$$

(or, equivalently[4] $z'\tilde{a} \geq 0$ and $z'p \leq 0$) with at least one strict inequality among these $E + 1$ inequalities. ∎

If there are no limits on the quantities exchanged, an opportunity for arbitrage cannot last, since operators will have an interest in exploiting it infinitely. This leads us to consider markets in which there are no opportunities for arbitrage.

A direct consequence of the *absence of opportunities for arbitrage* is that the value of a portfolio depends only on the payoff it generates. Indeed, assume that two portfolios, z^1 and z^2, generate the same payoffs but do not have the same value. Then, for example, if

$$p'z^1 < p'z^2,$$

portfolio $z^1 - z^2$ constitutes an opportunity for arbitrage.

2 In practice, purchase and sale prices differ to varying degrees, the difference being a *bid-ask spread*. Exercise 2.3 deals with a simple example of arbitrage relationships in this circumstance.
3 Two slightly different notions of arbitrage opportunity may be considered, depending on whether the profit is immediate or deferred. The relationships between these notions are examined in Exercise 3.2.
4 We adopt the following conventions for vector notation: $z \geq 0$ means that each element of z is positive or nil, $z > 0$ is equivalent to $z \geq 0$, except that at least one component is strictly positive. Finally, $z \gg 0$ indicates that all elements are strictly positive.

Valuation by arbitrage follows from this remark: A security j with revenue $\tilde{a}_j$ is "replicated" by a portfolio z comprising other securities if the payoff yielded by z is identical to that from j in all states:

$$a_j(e) = \sum_{k \neq j} z_k a_k(e) \ \forall e.$$

In this case, the security is said to be *redundant*. The price of security j must be equal to the value of the portfolio that replicates it, so as to eliminate any opportunity for arbitrage. We thus obtain a relationship between the price of the replicated security and those of the other securities in the replicating portfolio, that is,

$$p_j = \sum_{k \neq j} z_k p_k.$$

Example 2.2   Price of a call option in a two-state model   Let us return to the first example with two states of nature, one risk-free investment, one stock and a call option on the stock at time 1 with strike price K. The option can be replicated with the stock and the risk-free asset. Consider the more interesting case in which the option is only exercised if the stock price is high, so that

$$(1 + h)S > K > (1 + b)S.$$

The income yielded by the option is then:

$$(1 + h)S - K \quad \text{in state } h,$$

$$0 \quad \text{in state } b.$$

For a portfolio z consisting of the risk-free asset and the stock to replicate the option, it must satisfy

$$z_1(1 + r) + z_2(1 + h)S = (1 + h)S - K,$$

$$z_1(1 + r) + z_2(1 + b)S = 0.$$

Since this system of equations has the solution:

$$z_1 = -\frac{(1 + b)[(1 + h)S - K]}{(1 + r)(h - b)}, \quad z_2 = \frac{(1 + h)S - K}{(h - b)S},$$

the price of the option, C, must be equal to $z_1 + z_2 S$, so that

$$C = \frac{r - b}{(1 + r)(h - b)}[S(1 + h) - K]. \tag{2.1}$$

Notice that this reasoning is valid on the condition that the underlying security is available and can be traded without limitations, without transaction costs and without storage costs. If we are dealing with options on wheat prices, replication involves storage costs and is asymmetrical in terms of buying and selling, as we saw in Chapter 1. ∎

Valuation using State Prices

There exists a useful tool for pricing all portfolio payoffs without explicitly referring to the composition of the portfolio. These are state prices that are used frequently – especially in the context of dynamic valuation. State prices play a role comparable to that of discount factors used in intertemporal analysis without uncertainty. Just as discount factors allow comparison of revenues at different times, state prices allow the comparison of revenues between different states of nature. The state price associated with a state e has a direct interpretation when a specific security, known as an Arrow–Debreu security or a contingent security, is traded. An Arrow–Debreu security associated with a state of nature e yields 1 dollar if e occurs, and nothing otherwise. If such a security exists, its price is the state price associated with e: It is the price today of 1 dollar tomorrow in state e. Thus, it is a contingent discount factor. Even if there are no Arrow–Debreu securities, state prices can be defined whenever there are no arbitrage opportunities.

Theorem 2.1 State prices *There are no arbitrage opportunities on markets $(\mathcal{E}, \tilde{a}, p)$ if, and only if, there exists a column[5] vector $q = [q(e)]_{e \in \mathcal{E}}$ of strictly positive elements, such that*

$$p_k = \sum_e q(e) a_k(e) \quad \forall k. \tag{2.2}$$

Vector q is called a vector of state prices. ∎

Corollary 2.1 Discounting with state prices *Let q be a vector of state prices and z a portfolio. Then,*

$$p'z = \sum_e q(e) c_z(e). \tag{2.3}$$

∎

5 This vector, while indexed by the states, is a column vector: Indeed it plays the role of a price.

According to Corollary 2.1,

The price today of a portfolio is equal to the sum of the portfolio incomes discounted by the state prices.

State prices allow the comparison of revenues across various states of nature. They make it possible to find the value today of any *replicable* income. A contingent income vector $(c(e))$ is said to be[6] *replicable* or *spanned* if there is a portfolio z that generates exactly the same payoff in each state e: $c(e) = c_z(e)$. Equivalently, the vector is a linear combination of revenues generated by existing assets. Expression (2.3) can be restated as saying: *The price payable today to obtain a replicable income vector tomorrow is equal to the sum of these incomes discounted by the state prices.*

The qualifier *replicable* is very important here. The terminology "state prices" may be confusing, and may sometimes lead to a misguided application of Eqn (2.3) for computing the "value" of an income vector $(c(e))$ that is not replicable. This point will be clarified when we distinguish between complete and incomplete markets.

Corollary 2.2   State prices and Arrow–Debreu prices   *Let q be a vector of state prices. If there exists a portfolio yielding 1 dollar in state e and 0 dollars otherwise, its price is equal to $q(e)$.*   ∎

Corollary 2.2 assumes that the Arrow–Debreu security contingent on e can be replicated by a portfolio. In this case, $q(e)$ is unique, of course, and can be interpreted as the price to be paid today to obtain 1 dollar in state e. Otherwise, this interpretation is false and, furthermore, $q(e)$ is not uniquely determined. As an example of such a situation, let there be three states of nature and two securities with

$$\tilde{a} = \begin{bmatrix} 1 & 1 & 0 \\ 1 & 1 & -1 \end{bmatrix}.$$

The price of the Arrow–Debreu security associated with state 1 cannot be determined by arbitrage. There is an infinity of state prices, $q(1)$, satisfying the property in Theorem 2.1.

Proof of Theorem 2.1   The demonstration relies on a strong version of the Farkas lemma – see Gale (1960, p. 49), for example, see the following lemma.

---

6 Note that the terminology is identical to that used for a redundant asset: the payoff of a redundant asset is spanned by a portfolio composed of other assets.

Lemma *Let A be a real $K \times L$ matrix. Then only one of the following properties obtains:*

1. *There exists one solution $x \gg 0$ to the equation $Ax = 0$.*
2. *There is one solution, z, in $\mathbb{R}^K$ to the inequality $z'A > 0$.*

Let $A = (\tilde{a}, -p)$ be a $K \times (E + 1)$ matrix created by stacking horizontally $\tilde{a}$ and $-p$. If property 2 from the lemma obtains, there exists a portfolio z, such that $z'\tilde{a} \geq 0$ and $z'p \leq 0$ with some strict inequality. This contradicts the absence of opportunities for arbitrage. Thus, property 1 obtains, and the last element of x can be set equal to 1 without loss of generality. Denoting by q the vector of the first E components, this gives

$$\tilde{a}q - p = 0,$$

which proves Eqn (2.2). The converse is obvious. ∎

1.4 Complete Markets

The notion of *complete markets* is useful for a thorough understanding of the fundamental limitations of valuation by arbitrage. Markets are complete when all revenue configurations are replicable through some portfolio.

Definition 2.2 Complete markets *Given $(\mathcal{E}, \tilde{a})$, markets are complete if, for all $\tilde{c} = [c(e)]_{e \in \mathcal{E}}$, there exists a portfolio z such that $\tilde{c} = \tilde{c}_z$, that is,*

$$c(e) = \sum_{1}^{K} z_k \tilde{a}_k(e) \quad \forall e. \qquad \blacksquare$$

For markets to be complete, there must be at least as many securities as there are states of nature. If there is one security contingent on each state of nature, markets are clearly complete: The income configuration $\tilde{c}$ is obtained by buying $c(e)$ units of each security contingent on state e. The cost of $\tilde{c}$ is thus simply equal to $\sum_e q(e)c(e)$. Indeed, if markets are complete, everything transpires as if such a full system of contingent securities existed, since there exists a portfolio yielding 1 dollar in state e and 0 otherwise. If we denote the value of this portfolio by $q(e)$, we are back to the previous case. Rather than working with the original securities, we can, by a linear transformation, revert to a complete system of contingent securities. The following property, the demonstration of which is left to the reader, characterizes complete markets.

Theorem 2.2   *Given* $(\mathcal{E}, \tilde{a}, p)$,

(1) markets are complete if and only if the rank of $\tilde{a}$ is E; and

(2) complete markets without opportunities for arbitrage are associated with a unique vector of state prices q, and all future income configurations $\tilde{c}$ have a present value given by the discounting formula:

$$\sum_e q(e)c(e).$$ ∎

In practice, eliminating possibly redundant securities, markets are complete if there are exactly as many linearly independent securities as there are states of nature. In this case, the square matrix $\tilde{a}$ has an inverse, and the vector of state prices, if any, is given by $q = \tilde{a}^{-1}p$. Thus, the condition of absence of opportunities for arbitrage is simply written as

$$q = \tilde{a}^{-1}p \gg 0.$$

All financial instruments whose payoffs can be written as a function defined on that state space can thus be valued with state prices.

Example 2.3   Let us return to Example 2.2 in which there are two states of nature h or b that determine the stock price increase ($b < h$). Markets are complete, and the state prices $q(h)$ and $q(b)$, if any, satisfy:

$$1 = q(h)(1+r) + q(b)(1+r),$$
$$S = q(h)S(1+h) + q(b)S(1+b),$$

whence:

$$q(h) = \frac{r-b}{(1+r)(h-b)}, \quad q(b) = \frac{h-r}{(1+r)(h-b)}.$$

The condition that state prices be positive is thus $b < r < h$ (which we could easily have established by reasoning directly).

The price C of a call option of strike price K is simply:

$$C = q(h)[S(1+h) - K] = \frac{r-b}{(1+r)(h-b)}[S(1+h) - K].$$

Here, again, we find Eqn (2.1), as in Example 2.2.   ∎

1.5   Risk-Adjusted Probability

When there exists a risk-free security, the pricing formula in terms of state prices is interpreted as a mathematical expectation with respect to a probability measure calculated by normalizing the state prices. Such a distribution is called *risk adjusted*. This formulation is very popular in finance, particularly in dynamic settings (see the end of this chapter).

By definition, a risk-free security yields the same payoff in all possible states at time 1: $1 + r$ dollars for 1 dollar invested at time 0, where r is the risk-free interest rate. When q is a vector of state prices, Eqn (2.2) applied to the risk-free security yields

$$1 = \sum_e q(e)(1 + r).$$

Since state prices are nonnegative, we can define a probability distribution $\bar{\pi}$ on $\mathcal{E}$ by

$$\bar{\pi}(e) = q(e)(1 + r).$$

Equation (2.2) then becomes

$$p_k = \frac{1}{1 + r} \sum_e \bar{\pi}(e) a_k(e).$$

Anticipating in further chapters, the revenue per dollar invested on security k, $\tilde{a}_k / p_k$, is called the (gross) *return* to security k. Note that the return to the risk-free security is $1 + r$. This immediately yields the following.

Corollary 2.3   Risk-adjusted probability   *If there exists a risk-free security, there are no arbitrage opportunities if and only if there exists a probability distribution $\bar{\pi}$ on $\mathcal{E}$, with positive probability on each state, such that the price of any security is equal to its discounted expected payoff:*

$$p_k = \frac{1}{1 + r} \sum_e \bar{\pi}(e) a_k(e) \quad \forall k,$$

where r is the risk-free rate.

Under this probability, the expected returns to securities are all equal:

$$\sum_e \bar{\pi}(e) \frac{a_k(e)}{p_k} = 1 + r \quad \forall k.$$

■

By construction, the risk-adjusted probability is simply a system of normalized prices. The terminology may be confusing. There is no immediate relationship with the probabilities of occurrence of the various states of nature – these have not yet been defined!

2 Intertemporal Arbitrage

The preceding results extend directly to an intertemporal framework with several periods. First, we specify the time structure.

2.1 Time Structure

There are several periods with a final date T: $t = 0, \ldots, T$. At time T, all securities are sold at given exogenous prices. Transactions may occur, dividends distributed, and information available at discrete times intervening between 0 and T. To formalize this situation, let us assume that there is a set of states of nature on each date from 1 to T.

As stated previously, a state of nature at a time t provides a full description of the economic environment at time t, that is, all known factors that may impact on securities prices and their future dividends at time t. Past events are assumed not to be forgotten. In other words, knowledge of the state at time t includes knowledge of the states through which the economy passed since time 0. In practice, e_t is written as $e_t = (e_{t-1}, \varepsilon_t)$, where ε_t represents the possible shocks occurring at date t. This structure is represented by a *tree* (using graph terminology). Figure 2.2 represents a model, called the binomial model, in which a state is followed by two possible states over four periods. We write $e_t < e_{t+1}$ if state e_t precedes e_{t+1}, and we say that e_{t+1} is a successor to state e_t. A state can only have one predecessor, but typically has several successors. Seen from date 0, the set of all possible states at time T can be very large. For example, if each state has two successors, there will be 2^T final states – as time elapses, information becomes more focused, and the number of possible future final states is divided by two at each date. More generally, the set of all paths emanating from a state e_t until T provides the full range of possible developments. We denote by $\mathcal{E}_t$ the set of all possible states at time t and $\mathcal{E} = \cup \mathcal{E}_t$ the set of all states. This latter set plays an analogous role to the set of states $\mathcal{E}$ (same notation) in the two-period model from the previous section.

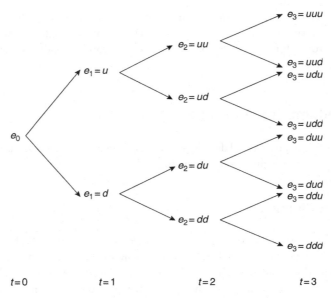

$t=0$ $\qquad$ $t=1$ $\qquad$ $t=2$ $\qquad$ $t=3$

Figure 2.2 A binomial tree structure.

2.2 Instantaneous Arbitrage

First, consider only portfolios constituted at time 0 and held until time T with no modification during the intervening dates.

The payoffs procured from the securities are described by extending the conventions of the two-period model. At all dates t, before the end of times, $t < T$, the income, in terms of the numeraire, paid to the owner of one unit of security k is $d_k(e_t)$ in state e_t. For example, for a bond, $d_k(e_t)$ is equal to the coupon paid in state e_t, possibly increased by reimbursement of the capital, if it matures before T. To account for assets representing claims that extend beyond time T, the income served at the last date is denoted by $a_k(e_T)$: It includes the (exogenously given) resale price at the last date. Thus, in the case of a stock, $d_k(e_t)$ represents the dividend paid out to stockholders in any state e_t prior to liquidation at time T, and $a_k(e_T)$ is the sum of the dividend and the resale price in any state at time T. We use the generic term "dividend" for d even though the terminology is only valid for stocks. For bonds, "coupon" would be the appropriate term.

By an immediate application of the absence of arbitrage opportunities, and in particular of Eqn (2.2) from Theorem 2.1, to all possible states at all times $\mathcal{E}$, there exist strictly positive state prices, $q = [q(e_t)]$, such that

$$p_k(e_0) = \sum_{e_t, t=1,\ldots,T-1} q(e_t)d_k(e_t) + \sum_{e_T} q(e_T)a_k(e_T). \qquad (2.4)$$

The intertemporal structure allows futures markets open at time 0 to be accommodated. For example, consider a futures market for time t for a fixed-income bond that yields a sure income stream, that is, one which is only a function of time, denoted by $d(t)$. This bond can be bought or sold for delivery at time t, at a price f agreed upon today and payable at t. Purchase of a bond on the futures market for t does not cost anything before that date and yields a revenue of $-f$, regardless of the states at time t and $d(\tau)$ for all states at the times τ subsequent to t. Thus, we have

$$f \sum_{e_t \in \mathcal{E}_t} q(e_t) = \sum_{\tau > t} \left[\sum_{e_\tau \in \mathcal{E}_\tau} q(e_\tau) \right] d(\tau).$$

The absence of opportunities for arbitrage provides a condition for consistency of futures prices with spot prices. Moreover, introducing futures markets may contribute to making markets complete. However, the potential is limited since, as in the Example above, futures markets are generally unconditional. Transactions are assumed to occur at time t, whatever state of nature e_t prevails at that time. Nonetheless, we have seen in Chapter 1 how, in the case of certainty, futures transactions are *replicable* by cash-and-carry type strategies, that is, by interventions on spot markets carried out today and at the term. This type of argument can be generalized to the case of uncertainty: the existence of spot markets in the future, *provided that the prices to be established on them are fully anticipated*, allow markets to be *dynamically* completed.

2.3 Dynamic Arbitrage

Assume that the *only* markets in place are the spot markets for securities that are open at all times.[7]

---

7 The introduction of futures markets in parallel to these spot markets would seriously complicate the notation and, to a lesser extent, the analysis. In the particular case of dynamically complete markets,

Thus, the *data* are

1 a succession of states of nature described by a tree;
2 securities $k = 1, \ldots, K$;
3 the sequence of dividends per unit of security $k, d_k(e_t)$ in state e_t, at all intermediate dates, and a final payoff $a_k(e_T)$ for the last date T; and
4 the sequence of security k spot prices $p_k(e_t)$. By convention, $p_k(e_t)$ is the spot price of the security purchased in the state e_t *after* distribution of the dividend $d_k(e_t)$, for all intermediate dates. By convention, as in the static model, the payoff $a_k(e_T)$ at the final date includes the resale price of the security, so that $p_k(e_T)$ can be set to zero.

This information is assumed known by the participants. This means in particular that the spot prices of the securities, $p_k(e_t)$, are perfectly foreseen, or, equivalently, that the prices of the securities are part of the definition of e_t.

The existence of spot markets for securities that are open in all states of nature and the assumption of *perfect foresight on prices* on these markets provide the framework for valuation by dynamic arbitrage. It is the most commonly used, both for discrete time (as here) and for continuous time. A portfolio constituted today is not necessarily maintained unaltered until time T. In particular, a stochastic revenue stream may be replicated with a program of acquisitions and sales during the intervening periods on the markets that will open, which is called a *dynamic portfolio strategy*.

Definition 2.3 *A portfolio strategy z defines the portfolio $z(e_t) = [z_k(e_t)]$ held in each state e_t after the transactions. Everything is liquidated at T, $z(e_T) = 0$ for all final states e_T.*

The value of the strategy z at time 0 is that of the initial portfolio:

$$p(e_0)'z(e_0) = \sum_{k=1}^{K} z_k(e_0)p_k(e_0),$$

and the income *generated in a state e_t at date t, $t = 1, \ldots, T - 1$, is given by*

$$c_z(e_t) = \sum_{k=1}^{K} [z_k(e_{t-1}) - z_k(e_t)]p_k(e_t) + \sum_{k=1}^{K} z_k(e_{t-1})d_k(e_t),$$

introduced further on, all futures transactions on an existing underlying security can be replicated by a sequence of cash-and-carry type operations on the spot market. Futures markets are thus redundant.

and at date T,

$$c_z(e_T) = \sum_{k=1}^{K} [z_k(e_{T-1})] a_k(e_T)$$

where e_{t-1} is the unique predecessor of e_t. ∎

Example 2.4 Some strategies, called *elementary* strategies, are very simple. They involve intervention only if a given state e_t occurs, and liquidating the purchased portfolio on the following date. If the portfolio consists of one unit of security k, the strategy viewed from time 0 consists of two opposing operations on the spot market for security k: At time t, if the state is e_t, one unit of the security is bought, and it is then resold on the following date whatever happens.

More generally, an elementary strategy is characterized by a vector $\theta(e_t)$ in $\mathbb{R}^K$ that describes the composition of the portfolio, and is written as

$$z(e_t) = \theta(e_t), \quad z(e_s) = 0 \text{ for } e_s \neq e_t.$$

The income generated by this strategy is[8]

$$c(e_t) = -\sum_{k=1}^{K} p_k(e_t)\theta_k(e_t), \tag{2.5}$$

$$c(e_{t+1}) = \sum_{k=1}^{K} [p_k(e_{t+1}) + d_k(e_{t+1})]\theta_k(e_t) \quad \text{if } e_{t+1} > e_t \tag{2.6}$$

$$c(e_s) = 0 \text{ for any other state.} \tag{2.7}$$

∎

An arbitrage opportunity is a strategy with an initial value that is negative or nil and that generates nonnegative revenues at all times and in all future states, with at least one strict inequality.

Definition 2.4 *An opportunity for arbitrage is a strategy z such that $c_z(e_t) \geq 0$ for all e_t, all $t > 0$, and $p(e_0)'z(e_0) \leq 0$, with at least one strict inequality.* ∎

---

8 The formula is valid for $t < T - 1$. When $t = T - 1$, the income generated by the strategy at date T is

$$c(e_T) = \sum_{k=1}^{K} a_k(e_T)\theta_k(e_{T-1}).$$

Intuitively, a short-term arbitrage opportunity in state e_t, between t and $t + 1$, should translate into an intertemporal opportunity for arbitrage. In addition, according to the principles of static arbitrage, the absence of opportunities for arbitrage in the short term implies the existence of state prices for the direct successors of e_t, e_{t+1}. We shall demonstrate that this is sufficient for constructing state prices as of time 0. A necessary and sufficient condition for the absence of opportunities for intertemporal arbitrage is the absence of short-term arbitrage opportunities in all states of nature.

Theorem 2.3 *Assume an economy in which the only markets are spot markets and in which prices are perfectly anticipated conditionally on the states of nature.*

1 *The three following properties are equivalent:*
  (a) There are no opportunities for arbitrage.
  (b) There exists a vector $q = [q(e_t), e_t \in \mathcal{E}]$ of strictly positive elements such that, for any strategy z,

$$p(e_0)'z(e_0) = \sum_{e_t, t=1,\ldots,T} q(e_t)c_z(e_t). \qquad (2.8)$$

  q is called the vector of state prices discounted at time 0.
  (c) For any state $e_t, t \geq 0$, there exists a vector $[q(e_{t+1}|e_t), e_{t+1} \in \mathcal{E}]$, of strictly positive prices for all direct successors of e_t, such that, for all k:

$$p_k(e_t) = \sum_{e_{t+1}|e_{t+1}>e_t} q(e_{t+1}|e_t)[p_k(e_{t+1}) + d_k(e_{t+1})],$$

$$t = 0, \ldots, T - 2 \qquad (2.9)$$

$$p_k(e_{T-1}) = \sum_{e_T|e_T>e_{T-1}} q(e_T|e_{T-1})a_k(e_T).$$

  The vector $[q(e_{t+1}|e_t)]$ gives prices for the successor states of e_t discounted in e_t.
2 *Given discounted state prices $[q(e_{t+1}|e_t)]$ for all e_t, the prices defined by*

$$q(e_{t+1}) = q(e_1|e_0) \cdots q(e_{t+1}|e_t), \qquad (2.10)$$

where $(e_0, e_1, \ldots, e_{t+1})$ is the unique path from e_0 to e_{t+1}, are state prices.
  Conversely, given state prices $[q(e_t)]$, the formula:

$$q(e_{t+1}|e_t) = \frac{q(e_{t+1})}{q(e_t)}$$

defines prices for the successor states of e_t for all e_t. ∎

The interpretation of Eqn (2.8) is the same as in the two-period model: *the value of a portfolio strategy in e_0 is equal to the discounted value of the revenue it generates.*

Similarly, the discounted state prices at some date, knowing the state e_t, link the price of a security with the income it generates at time $t + 1$. According to Eqn (2.9), *the price of security k in state e_t is equal to the discounted value, measured with the discounted state prices in e_t, of the income (dividends + resale price) it generates at time $t + 1$.*

Proof of Theorem 2.3

1 (a) $\Rightarrow$ (c) This results from applying Theorem 2.1 to the elementary strategies of state e_t.

(c) $\Rightarrow$ (b) Let us define the prices $[q(e_t)]$ by Eqn (2.10). We multiply (2.9) by $q(e_t)\theta_k(e_t)$ and sum over k. This yields:

$$q(e_t)[p(e_t)'\theta(e_t)] = \sum_{e_{t+1}|e_{t+1}>e_t} q(e_{t+1})[p(e_{t+1}) + d(e_{t+1})]'\theta(e_t),$$

$$t = 0, \ldots, T - 2$$

$$q(e_{T-1})[p(e_{T-1})'\theta(e_{T-1})] = \sum_{e_T|e_T>e_{T-1}} q(e_T)a(e_T)'\theta(e_{T-1}).$$

Using (2.5), we see that (2.8) obtains for all elementary strategies. Observe that any portfolio strategy z is a sum of elementary strategies $\theta(e_\tau)$, setting

$$\theta(e_0) = z(e_0), \quad \theta(e_t) = z(e_t) - z(e_{t-1}) \quad \text{for } t > 0.$$

By linear combination, (2.8) is true of all portfolio strategies. This also demonstrates that q is a system of state prices.

(b) $\Rightarrow$ (a) directly.

2 The first part has already been demonstrated. Conversely, applying (2.8) to elementary strategies associated with state e_t, dividing by $q(e_t)$, yields (2.9). ∎

Equation (2.8) allows any revenue stream that can be replicated by a portfolio strategy to be valued. Drawing on the static model, this leads to the introduction of the notion of *dynamically complete markets*. In such markets, any income stream can be replicated by a portfolio strategy. Consequently, (2.8) permits a rigorous interpretation of state prices, on one hand, and of the valuation of any financial instrument, on the other.

Definition 2.5 *Markets are* dynamically complete *if any income stream,* $(c(e_t), t \geq 1)$*, can be replicated by a portfolio strategy: for any stream* c*, there exists* z *such that*

$$c(e_t) = c_z(e_t) \ \forall e_t, \ t = 1, \ldots, T. \qquad ■$$

Let us interpret state prices in the case of complete markets. According to (2.8), the cost of a strategy that yields 1 dollar in state e_t and nil in any other state is necessarily equal to $q(e_t)$. Consequently, $q(e_t)$ is the price to be paid at $t = 0$ to obtain 1 dollar in state e_t. It is strictly positive and uniquely defined. When markets are incomplete, this interpretation is only valid if such a strategy exists. The most important practical point is that markets are dynamically complete whenever there are enough securities in each state to generate any vector of state-contingent revenues for the *immediately* succeeding states. Compared with the static perspective at the initial date, which requires considering all paths that the economy might follow, the use of dynamic strategies allows a considerable reduction in the number of securities required for complete markets. When it is a matter of a derivative written on an underlying security, the relevant states correspond to the various prices of the security, which are naturally organized into a tree describing the possible evolution of this price. If markets are complete in each period – and this condition imposes a strong constraint on the choice of the tree – it is technically simple to assign a price to each new derivative for each price stream. We shall illustrate these techniques with the binomial model of Cox et al. (1979).

Valuing an Option in the Binomial Model

We take up Example 2.2 extended to several periods. In each period, a risk-free security with a constant return of r between two successive dates and the risky stock can be traded. A state e_t is followed by two successors, (e_t, h) and (e_t, b), corresponding to stock price growth rates of h and b, respectively. In other words, if $S(e_t)$ is the stock price in state e_t, its price will be $S(e_t)(1 + h)$ in state (e_t, h) or $S(e_t)(1 + b)$ in state (e_t, b).

Consider a derivative on this stock, say a European option maturing at T with a strike price of K. From the perspective of time 0, there is a large number of final states. However, markets are dynamically complete: Since each state is followed by two successors, the risky stock and the risk-free security suffice to complete the markets (their payoffs are never proportional since b and h differ).

To value the option using (2.8), we need to evaluate the state prices. For this, it is convenient to first compute the state prices between two successive dates, and then apply (2.10).

1 *Calculation of the state prices $q(e_{t+1}|e_t)$*   We apply (2.9) to the two assets in e_t, knowing that the two following states are characterized by h and b:

$$1 = q(h|e_t)(1 + r) + q(b|e_t)(1 + r),$$

$$S(e_t) = q(h|e_t)S(e_t)(1 + h) + q(b|e_t)S(e_t)(1 + b).$$

Thus, it follows that state prices are independent of e_t and are given by the same expression as in the two periods model in Example 2.2:

$$q(h) = \frac{r - b}{(1 + r)(h - b)}, \quad q(b) = \frac{h - r}{(1 + r)(h - b)}.$$

2 *Calculation of the state prices q discounted in 0*   A state e_t is characterized by the succession of growth rates, high or low, realized from date 0 up to t. The state price, which is the product of the intermediate prices, is equal to $q(h)^i q(b)^{t-i}$ if there were exactly i times h and $t - i$ times b between 0 and t. Consequently, it is independent of the order in which the jumps occurred.

3 *The price at $t = 0$ of an option maturing at T and with a strike price of K*   The option does not distribute intermediate dividends, and at time T, it pays out $[S(1 + h)^i(1 + b)^{T-i} - K]^+$ (we denote $\alpha^+ = \max(\alpha, 0)$) if there were i high yields between 0 and T. Setting $\bar{\pi} = (r - b)/(h - b)$ and grouping all the states in which the yield was high i times, we obtain

$$C = \frac{1}{(1 + r)^T} \sum_{i = 0,\dots,T} \frac{T!}{(T - i)!i!} \bar{\pi}^i (1 - \bar{\pi})^{T-i}$$

$$\times [S(1 + h)^i(1 + b)^{T-i} - K]^+,$$

where $\bar{\pi}$ can be interpreted as a probability of occurrence of h, since it is between 0 and 1.

In the Cox–Ross–Rubinstein model, the option price is equal to the expectation, given the (risk-adjusted) probability $\bar{\pi}$, of its final value discounted at the risk-free rate.

This result can be generalized when the risk-free rate varies with the state of nature (see the following section).

4 *Hedging strategies*   The use of state prices allows the option price to be computed very easily. Often a financial institution also wishes to calculate the portfolio strategy that replicates the option. Indeed, having sold the option and

unwilling to assume the associated risk, a replicating portfolio strategy serves as a hedge: It exactly gives the payoffs that the institution is required to pay to the option holders. The following algorithm accomplishes this:

(a) Starting from the "end" of the tree, in any state e_{T-1} preceding maturity, compute the value of the option $C(e_{T-1})$ in these states and the portfolio $z(e_{T-1})$ that replicates it.

(b) For any state e_{T-2} at $T-2$, we know from step (a) the option price in the two successor states: $C(e_{T-2}, h)$ and $C(e_{T-2}, b)$. The value of the option in e_{T-2} follows:

$$C(e_{T-2}) = q(h)C(e_{T-2}, h) + q(b)C(e_{T-2}, b),$$

This is also the value of the portfolio $z(e_{T-2})$ that will be worth $C(e_{T-2}, h)$ and $C(e_{T-2}, b)$ in the two following states. This portfolio permits the purchase of the replicating portfolio in the two succeeding states.

(c) Continue "up" the tree in the same fashion until time 0.

This Example illustrates two points:

1 The usefulness of the valuation formula (2.8): If we only seek to value the option, it is much simpler to compute the state prices than to replicate the option. The valuation, however, is only valid when such a replicate exists, which follows automatically if markets are dynamically complete.

2 The flexibility provided by the algorithm: It allows to price and replicate all derivatives written on the stock. For example, consider an American option (recall that such an option can be exercised at various dates before maturity). In each state, compare the value of the option if it is not exercised with the profit generated by exercising it immediately: This simultaneously determines the value of the option as the greater of these two terms, and the optimal exercise strategy.

Example 2.5 *Valuation of an option with a sliding strike price* The binomial tree allows the valuation of options with complex characteristics, known as "exotics." Here we propose the valuation of an option on stocks with the following features:

1 The strike price is periodically redefined as a percentage of the stock price, unless it reaches a floor fixed at the time of issue.

2 The option can be exercised at certain predetermined periods.

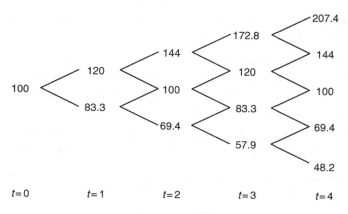

$t=0$ $t=1$ $t=2$ $t=3$ $t=4$

Figure 2.3 Binomial model.

Figure 2.3 represents the possible evolution of the stock price over four periods, in which we have set $h = 0.20$ and $1 + b = 1/(1 + h)$. If the risk-free rate r is equal to 0.05, the risk-adjusted probability of the high state $\bar{\pi}$ is equal to 0.591.

Consider an option with a strike price of 95 at time 0, revisable at $t = 2$, and whose new value will be the greater of 90 (the floor) or 95 percent of the stock price. The option can only be exercised on even dates, $t = 2, 4 \ldots$ and at the strike price determined two periods previously. Thus, 95 is the strike price that will prevail if it is exercised at time 2. At this time, the strike price (which is to be exercised at $t = 4$) is adjusted to 136.8 if $S = 144$, maintained at 95 if $S = 100$, and lowered to 90 if $S = 69.4$.

The calculation of the option value proceeds in several steps, starting from the end of the tree. The retention value of the option at a given date is defined as the value yielded by the option if it is not exercised immediately.

Step 1: We start at $t = 2$ in one of the three possible states.

Assuming that we keep the option, it can only be exercised at $t = 4$ and at a known strike price. Thus, computing the retention value is a simple matter.

This allows the exercise strategy to be determined at $t = 2$. To know whether it is preferable to exercise the option immediately or hold on to it, all that is needed is to compare the retention value with the profit yielded by exercising it now.

For example, assume that $S = 144$. The retention value is equal to

$$\bar{\pi}^2(207.4 - 136.8) + 2\bar{\pi}(1 - \bar{\pi})(144 - 136.8) = 28.14,$$

while exercising it immediately yields $144 - 95 = 49$: The option is exercised! Similarly, we find that

1 if $S = 100$: the retention value, $\bar{\pi}^2(144 - 95) + 2\bar{\pi}(1 - \bar{\pi})(100 - 95) = 19.53$, is larger than the exercise value, 5 (the option is not exercised); and
2 if $S = 69.4$: the retention value, $\bar{\pi}^2(100 - 95) = 1.75$, is larger than the exercise value, 0 (the option is not exercised), respectively.

The option value at $t = 2$, before possibly being exercised, is the maximum of the two quantities, or 49 if $S = 144$, 19.53 if $S = 100$, and 1.75 if $S = 69.4$.

Step 2: We can now easily compute the option price at $t = 0$. It is the discounted sum, computed with the state prices, of its value at time 2:

$$\bar{\pi}^2 49 + 2\bar{\pi}(1 - \bar{\pi})19.53 + (1 - \bar{\pi})(1 - \bar{\pi})1.75 = 26.98. \qquad \blacksquare$$

2.4 Probabilistic Formulation: Risk-Adjusted Probability

The notion of risk-adjusted probability introduced in the two-period model (Section 1.5) is particularly useful in a dynamic framework. Indeed, after normalization, the formula (2.10) for constructing the state prices is transformed into the Bayesian formula for conditional probabilities.

Consider a T-period model. Assume that there exists a short-term risk-free security at all dates. Its return between t and $t + 1$, knowing the state e_t, is independent of the successor e_{t+1} of e_t and is denoted by $r(e_t)$. Note that $r(e_t)$, which is the short-term *risk-free* rate, depends upon state e_t and may vary over time: The security is riskless only between two successive periods, once the state is known.

Theorem 2.4 *Assume an economy with a risk-free short-term security in each period. The three following properties are equivalent:*

1 *There are no opportunities for arbitrage;*
2 *There exists a strictly positive probability distribution $\bar{\pi}$ for the tree, such that the value of any strategy is equal to the expectation under $\bar{\pi}$ of the discounted sum at the risk-free rate for the future incomes it generates:*

$$p(e_0)'z(e_0) = \sum_{e_t, t=1,\ldots,T} E_{\bar{\pi}} \prod_{\tau=1}^{t} \frac{1}{1 + r(e_{\tau-1})} c_z(e_t);$$

3 *There exists a strictly positive probability distribution for the transition from any state* e_t *to its successors* $\bar{\pi}(.|e_t)$ *such that, for any k and* e_t,

$$p_k(e_t) = \frac{1}{1 + r(e_t)} E_{\bar{\pi}}[p_k(e_{t+1}) + a_k(e_{t+1})|e_t], \quad t = 0, \dots, T - 2$$

$$p_k(e_{T-1}) = \frac{1}{1 + r(e_{T-1})} E_{\bar{\pi}}[a_k(e_T)|e_{T-1}].$$

$$(2.11)$$

∎

Comments: As in the two-period model, $\bar{\pi}$ is called the risk-adjusted probability. This probability is particularly useful in the dynamic model and in continuous time, which is obtained in the limit when the interval separating successive transactions is allowed to tend toward zero. In this situation, powerful tools developed for stochastic processes can be used.

For a security k that does not distribute any dividends before the final period, assuming that the interest rate is constant and equal to r, Eqn (2.11) is often written as

$$(1 + r)^{-t} p_k(e_t) = E_{\bar{\pi}}[(1 + r)^{-t-1} p_k(e_{t+1})|e_t].$$

The term $(1 + r)^{-t} p_k(e_t)$ is the security price in state e_t counted in terms of dollars at time 0, for short the discounted price. Thus, the above expression says that the expectation at time $t + 1$ of the discounted security price, conditional on the state at date t, is equal to its value in state e_t. The risk of loss compensates for the chance of profit in mathematical expectation. In mathematical terms, the discounted security price is a martingale.[9]

Proof of Theorem 2.4 All that is required is Theorem 2.3 and to define $\bar{\pi}$ from the state prices $[q(e_t)]$ with

$$\bar{\pi}(e_t) = \frac{q(e_t)}{\sum_{\text{states at time } t} q(e)},$$

and the transition probabilities from the transition prices with

$$\bar{\pi}(e_{t+1}|e_t) = q(e_{t+1}|e_t)[1 + r(e_t)].$$

∎

9 Mathematically, a stochastic process $\tilde{x}_t$ is a martingale if the expectation of x_{t+1} conditional on the information available at time t is equal to x_t:

$$E_t x_{t+1} = x_t.$$

BIBLIOGRAPHICAL NOTE

Arbitrage theory was pioneered in the works of Ross (1976a,b, 1978), who under-stood the importance of valuing a security, of being able to replicate it with existing assets. Its application to options can be found in Cox et al. (1979). Our presenta-tion of the static version in this chapter resembles that in Varian (1987), though we also call on a strong version of the separation theorem developed in Gale (1960). Cox et al. (1985) developed the dynamic interpretation in discrete time. We delib-erately ignored the technical difficulties associated with continuous time models in order to focus on the basic concepts and economic principles. Readers who wish to learn more on this subject are referred to Demange and Rochet (1992) or Duffie (1988). Finally, Hull (1997) is a reference on valuing derivatives and the associated hedging issues.

Cox, J., J. Ingersoll, and S. Ross (1985). "A theory of the term structure of interest rates," *Econometrica*, **53**, 385–408.

Cox, J., S. Ross, and M. Rubinstein (1979). "Option pricing : a simplified approach," *Journal of Financial Economics*, 7, 229–263.

Demange, G. and J.-C. Rochet (1997/1992). *Méthodes mathématiques de la finance*, 2nd edn, Economica, Paris.

Duffie, D. (1988). *Security markets: stochastic models*, Academic Press, San Diego.

Gale, D. (1960). *The theory of linear economic models*, McGraw-Hill, New York.

Hull, J.C. (1997). *Options, futures, and other derivatives*, Prentice Hall, NJ.

Ross, S. (1976a). "Risk, return, and arbitrage." In I. Friend and J. Bicksler, eds., *Risk and return in finance*, Ballinger, Cambridge, 189–218.

Ross, S. (1976b). "Options and efficiency," *Quarterly Journal of Economics*, **90**, 75–89.

Ross, S. (1978). "A simple approach to the valuation of risky streams," *Journal of Business*, **51**(3), 453–475.

Varian, H.R. (1987). "The arbitrage principle in financial economics," *The Journal of Economic Perspectives*, **1**(2), 55–72.

Exercises

2.1 *Options and complete markets*   The notion of complete markets is essential to valuation by arbitrage. The following examples are designed to illustrate the notion that it may be possible to complete markets by authorizing the negotiation of options on preexisting assets.

1 In a two-period model with three states of nature e_1, e_2, and e_3, consider a single asset with payoffs $\tilde{a}_1$ given by (4,3,1).

Show that the introduction of two call options with different strike prices on the asset allows the market to be completed.

How would this result be changed if the revenue a_1 in state e_3 was no longer 1, but 3? Explain your results.

2 Consider a second scenario in which the market is comprised of two assets. The states of nature in the second period are e_1, e_2, e_3, and e_4, and the revenue vectors are

	e_1	e_2	e_3	e_4
a_1	1	1	2	2
a_2	1	2	1	2

Is it possible to complete this market by introducing options on a_1 and a_2? Explain your results.

3 Prove that it is possible to constitute a portfolio (or fund) with the two assets so that call options on this fund allow for completion of the market.

Note: Question 1 illustrates the following, more general, result: Options on the securities can complete market only if the securities allow the different states of nature to be distinguished. Question 2 reveals that the converse is not trivial. Indeed, the condition that the income from the available securities allows a distinction to be made between the various states is necessary and sufficient for the existence of a *portfolio* of initial securities for which call (or put) options allow the market to be completed (see Ross 1976b).

2.2 Consider a firm whose underlying value per share increases either by h or b between $t = 0$ and $t = 1$ and between $t = 1$ and $t = 2$, where $h > b$. At date 1 it pays out a dividend of d, so that if the share price at $t = 0$ is 1, the share price after the dividend is paid evolves as follows:

$$p(e_0) = 1$$

$$p(e_1) = (1 + h - d)$$

$$p(e_2) = (1 + b - d)$$

$$p(e_3) = (1 + h - d)(1 + h)$$

$$p(e_4) = (1 + h - d)(1 + b)$$

$$p(e_5) = (1 + b - d)(1 + h)$$

$$p(e_6) = (1 + b - d)(1 + b)$$

$$t = 0 \qquad\qquad t = 1 \qquad\qquad\qquad t = 2$$

The risk-free interest rate is r.

1 Compute the state prices associated with e_1 and e_2, at time $t = 0$. Verify that they are independent of the dividend. Under what conditions are there no opportunities for arbitrage? Similarly, at e_1 and e_2, compute the state prices of the two possible successor states.

2 Consider a call option that can be exercised at $t = 2$, with a strike price of K, and with $(1 + h - d)(1 + b) < K < (1 + h - d)(1 + h)$. Find an expression for its price at $t = 0$.

3 Consider a call option that can be exercised at $t = 1$ *before* distribution of the dividend, or at $t = 2$ at the strike price K. Under what condition on d is it advantageous to exercise this option at $t = 1$?

4 Compute both option prices at $t = 0$ for

$$h = 0.05, \quad b = 0.01, \quad r = 0.02, \quad d = 0.04, \quad K = 1.04.$$

2.3 *Arbitrage and transaction costs*   The organization of markets creates operating costs that are supported by the participants. The purpose of this exercise is to examine some of the interactions between these costs and arbitrage operations.

Consider a two-period model in which there are two states of nature and two securities. The first security is risk free indexed with 0. To simplify, the interest rate is nil, so that 1 dollar invested in it yields 1 dollar in each state of nature. The other security yields $a(1)$ in state 1 and $a(2)$ in state 2, with $a(2) > a(1) > 0$. The purchase price of this security is denoted by p_1^+, which may be greater than its sale price, p_1^-.

We wish to value another security, defined by a contingent revenue stream $[b(1), b(2)]$ in the two states of nature, where $b(2) > b(1)$. This security is exchanged on a market with no transaction costs: There is a single buy and sell price, p_2.

1 In the absence of opportunities for arbitrage, calculate the state prices $q(e_1)$ and $q(e_2)$ when $p_1^+ = p_1^-$. Use this to derive the price of security 2. Now assume that $p_1^+ > p_1^-$.

(a) Determine the portfolio (z_0, z_1) of assets 0 and 1 that replicates the asset b. Verify that $z_1 > 0$.

(b) In the absence of opportunities for arbitrage, determine upper and lower bounds $\bar{p}_2$ and $\underline{p}_2$ for the price of asset 2.

2 Here we examine how the Arrow–Debreu formula for asset valuation (Theorem 2.2) can be extended.

(a) Calculate the bounds for the prices of the Arrow–Debreu assets: $(q^+(e_i), q^-(e_i))$ for the asset yielding 1 in state i.

(b) Assume that $b(1) > 0$. Show that the pricing formula:

$$p_2^+ = q^+(e_1)b(1) + q^+(e_2)b(2), \, p_2^- = q^-(e_1)b(1) + q^-(e_2)b(2),$$

yields upper and lower bounds for the asset price, but that these bounds can be improved upon.

part 2

Exchanging Risk

Before delving into the heart of the material, it is useful to briefly review an intertemporal economy without uncertainty. The determinants of the demand for savings, as well as the optimality properties of the equilibrium on the market for loans, are briefly recapitulated in the first section. This allows us to explain the problems encountered when future is uncertain and to put the material in the following chapters into perspective.

1 The Model with Certainty

We adopt the simplest possible framework: There is a single good[1] that cannot be stored and is available "today," at $t = 0$, and "tomorrow," at $t = 1$. Consumers live during both periods. They have resources during each period. To illustrate, think of current resources as wage income and future resources as pension income. Future resources are assumed known in the current period with no shadow of uncertainty. Some exchanges between the members of this economy are likely to be profitable. Some expect to have a more generous pension income than required, while confronting substantial child-rearing costs in the present. They wish to have part of their future resources available today. Conversely, others are worried about their future and want to save. A market for lending and borrowing allows mutually beneficial exchanges between these two periods. To describe the functioning of this market, we first examine the behavior of a typical individual, and then how equilibrium is established.

1.1 Individual Demand for Savings

Consider an individual with resources ω_0 at $t = 0$ who receives ω_1 at $t = 1$ with certainty.

Lending and borrowing is possible at the rate r, $r > -1$. Savings of z, where negative z indicates borrowing, yields the consumption profile (c_0, c_1) at times 0 and 1:

$$c_0 = \omega_0 - z, \quad c_1 = \omega_1 + (1 + r)z. \tag{P2.1}$$

1 The analysis can be easily extended to the case of several goods, in the following setup. First, in addition to the market of lending and borrowing the numeraire, spot markets for all the goods exist at both periods. Second, the relative prices that prevail at $t = 1$ are correctly anticipated.

Eliminating z, the budget constraints for each date (P2.1) *imply* that the profile satisfies

$$c_0 + \frac{c_1}{1+r} = \omega_0 + \frac{\omega_1}{1+r}. \tag{P2.2}$$

This equation is known as the *intertemporal budget constraint*. The price of one unit of the good at time 1, in terms of the good at time 0, equals $1/(1+r)$. To increase consumption by one unit at time 1, $1/(1+r)$ units of consumption must be forfeited at time 0. The term on the left-hand side of the budget constraint is the value of the consumption profile, while the right-hand side is that of the income profile. Since the good at time 0 serves as the numeraire, we say that these values are *discounted at time 0*. *If there are no limits on savings or borrowing*, any profile satisfying the intertemporal budget constraint can be obtained by adjusting savings, z.

Individuals have *preferences* that describe their relative tastes over current and future consumption (c_0, c_1). Faced with the rate r, a consumer chooses the consumption profile he prefers from among those satisfying the intertemporal budget constraint (P2.2): Such a profile is called *optimal*.

Preferences are represented by a real-valued utility function $U(c_0, c_1)$ defined on $\mathbb{R}_+^2$. The function U is assumed increasing in all arguments, continuously differentiable, and strictly concave. Often it is also assumed to be additive across periods of the form

$$U(c_0, c_1) = u(c_0) + \delta u(c_1).$$

Albeit restrictive, this formulation is convenient, especially when generalizing the model to more than two periods. The *psychological discount factor*, δ, positive and less than one, captures the consumer's preference for the present. The *psychological discount rate j* is defined by:

$$\delta = \frac{1}{1+j}.$$

A consumption profile (c_0, c_1) is *optimal* when it maximizes utility $U(c_0, c_1)$ subject to the intertemporal budget constraint (P2.2). An optimal profile is characterized by (P2.2) and the equality between the marginal rates of substitution and the ratio of the good price during the two periods[2]:

$$\frac{U_0'(c_0, c_1)}{U_1'(c_0, c_1)} = 1 + r, \qquad\qquad\qquad \text{(P2.3)}$$

where $U_t'(c_0, c_1)$, the partial derivative $\partial U(c_0, c_1)/\partial c_t$, is the marginal utility of consumption c_t, for t equal to 0 or 1.

The rationale for this property of the optimal consumption profile is as follows. Consider a consumption profile (c_0, c_1) that satisfies (P2.2). A variation in consumption of $[dc_0, -(1+r)dc_0]$ satisfies the budget constraint and, for small variations, translates into a change in utility approximately equal to

$$[U_0'(c_0, c_1) - U_1'(c_0, c_1)(1+r)]dc_0.$$

If the term within the square brackets is positive (negative), the consumer will increase (decrease) consumption today. Condition (P2.3) is necessary. It is also sufficient owing to the strict concavity of the function U: Together with the budget constraint (P2.2), condition (P2.3) provides a unique solution to the consumer's program.

In the (c_0, c_1) plane, the consumer's budget constraint is the line through the point $\Omega = (\omega_0, \omega_1)$, with slope equal to $-(1+r)$ (Figure P2.1). The optimum occurs at the point of tangency of the indifference curve with the budget line.

In the case of additive utility, (P2.3) simplifies to

$$\frac{u'(c_0)}{u'(c_1)} = \frac{1+r}{1+j}. \qquad\qquad\qquad \text{(P2.4)}$$

Since marginal utility is decreasing, we have

$$c_0 > c_1 \iff r < j.$$

Current consumption exceeds future consumption if, and only if, the interest rate r is less than the psychological discount rate j.

An increase of dr in the interest rate has several impacts – not necessarily all in the same direction – on consumption today and its complement, savings. Traditionally, a distinction is made between an *income* effect and a *substitution* effect. To see this, the *compensating variation* dW is defined as the change in discounted

---

2 We only consider situations in which there is no corner solution, that is, the consumer chooses strictly positive levels of consumption in each of the two periods. This is the case if the utility function satisfies the Inada condition: For all $c_1 > 0$ $\lim_{c \to 0} U_0'(c, c_1) = \infty$ and for all $c_0 > 0$ $\lim_{c \to 0} U_1'(c_0, c) = \infty$.

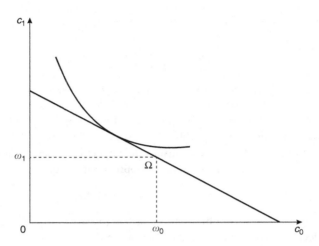

Figure P2.1　The consumer.

income necessary to enable the consumer to maintain the same consumption profile as in the reference situation. Differentiating (P2.2) yields

$$dW = \frac{\omega_1 - c_1}{(1+r)^2}dr = \frac{c_0 - \omega_0}{(1+r)^2}dr.$$

dW is negative when the consumer is saving (i.e., consumption in period 1 exceeds income in the same period) because, for a given level of savings, more can be consumed during the second period if the interest rate increases. Similarly, dW is positive when he is dissaving. To compute the variation in consumption levels (dc_0, dc_1), we differentiate[3] (P2.2) and (P2.4) in terms of dr. This yields:

$$dc_0 + \frac{dc_1}{1+r} = -dW,$$

$$u''(c_0)dc_0 - \frac{1+r}{1+j}u''(c_1)dc_1 = \frac{u'(c_1)}{1+j}dr,$$

3 Formally, the implicit function theorem applied to the system comprised of (P2.2) and (P2.4) yields the consumption profile in terms of the exogenous variables of the model.

and, after eliminating dc_1,

$$\left[u''(c_0) + \frac{(1+r)^2}{1+j} u''(c_1) \right] dc_0 = \frac{u'(c_1)}{1+j} dr - \frac{(1+r)^2}{1+j} u''(c_1) dW.$$

The variation in current consumption is decomposed into the two terms on the right-hand side of the above equation. The first is the *substitution* effect. It follows from the equality of the marginal rate of substitution with the price ratio between consumptions today and tomorrow, as given by (P2.4). As the interest rate increases, its impact is always to reduce consumption today or, equivalently, to increase savings. The second is the *income* effect. When the consumer is dissaving ($dW > 0$), it operates in the same direction as the substitution effect; hence, a rise in the interest rate unambiguously increases savings. In the more common case of positive savings, the two effects work in opposite directions, and any further conclusions require more information on preferences and the intertemporal structure of resources (we will illustrate this with isoelastic functions).

1.2 Equilibrium, Optimum

Now consider the economy as a whole. Consumers are indexed with i and characterized by their resources at both periods (ω_0^i, ω_1^i) and preferences U^i.

Definition P2.1 *Equilibrium is given by an interest rate r and a consumption profile* (c_0^i, c_1^i) *for each individual i, such that*

1 (c_0^i, c_1^i) *maximizes U^i subject to the budget constraint of agent i;*
2 *the scarcity constraints are satisfied:*

$$\sum_i c_0^i = \sum_i \omega_0^i \quad and \quad \sum_i c_1^i = \sum_i \omega_1^i. \qquad \blacksquare$$

When one of the scarcity constraints is satisfied, the fact that all the individual budget constraints are met ensures that the other scarcity constraint is satisfied as well (Walras' law). The definition can be interpreted as describing equilibrium on the market for borrowing and lending at time 0: Agent i's savings are equal to $\omega_0^i - c_0^i$, and aggregate borrowing equals aggregate lending.

It is easy to demonstrate that an equilibrium exists. Furthermore, the allocation of resources in equilibrium is Pareto optimal: It is impossible, given scarce resources, to increase everyone's utility. The proof of the optimality of the equilibrium is very simple: If one individual's utility is increased, the discounted value of his consumption profile (as calculated at the equilibrium discount rate r) must be greater than at equilibrium. To improve everyone's position vis-à-vis the equilibrium situation, it is thus necessary that the value of each person's consumption exceeds that of his available resources. Summing over all individuals, the value of aggregate consumption exceeds that of available resources, which is impossible at a feasible allocation.

Example P2.1 Consider a consumer with an additive utility function U, where u is given by

$$u(c) = \frac{c^{1-\gamma}}{1-\gamma}, \quad \text{if } \gamma > 0, \ \gamma \neq 1,$$

or

$$u(c) = \ln c, \quad \text{if } \gamma = 1.$$

The case $\gamma = 1$ corresponds to the logarithmic specification. The function u is *isoelastic*, since its elasticity with respect to consumption, that is, the derivative of its log with respect to $\log c$, is constant – independent of the level of consumption. Optimal consumption is characterized by (P2.2) and

$$\frac{u'(c_0)}{u'(c_1)} = \frac{c_0^{-\gamma}}{c_1^{-\gamma}} = \frac{1+r}{1+j},$$

which yields

$$c_0 = \alpha(r)\left(\omega_0 + \frac{\omega_1}{1+r}\right), \quad \text{where } \alpha(r) = \left[1 + \frac{1}{1+r}\left(\frac{1+r}{1+j}\right)^{1/\gamma}\right]^{-1}.$$

$$(P2.5)$$

Current consumption is a fraction of intertemporal income, with a factor of proportionality equal to $\alpha(r)$.

If $\gamma < 1, \alpha(r)$ decreases with r: Current consumption declines and savings rise with r.

If $\gamma > 1, \alpha(r)$ increases with r: The direction of the variation thus depends on the structure of resources or, specifically, on the ratio ω_1/ω_0. If this ratio is very small, for example, nil, the consumer expects no future resources and her savings diminish with the yield to savings, r. Conversely, if this ratio is very high, the consumer dissaves. Borrowing decreases (savings increase) when the interest rate rises, owing to higher interest charges.

Now consider an economy in which all individuals have the same isoelastic utility function with parameter γ and the same psychological discount rate j. According to (P2.5), the equilibrium interest rate solves:

$$\alpha(r) \sum_i \left(\omega_0^i + \frac{\omega_1^i}{1+r} \right) = \sum_i \omega_0^i.$$

This equation only depends on aggregate resources or, more precisely, on their growth rate g defined as $1 + g = \sum_i \omega_1^i / \sum_i \omega_0^i$. It can be written as

$$\alpha(r) \left(1 + \frac{1+g}{1+r} \right) = 1.$$

Using the properties of α, one can easily verify that there is a unique equilibrium if $\gamma < 1$, and that the equilibrium interest rate increases with the growth rate g. If $\gamma > 1$, several equilibria may exist. ∎

2 Introducing Uncertainty

Financial markets allow the exchange of goods available at different times. Without uncertainty, as in the just described framework, a single market is sufficient for all relevant exchanges to be possible. In other words, in the sense defined in Chapter 2, markets are *complete* since there is only one state of nature at $t = 1$. As we have just seen, equilibrium ensures an optimal allocation of resources. How does this result generalize when future resources are uncertain? Following the same reasoning as in the previous section, several questions arise.

First, future consumption is typically risky. This calls for a description of individuals', or investors', choices when prospects are risky (Chapter 3). Under uncertainty, utility reflects the individual's *attitude toward risk* and the evaluation of the risk. This evaluation is likely to be affected by the available information.

Second, the consumption or expenditure profiles that are attainable by trading depend on the available financial instruments. A risk-free asset allows wealth to be transferred between two periods in a very specific way. Assets that enable income transfers between two states of nature tomorrow are valuable because they allow the sharing of risky resources. They facilitate, for instance, risk-taking by entrepreneurs by limiting their liability, at least partially, toward investors. As described in Chapter 1, various assets perform this type of operation: Corporate stock yields an income that is correlated with fluctuations in activity, while futures contracts allow risk at term to be shared with no prior exchange of funds. Savings behavior thus becomes inextricably linked to the assets comprising the *portfolio choice*, which determines the (risky) future consumption profile. Chapter 4 is devoted to a detailed examination of a typical investor's portfolio choice in terms of his preferences, the risks of the resources linked to his activities, and the securities that can be exchanged on the markets.

From the perspective of society as a whole, it is important to establish under what conditions existing financial markets make a Pareto efficient allocation of risky resources possible. Chapter 5 introduces the main principles: Mutualization of individual risks and optimal allocation of macroeconomic risks. Again the notion of complete markets turns out to be essential, allowing a link to be established between the risk-adjusted probability of Chapter 2 and the "fundamentals," namely the objective probability of the occurrence of states of nature, resources, and risk aversion. Also, the role of options as a tool to complete markets is outlined. Chapter 6 more closely examines standard specifications of the economy that permit an explicit resolution of the equilibrium allocation and prices: The CAPM and Consumption-based Capital Asset Pricing Model (CCAPM). The returns of financial assets at equilibrium and risk premiums can be computed.

The two final chapters of Part 2 are devoted to extensions to the basic model. Chapter 7 uses simple examples to address issues related to the information available to agents. In the preceding chapters, all agents had the same exogenous expectations concerning the future, represented by a single (objective) probability associated with the occurrence of the states of nature. We show how, when investors have distinct expectations, a market equilibrium may exist only under a great deal of consistency between these expectations. We study how the arrival of news interacts with the functioning of the markets and the associated risk allocation. Finally, through the notion of *rational expectations* equilibrium, the issue of whether and how prices convey private information is addressed. Chapter 8 deals with an infinite time horizon – in contrast to the preceding material that was mostly limited to two-period models. This is the occasion to describe a model for the stochastic evolution of the spot curve and to make explicit the difficulties encountered by the theory in trying to explain the gap between the returns of bonds and stocks.

BIBLIOGRAPHICAL NOTE

For a deeper understanding of basic microeconomic theory, the reader can refer to microeconomic textbooks appropriate for Masters or PhD level courses. For the Masters level, Varian (1990) is recommended. Mas Colell et al. (1995) and Kreps (1990) provide a more advanced coverage. Debreu's book (1959), which is quite abstract but fundamental, examines the relationships between equilibrium and Pareto optimality. Debreu demonstrates how general equilibrium theory can be applied to a world with uncertainty. Two crucial assumptions are needed: Uncertainty is represented by exogenous states of nature and markets should be complete.

Debreu, G. (1959). *Theory of value*, Wiley, New York.

Kreps, D. (1990). *A course in microeconomic theory*, Princeton University Press, New Jersey.

Mas Colell, A., M. Whinston, and J. Green (1995). *Microeconomic theory*, Oxford University Press, New York.

Varian, H. (1990). *Intermediate microeconomics, a modern approach*, Norton, New York.

Investors and their information / 3

By operating on financial markets, investors modify the risk profile of their future resources. Futures markets allow a farmer to safeguard against the risk associated with fluctuating crop prices, and options make it possible to insure against sudden price drops or, conversely, to profit from them. Interventions in these markets are linked to incomes the investor hopes to receive from real activities: Labor income, the sale of agricultural produce, revenue from a privately held, unlisted company, and the like. However, current or future real resources are not the only determinants of investor behavior: Two individuals with identical incomes rarely choose the same portfolios. A priori, two other factors play a key role: The investor's assessment of risk, whether on her nonfinancial resources or on the securities she can trade, and the extent of her risk tolerance – or her attitude vis-à-vis risk. It is common to evaluate the risk of a random variable by its variance. Is it justified? Thus, a first task is to model how an investor faced with a risky environment behaves.

Section 1 of this chapter introduces some fundamental concepts, such as stochastic dominance, von Neumann Morgenstern utility functions, and risk aversion. The underlying assumption is that the investor's preferences are based on the probability distribution of future income.

The choice of a portfolio determines, in conjunction with other sources of revenues, the agent's overall future stochastic income. Thus, comparing two portfolios is tantamount to comparing two stochastic revenue flows. This leads to a description of investors' criteria for investing in the stock exchange. Section 2 illustrates these criteria in the case where there is a single risky asset. A detailed examination of investments in multiple securities is postponed until the next chapter.

In a similar way as in Chapter 2, the notion of "subjective" opportunities for arbitrage can be defined. Section 3 establishes a link between the absence of such opportunities and the existence of an optimal portfolio. How do individuals determine the probability distribution of risky incomes? A probability, often called subjective, appears in a von Neumann Morgenstern setup. Section 4 investigates how Bayesian learning shapes the evolution of subjective expectations and their possible convergence toward an objective probability.

Finally, we address the issue of information, which is an essential concept on financial markets. As information, or *signals*, become available, the subjective probability of events changes. The Blackwell criterion allows the informational content of various signals to be partially ranked and their value to be identified.

1 Choice Criteria

Agents' choices feature elements of consistency when circumstances are modified, for example, when the securities payoffs change, when new assets are introduced, or when an investor's expected wealth is modified. We present here an analysis of choice that accounts for this consistency: *the agent's preferences bear on the probability distribution of future revenues.*

The probability distribution of a future income $\tilde{c}$ is characterized by a function F defined from $\mathbb{R}$ into $[0, 1]$ that specifies for each value c the probability that the realized income is lower than this value:

$$F(c) = \Pr(\tilde{c} \leq c).$$

The function F is nondecreasing and right continuous. The investor's preference relationship, denoted by $\succ$, ranks these distribution functions.

One natural hypothesis is that the investors' preferences on these probability distributions are increasing in the sense of *first-order stochastic dominance*. A distribution F is said to first-order dominate a distribution G if, for any c,

$$F(c) \leq G(c).$$

A necessary and sufficient condition[1] for F to first-order dominate G is that for any piece-wise differentiable increasing function v,

$$\int v(c) \mathrm{d}F(c) \geq \int v(c) \mathrm{d}G(c).$$

1 It can be seen that the condition is sufficient by letting v be equal to 0 on the interval $(-\infty, c]$ and to 1 elsewhere. To verify that it is necessary, integrate by parts.

In other words, if F dominates G, then any investor maximizing the mathematical expectation of an increasing utility function of income prefers F to G.

First-order stochastic dominance yields a very incomplete ranking of probability measures. Hence, the criterion is usually not very operational: Typically, choices are on probability distributions that cannot be compared in terms of stochastic dominance. To go beyond this measure, a very commonly used formulation is the von Neumann Morgenstern criterion.

1.1 Von Neumann Morgenstern Utility and Risk Aversion

Given certain axioms, preferences over probability distributions can be represented by a function v, a von Neumann Morgenstern index, defined from $\mathbb{R}$ into $\mathbb{R}$. Investors classify random revenue flows $\tilde{c}$ according to the expected value of this index $Ev(\tilde{c}) = \int v(c)dF(c)$. In other words,

$$F \succ G \Leftrightarrow \int v(c)dF(c) > \int v(c)dG(c).$$

Among all rankings of probability distributions, those of the von Neumann Morgenstern form are quite specific. They correspond to a linearity of choices in probability.

In this book we assume that the agents' choices satisfy the von Neumann Morgenstern hypothesis.

The concavity of the von Neumann Morgenstern utility index v reflects intuitive concepts of *risk aversion*.

First, investors have *risk neutral* preferences if they are only interested in the mathematical expectations of their incomes. As a result, they are indifferent between the prospect of a stochastic income $\tilde{c}$ and its certainty equivalent, $E\tilde{c}$. Such preferences are represented by the linear index: $v(c) = c$.

Most often however, individuals prefer to a stochastic prospect, $\tilde{c}$, the sure income, $E\tilde{c}$, with the same mathematical expectation. Such investors are called *risk averse*. This property is equivalent to the strict concavity of the function v. Indeed, when individuals are risk averse, for any c_1, c_2, and π in $]0, 1[$, they prefer the sure income $\pi c_1 + (1 - \pi)c_2$ to the lottery "receive c_1 with probability π or receive c_2 with probability $1 - \pi$." Thus,

$$\pi v(c_1) + (1 - \pi)v(c_2) < v[\pi c_1 + (1 - \pi)c_2)],$$

which is the definition of the concavity of v. Conversely, if v is strictly concave, according to Jensen's inequality,

$$Ev(\tilde{c}) \leq v(E\tilde{c}).$$

Furthermore, the inequality is strict when $\tilde{c}$ is not certain.

The *risk premium* is defined as the amount of money the agent is willing to pay to be fully insured. Thus, this premium, ρ, satisfies the equality

$$Ev(\tilde{c}) = v(E\tilde{c} - \rho).$$

Local measures of risk aversion use a single number to describe the preferences of an agent whose stochastic income is close to the value of the sure amount c. Furthermore, often as a first approximation, only the variance of the income matters to evaluate the risk premium. To see this, consider a small random deviation $d\tilde{c}$ (small in the sense that any realization of $d\tilde{c}$ is less than some small, positive ε). The expansion:

$$Ev(c + d\tilde{c}) = v(c) + v'(c)Ed\tilde{c} + \tfrac{1}{2}v''(c)Ed\tilde{c}^2 + o(\varepsilon^2)$$

allows us to compare various types of deviations. A $d\tilde{c}$ with an expected value of zero and a variance σ^2 translates into a utility loss (v'' is negative) of $|v''(c)|\sigma^2/2$. From the consumer's point of view, this is equivalent to a decline in sure income of

$$-\frac{v''(c)}{v'(c)}\frac{\sigma^2}{2}.$$

This amount also reflects the risk premium that must be given an investor whose sure income is c to compensate for accepting the risk $d\tilde{c}$. This calculation motivates the definition of the coefficient of *absolute risk aversion* $R_a(c)$:

$$R_a(c) = -\frac{v''(c)}{v'(c)}.$$

This coefficient is (twice) the amount the investor is prepared to pay for sure to avoid increasing the variance of his income by one unit. One also often speaks of *risk tolerance* , which is defined as the reciprocal of absolute risk aversion:

$$T(c) = \frac{1}{R_a(c)} = -\frac{v'(c)}{v''(c)}.$$

It is sometimes interesting to consider small deviations that are proportional to the initial reference income: add to the sure income c the stochastic income $d\tilde{c}$ with expectation nil and variance $\sigma^2 c^2$. A similar calculation as above shows that from the individual's perspective, this is equivalent to a decline in sure income, computed as a proportion of initial income, equal to

$$-\frac{cv''(c)}{v'(c)}\frac{\sigma^2}{2}.$$

This calculation motivates the definition of *relative risk aversion* $R_r(c)$:

$$R_r(c) = -\frac{cv''(c)}{v'(c)}.$$

1.2 Standard von Neumann Morgenstern Utility Functions

The measures of risk aversion in general depend on the level of the reference sure income c. Often, for simplicity, either absolute or relative risk aversion is assumed to be constant. This leads to the following classes:

1 Constant absolute risk aversion (CARA), or exponential, utility:

$$v(c) = -\exp(-\rho c), \quad \text{for positive } \rho.$$

$R_a(c) = \rho, R_r(c) = \rho c$. Absolute risk aversion is constant and relative risk aversion is increasing with income. The function is defined for any, positive or negative, income.

2 Constant relative risk aversion (CRRA), or isoelastic, utility[2]:

$$v(c) = \begin{cases} \dfrac{c^{1-\gamma}}{1-\gamma}, & \text{for } \gamma \geq 0, \gamma \neq 1 \text{ or} \\ \log c. \end{cases}$$

The case of $\gamma = 0$ corresponds to a risk neutral investor. As γ tends toward 1, we obtain the log. We have: $R_a(c) = \gamma/c, R_r(c) = \gamma$. Absolute risk aversion is decreasing with income and relative risk aversion remains constant. These functions are only defined for positive income.

3 CARA and CRRA utilities belong to the family of hyperbolic absolute risk aversion (HARA) utilities, characterized by an affine risk tolerance:

$$v(c) = \frac{1-\alpha}{\alpha}\left(\frac{ac}{1-\alpha}+b\right)^{\alpha}, \quad b \geq 0.$$

---

2 The elasticity of the utility of consumption, $\log v$, with respect to $\log c$, is constant.

It is important to only consider v on the domain that is relevant to the definition, $ac/(1 - \alpha) + b > 0$, where it is increasing and concave.[3] Risk tolerance,

$$T(c) = \frac{1}{R_a(c)} = \frac{c}{1 - \alpha} + \frac{b}{a},$$

is affine. Absolute risk aversion is increasing when α is less than 1 and decreasing when α is greater than 1. The CARA and CRRA functions are limiting cases (the exponential form is obtained by letting α tend to $-\infty$ for $b = 1$, and the isoelastic form when $b = 0$ and $\alpha < 1$).

2 The Investor's Choice

Uncertainty is modeled by a state of nature space, as in the previous chapter. The random incomes from which an investor can choose depend on his nonfinancial resources and on the available securities on the market.

2.1 Markets and Budget Constraints

There are two periods, $t = 0$, or today, when the decisions are made, and $t = 1$, when all uncertainty is resolved. From the perspective of time 0, the uncertainty at time 1 is represented by a finite number of possible circumstances: the states of nature $e, e = 1, \ldots, E$.

The investor may buy or sell on the stock exchange, as described in Chapter 2. However, the risk-free security, which is to have a special role, is singled out and indexed[4] by $*$.

1 K risky financial assets, indexed by k, can be traded at $t = 0$ at price p_k, $k = 1, \ldots, K$. A unit of the asset k is characterized by a stochastic payoff, $\tilde{a}_k = a_k(e)$, $e = 1, \ldots, E$, to which its possession confers a right at time 1, and

---

3 It is worth bearing in mind that, for whole values of α greater than 1, for example, the quadratic case, $\alpha = 2$, the function v is well defined over all $\mathbb{R}$. However, it is only increasing in c when $ac/(1 - \alpha) + b > 0$.

4 The assumption that a risk-free security is available may be debatable, particularly if the investor's horizon is long (e.g., because of inflation). To handle a situation without such a security, one can impose the constraint that the positions on this security be nil, $z_* = 0$.

which is determined by the realized state. $\tilde{a}$ designates the matrix $K \times E$ of elements $a_k(e)$.

2 The riskless security yields one unit of currency regardless of the state of nature. Its revenue vector, denoted by 1_*, is thus an E-dimensional row vector of ones. Its price is $p_* = 1/(1+r)$.

Trades are unconstrained: transaction costs are nil, short sales are allowed, and there are no limits on buys or sales.

At time 0, before the markets open, the investor owns an initial resource ω_0 and a portfolio composed of $z_*(0)$ units of riskless security and $z_k(0)$ units of the risky security k, $k = 1, \ldots, K$. He expects to receive an *exogenous* stochastic nonfinancial income flow at time 1, $\tilde{\omega} = (\omega(e), e = 1, \ldots, E)$, completely described by the states of nature.

A portfolio (z_*, z), where $z = (z_k)_{k=1,\ldots,K}$, costs $p_* z_* + p' z$ at $t = 0$ and yields a future financial income in state e equal to $z_* + \sum_k a_k(e) z_k$. Thus, if the investor final portfolio after trades is (z_*, z), his consumptions $(c_0, \tilde{c})$ at times 0 and 1, respectively, are given by

$$c_0 + p_* z_* + p' z = \omega_0 + p_* z_*(0) + p' z(0), \tag{3.1}$$

and in state e at time 1,

$$c(e) = \omega(e) + z_* + \sum_{k=1}^{K} a_k(e) z_k, \tag{3.2}$$

which, in vector notation, is

$$\tilde{c} = \tilde{\omega} + z_* 1_* + z' \tilde{a}. \tag{3.3}$$

also noted, with a slight abuse of notation:

$$\tilde{c} = \tilde{\omega} + z_* + z' \tilde{a}.$$

There are *redundant* securities when a given random income profile $\tilde{c}$ can be obtained with an infinite number of different portfolios. Such a situation is observed when the security payoffs, the (row) vectors 1_* and $\tilde{a}_k$, are collinear. With no loss of generality, one can then pursue the analysis with a subset,

$k = *, 1, \ldots, K$, of nonredundant securities.[5] Formally, throughout this book, we assume the following.

Hypothesis 3.1 **(Nonredundancy)** *The $K + 1$ row vectors 1_* and $(\tilde{a}_k)_{k=1,\ldots,K}$ are linearly independent.* ∎

The investor is assumed unable to influence prices, either directly or indirectly – and takes them as given.

The investor's preferences over consumption at the two periods are separable. For consumption in period 1, they are represented by a von Neumann Morgenstern utility function v: The utility level associated to $(c_0, \tilde{c})$ is given by

$$u(c_0) + E[v(\tilde{c})],$$

where the symbol E designates the mathematical expectation taken over the probability measure representing the investor's expectations. His expectations are formally represented by a probability distribution, π, over the states of nature, so that

$$E[v(\tilde{c})] = \sum_e \pi(e)v(c(e)).$$

Actually, for the study of investment behavior, what counts is the derived probability distribution ψ on nonfinancial future income $\tilde{\omega}$ as well as the revenues yielded by securities $\tilde{a}$. In other words, the states can be identified with the values taken by $(\tilde{\omega}, \tilde{a})$.[6]

The investor chooses (z_*, z) so as to maximize

$$u(c_0) + \int v(\tilde{c})\psi(d\omega, da_1, \ldots, da_K),$$

where c_0 and $\tilde{c}$ are given by (3.1) and (3.2).

---

5 The redundant securities can be priced by arbitrage in terms of the selected $K + 1$ securities. The eventual initial holdings in redundant securities also can be translated into the nonredundant fundamental basis.

6 In the framework we have just presented, the distribution ψ is discrete, since incomes depend on a finite number of states. The analysis can easily be extended to a continuum of states, making it possible to handle the situation in which the distribution is absolutely continuous with respect to the Lebesgue measure, as in models in which the distributions of incomes are normal.

In the absence of randomness, this reduces to the consumption–savings decision discussed in the introduction in Part 2. Here, the choice of (z_*, z) simultaneously determines consumption today and its complement (possibly negative) savings, as well as the allocation of savings to various assets.

To see this more clearly, let us denote the value of the initial, financial and nonfinancial, resources at date 0 by V_0: $V_0 = \omega_0 + p_* z_*(0) + p'z(0)$. From the budget constraint (3.1) at time 0, the value of the end-of-period portfolio, including the investment in the risk-free security, is equal to savings $V_0 - c_0$. Thus, the investor's problem can be seen as choosing how much to save (or equivalently how much to consume today) and allocating savings among the available securities.

This second problem is often studied separately, by considering the allocation of a given amount of cash on the available securities: this is called the *portfolio choice*. To focus on the portfolio choice, it suffices to adapt the model by assuming no utility for current consumption (c_0 is nil).

Finally, in the presence of a risk-free security, the choice between the risk-free security and the risky ones has been much studied. This choice becomes clear by eliminating the variable z_* from the budget constraints as follows. Recall that $p_* = 1/(1 + r)$. Drawing z_* from (3.1) and plugging it into (3.2) gives the difference between consumption and nonfinancial income in period 1:

$$c(e) - \omega(e) = (V_0 - c_0)(1 + r) + \sum_{k=1}^{K} [a_k(e) - p_k(1 + r)]z_k,$$

or, in vector notation,

$$\tilde{c} - \tilde{\omega} = (V_0 - c_0)(1 + r)1_* + z'[\tilde{a} - p(1 + r)1_*]. \tag{3.4}$$

The right-hand side is interpreted as follows: the first term is the value of savings if it is all invested in the riskless asset, and the second is the income yielded by a risky portfolio entirely financed by borrowing. The term $a_k(e) - p_k(1 + r)$ is the income of one unit of security k net of its cost, evaluated at time 1.

As an illustration, we examine a simple portfolio choice, in which there is only one risky security.

2.2 The Demand for One Risky Security and Risk Aversion

The investor's preferences determine his asset demand. A classic example, which illustrates the usefulness of risk aversion measures, is how the investor's demand for risky securities depends on his wealth. It is sometimes observed that this demand increases with wealth, while the proportion of risky securities in the portfolio decreases. When there is only one risky asset, this behavior can be derived from simple properties of risk aversion.

Consider the following portfolio choice problem. An individual invests ω_0 in two securities, one risk-free and one risky. He expects no resources next period (the analysis straightforwardly extends if he expects a sure resource). His preferences are given by a von Neumann Morgenstern utility function v over second period consumption. He is strictly risk averse: v is strictly concave, with a strictly negative second derivative. Hence, the optimal portfolio maximizes $E[v(z_* + z_1 \tilde{a}_1)]$ under the budget constraint $z_*/(1+r) + p_1 z_1 = \omega_0$; or equivalently, eliminating z_*, z_1 maximizes

$$E[v(\omega_0(1+r) + z_1(\tilde{a}_1 - p(1+r)))].$$

This function is derivable and concave in z_1, with a derivative given by

$$Ev'(\tilde{c})(\tilde{a}_1 - p_1(1+r)),$$

where

$$\tilde{c} = \omega_0(1+r) + z_1(\tilde{a}_1 - p_1(1+r)).$$

Therefore, the first-order condition,

$$Ev'(\tilde{c})(\tilde{a}_1 - p_1(1+r)) = 0, \qquad (3.5)$$

characterizes an optimal solution.

Note that an optimal portfolio may not exist. For example, if the excess return is surely strictly positive, that is, if $\tilde{a} - p(1+r) > 0$, the derivative is always positive: the investor is willing to take infinite position on the risky security by borrowing. The existence problem is studied in the next section. We now discuss the case where there is an optimal portfolio.

The derivative at $z_1 = 0$ is equal to $v'(\omega_0(1+r))E[\tilde{a}_1 - p_1(1+r)]$. This readily gives the following:

The investor invests a positive quantity in the risky asset if and only if the expectation of the excess payoff, $E[\tilde{a}_1 - p_1(1+r)]$, is positive, that is, if the expectation of the security payoff is larger than its price discounted at time 1.

The intuition is the following: under the above condition, by investing marginally in the risky security, the investor takes a small risk in exchange of a strictly positive expected return.[7] Also, when $E\tilde{a} = p_1(1 + r)$, it is optimal to invest everything in the sure asset: Taking a position on the risky security does not change the expected portfolio payoff but makes it risky. Therefore, by Jensen's inequality, this always lowers expected utility.

Whether the amount invested in the risky security is larger than the initial wealth, in which case $z_0 < 0$ and the investor borrows, depends on the distribution of the excess return, and risk aversion. Theorem 3.1 assumes that an optimal portfolio exists, and that the investor does not borrow any of the securities. It examines how the demand for the risky asset varies with ω_0.

Theorem 3.1 *Assume that the optimal portfolio includes positive quantities of both securities: the amount invested in the risky security is positive but less than the invested wealth ω_0.*

1 *If the index of absolute risk aversion is decreasing, the amount invested in the risky asset z_1 increases with ω_0,*
2 *If the index of relative risk aversion is increasing, the share of wealth invested in the risky asset declines with ω_0.* ∎

Proof of Theorem 3.1   The first order condition (3.5) implicitly determines z_1, the demand for the risky asset, as a function of the parameters, in particular ω_0. The equation is of the form $F(z_1, \omega_0) = 0$, where F is differentiable. To apply the implicit function theorem in order to find how z_1 varies with ω_0, it suffices that the partial derivative with respect to z_1 is not nil. Indeed, this derivative is equal to $Ev''(\tilde{c})(\tilde{a}_1 - p_1(1 + r))^2$, which is strictly negative by strict concavity of v. Differentiating with respect to ω_0, we obtain

$$Ev''(\tilde{c})(\tilde{a}_1 - p_1(1 + r))^2 \frac{dz_1}{d\omega_0} + Ev''(\tilde{c})(\tilde{a}_1 - p_1(1 + r))(1 + r) = 0.$$

Since the coefficient of $dz_1/d\omega_0$ is negative, the sign of the derivative $dz_1/d\omega_0$ is that of

$$Ev''(\tilde{c})(\tilde{a}_1 - p_1(1 + r)).$$

To demonstrate that this expression is positive, we use the assumption of decreasing absolute risk aversion and the first-order condition. Since $z_1 > 0$ and

---

7 Note that this argument is not valid if the investor has risky nonfinancial resources.

$\tilde{c} = \omega_0(1 + r) + (\tilde{a}_1 - p_1(1 + r))z_1$, we have, for $\tilde{a}_1 < p_1(1 + r)$,

$$-\frac{v''(\tilde{c})}{v'(\tilde{c})} = R_a(\tilde{c}) > R_a(\omega_0(1 + r)).$$

Multiplying this inequality by the positive expression $(p_1(1 + r) - \tilde{a}_1)$ gives

$$v''(\tilde{c})(\tilde{a}_1 - p_1(1 + r)) > R_a(\omega_0(1 + r))v'(\tilde{c})(\tilde{a}_1 - p_1(1 + r)).$$

An analogous calculation yields the same result for $\tilde{a}_1 > p_1(1 + r)$. Taking the mathematical expectation, the expression on the right-hand side is equal to zero, under the first-order condition, which yields the desired result.

As to the second part of the theorem, we must show that the ratio $p_1 z_1 / \omega_0$ is a decreasing function of ω_0 or, taking logs, that

$$\frac{\omega_0}{z_1} \frac{dz_1}{d\omega_0} < 1.$$

Using the expression for the derivative, this inequality can be written as

$$-\frac{\omega_0}{z_1} Ev''(\tilde{c})(\tilde{a}_1 - p_1(1 + r))(1 + r) > Ev''(\tilde{c})(\tilde{a}_1 - p_1(1 + r))^2,$$

or, rewriting and using the budget constraint,

$$Ev''(\tilde{c})(\tilde{a}_1 - p_1(1 + r))\tilde{c} < 0.$$

This inequality follows from increasing *relative* risk aversion, using the same argument as in the first part of the proof. ∎

In the case of a constant risk aversion utility, the amount invested in the risky asset is independent of the investor's wealth. To see this, let $v(c) = -\exp(-\rho c)$. Using the expression for $\tilde{c}$, we have

$$v'(\tilde{c}) = \rho \exp[-\rho\omega_0(1 + r)] \exp[-\rho z_1(\tilde{a}_1 - p_1(1 + r))].$$

Thus, the first-order condition is independent of ω_0:

$$E(\tilde{a}_1 - p_1(1 + r)) \exp[-\rho(\tilde{a}_1 - p_1(1 + r))z_1] = 0,$$

and the optimal portfolio as well.

It turns out that Theorem 3.1 is not very robust: It cannot be generalized to the case of several risky assets. The theoretical properties of the demand for risky assets are very sensitive to the assumptions made on the utility functions.

3 Subjective Expectations and Opportunities for Arbitrage

As previously discussed, the existence of an optimal portfolio is not guaranteed. From the preceding chapter, however, we may suspect that if an arbitrage opportunity can be exploited at any scale, no portfolio is optimal: to any (finite) portfolio, the investor prefers another one with larger speculative positions. Our purpose here is to explore the relationships between a well-defined investor's behavior and arbitrage opportunities.

To this end, it suffices to consider a portfolio choice problem (since the general problem encompasses such a choice). To simplify the presentation, assume that all income comes from savings at time 1 ($\tilde{\omega}$ is nil). Also, there is a risk-free asset. One dollar invested in the risk-free asset yields $(1 + r)$ dollars tomorrow. The subjective probability distribution of future income only bears on the payoffs of the risky securities. Consequently, the investor's criterion is

$$\int v \left(z_* + \sum_{k=1}^{K} \tilde{a}_k z_k \right) \psi (da_1, \ldots, da_K),$$

under the budget constraint,

$$\frac{z_*}{1 + r} + p'z = \omega_0,$$

1 the function v is continuously differentiable, strictly increasing, strictly concave from $\mathbb{R}_+$ into $\mathbb{R}$, and strictly positive;
2 the risky security payoffs are not negative: the probability distribution ψ is defined on $\mathbb{R}_+^K$. Furthermore, its support ψ is not reduced to a single point.

As in the previous example, if the discounted price of a security is expected by the investor to be less than its payoff with probability 1, then it is in the investor's interest to run up an unlimited debt in the sure asset to buy the risky asset, regardless of the shape of her utility function. Similarly, if the discounted price is higher, the investor will profit with probability 1 if she short sells the risky asset and invests the proceeds of that sale in sure assets. These operations can be made at any arbitrary large scale if there are no constraints when borrowing sure assets or on short selling risky securities. From the investor's point of view, there is an opportunity for arbitrage. This leads to the following definition that is a transposition of the one presented in Chapter 2 to a framework that no longer deals with states of nature, but rather with probabilities, the investor's beliefs.

Definition 3.1 *The agent has an opportunity for arbitrage if there exists a portfolio* (z_*, z), *such that:*

$$\frac{z_*}{1+r} + p'z \le 0, \quad z_* + \sum_{k=1}^{K} \tilde{a}_k z_k \ge 0,$$

with a strict inequality at date 0, or with positive probability at date 1. ∎

The absence of opportunities for arbitrage imposes a consistency condition between prices and expectations. Referring back to Chapter 2, let the states of nature be in a one-to-one correspondence with the values taken by $\tilde{a}$. There is a finite number of states if the support of beliefs ψ is finite. Consequently, from Theorem 2.1, there are no opportunities for arbitrage if, and only if, there exist strictly positive state prices $q(e)$ such that, for all k,

$$p_k = \sum_e q(e) a_k(e). \tag{3.6}$$

The sum of the state prices must be equal to $1/(1 + r)$ (applying this equation to the riskless security). Therefore, the vector of prices $(1 + r)p$ is a convex combination with strictly positive weights of the payoffs $\tilde{a} = (\tilde{a}_k)$ that the investor thinks possible. In mathematical terms, and in order to treat more general cases, condition (3.6) can be put equivalently: the vector of prices $((1 + r)p)$ belongs to the *relative* interior of the convex envelope of the values of $\tilde{a}$ that can be reached with positive probability, that is, the relative interior of the convex envelope[8] of the support of the probability distribution ψ. This property is general and even valid when the state space is infinite, as stated by Theorem 3.2 (even though we only present an illustrative demonstration in a very simple situation[9]).

---

8 The convex envelope is the set of all convex combinations formed from points in the support of ψ. In the vector space generated by these points, the convex envelope has a nonempty interior, which is called the relative interior of the convex envelope. For example, consider the convex envelope of two points, a and b, the segment $[a, b]$, in a *multi*dimensional space. Whereas the interior of the segment is empty, the relative interior is nonempty, and is (a, b).

9 In the general case, the proof consists of applying a separation theorem in $\mathbb{R}^K$ to the convex envelope of the support of ψ and the point p.

Theorem 3.2 *The three following properties are equivalent:*

1 *The investor has no opportunities for arbitrage.*
2 *The investor's program has a solution.*
3 *The price vector $(1 + r)p$ belongs to the relative interior of the convex envelope of the belief's support.* ∎

Condition 3 generalizes the existence of state prices to the probabilistic context. The equivalence between Conditions 1 and 2 means that the absence of opportunities for arbitrage from the point of view of an investor is equivalent to his asset demand being well defined. This is a prerequisite for any study of the stock market.

Proof of Theorem 3.2 We prove the theorem for the case of a single risky asset ($K = 1$) and, without loss of generality, for $r = 0$. Given initial wealth ω_0, the choice of z_1 yields the final income: $\omega_0 + z_1(\tilde{a}_1 - p_1)$.

2 ⇒ 3 If the price does not belong to the interior of the convex envelope of the support of the distribution ψ, we have either $\tilde{a}_1 - p_1 \geq 0$ or $\tilde{a}_1 - p_1 \leq 0$ with probability 1. Since the probability distribution is nondegenerate (otherwise the two assets would be redundant!), in the first case, it is optimal to increase z_1 to $+\infty$, and in the second case to short sell it without limit.

3 ⇒ 2 On the other hand, assume that the price falls within the interior of the convex envelope of the support of ψ. Let us denote the lower and the upper bounds of this support by $\underline{a}_1$ and $\bar{a}_1$, respectively. Thus, by assumption, $\underline{a}_1 < p_1 < \bar{a}_1$. Since the utility function is not defined for negative wealth, the investor chooses portfolios z_1 such that

$$\omega_0 + (\underline{a}_1 - p_1)z_1 \geq 0 \quad \text{and} \quad \omega_0 + (\bar{a}_1 - p_1)z_1 \geq 0.$$

The objective function is defined for z_1 in a compact interval. Since it is continuous (dominated convergence), it is bounded and reaches a maximum.

3 ⇔ 1 The third property directly implies that there are no opportunities for arbitrage: Any nonzero portfolio yields a wealth less than ω_0 with strictly positive probability. Conversely, if there is an opportunity for arbitrage, let us say $\bar{z} > 0$, then $(\tilde{a}_1 - p_1)$ is never less than 0, and strictly greater with positive probability. Owing to the fact that the utility function is strictly increasing, there does not exist an optimal portfolio z°: the portfolio $z^{\circ} + \bar{z}$ is strictly preferred to z° (the same reasoning applies when the opportunity for arbitrage involves selling). ∎

Remark 3.1 The results in this section were derived under the assumption that consumption is restricted to be positive or nil. Under this assumption, the set of feasible portfolios is bounded. The preceding results do not always hold if consumption has no lower bound. An optimal portfolio may not exist even in the absence of opportunities for arbitrage if the investor is prepared to accept unbounded losses. To analyze this type of situations, joint assumptions on the utility function and the distribution of payoffs are needed (cf. Leland 1972).

4 Convergence of Expectations: Bayesian Learning

Beliefs[10] are often assumed to be accurate and to reflect the "true" probability according to which various events are drawn. How can investors acquire this knowledge?

A realistic framework is learning, as illustrated by the following experiment. An urn contains red and black balls. The total number of balls is known, but the proportion of red and black ones is not. Will an individual who repeatedly draws balls, with replacement after each draw, learn the proportion? To address this question, assume that the individual has an a priori distribution μ of the proportion ψ of red balls, and that he revises this distribution as the draws progress. The evolution of the individual's belief depends on the observations and the manner in which they are processed to revise his a priori distribution.

We study an analogous situation in a financial market: Securities payoffs are drawn from a distribution that is constant over time, which is called the "objective" distribution. Consider an investor who does not know the objective distribution but has an a priori idea about it (this "idea" will be formalized below). Furthermore, he observes a succession of independent draws from this distribution. Clearly, this situation is the most conducive to learning and the convergence of beliefs. If agents' beliefs do not converge toward a true distribution within this framework, it is useless to attempt to broach more realistic, but more complex, situations.

Payoffs $\tilde{a}$ are drawn from a distribution ψ^*. Now, consider an investor who is aware of the existence of this objective probability, but who does not know its value. The Bayesian approach allows this ignorance to be formalized: The

---

10 Sections 4 and 5 of this chapter are not indispensable for understanding the remainder of the book and can be omitted during a first reading.

investor postulates an a priori probability distribution on what he does not know, the distribution ψ^* in this case. This means that the a priori is a probability distribution on payoffs distributions.

We shall make several assumptions allowing us to remain within the discrete context:

1 the vector $\tilde{a}$ may take a finite number of distinct values; $\psi^*(a)$ is the probability that the value a will occur.
2 the investor only considers a finite number of income distributions, ψ, as possible. His a priori judgment (also called beliefs or priors) is represented by a discrete distribution μ_0 that assigns the probability $\mu_0(\psi) > 0$ to the distribution ψ.
3 all the distributions ψ over payoffs, like the objective distribution, are discrete. We note $\mathcal{A}$ the (discrete) set of values of $\tilde{a}$, the probability of which is strictly positive in at least one of the contemplated distributions, that is, the union of the supports of ψ.

If the investor is sure about the distribution and if he is correct, one has: $\mu_0(\psi^*) = 1$ (μ_0 is then the Dirac mass on ψ^*). The question examined here is whether his opinion will eventually converge to correct beliefs under Bayesian learning.

From his prior μ_0, the investor infers a probability of occurrence for the payoffs in $\mathcal{A}$. Let us denote by ϕ this probability over $\mathcal{A}$. By composition of probabilities,[11]

$$\phi(a) = \Pr(a|\mu_0) = \sum_{\psi} \psi(a)\mu_0(\psi).$$

At discrete points in time $t = 1, \ldots$, traded assets yield revenues a_t drawn independently from the objective probability distribution ψ^*. The investor revises his current beliefs on the basis of the new observation by applying the Bayesian decision rule. Given the *beliefs* at time t, μ_t, and the derived distribution of payoffs, ϕ_t, observing a_t yields the revised beliefs

$$\mu_{t+1}(\psi) = \Pr(\psi|_t, \mu_t) = \frac{\Pr(\psi \text{ and } a_t|\mu_t)}{\Pr(a_t|\mu_t)} = \frac{\Pr(a_t|\psi, \mu_t)\Pr(\psi|\mu_t)}{\Pr(a_t|\mu_t)}.$$

Since

$$\Pr(a_t|\psi, \mu_t) = \psi(a_t), \quad \Pr(\psi|\mu_t) = \mu_t(\psi), \quad \text{and} \quad \Pr(a_t|\mu_t) = \phi_t(a_t),$$

11 In what follows, Pr means "probability of."

we obtain Bayes's formula:

$$\mu_{t+1}(\psi) = \frac{\psi(a_t)}{\phi_t(a_t)}\mu_t(\psi). \tag{3.7}$$

Theorem 3.3 *Assume that the investor's initial a priori belief assigns a non-nil weight to the true probability: $\mu_0(\psi^*) > 0$. When t tends to infinity, the sequence ϕ_t converges toward the objective probability ψ^*, and the sequence of revised distributions μ_t converges to the Dirac mass on the objective probability.* ■

The assumption that $\mu_0(\psi^*) > 0$ says that the true probability is not excluded a priori. This "grain of a truth" assumption is crucial: Beliefs evolve, but they only assign a positive weight to those probabilities ψ that were initially considered possible, as shown below.

Proof of Theorem 3.3   Consider ψ, with $\psi \neq \psi^*$. The distributions ψ that the investor thinks not to be possible at time 0 remains not possible afterward: $\mu_t(\psi) = 0$ for the values of ψ that do not belong to the support of μ_0. We shall demonstrate that $\mu_t(\psi)$ tends toward 0 if $\mu_0(\psi) > 0$. Since $\sum_\psi \mu_t(\psi) = 1$, where the sum is over all values of ψ such that $\mu_0(\psi) > 0$, this implies that $\mu_t(\psi^*)$ tends to 1, which is the desired result.

Only values for the payoffs a in the support of ψ^* are observed. Applying Eqn (3.7) to ψ^* gives by induction that $\mu_t(\psi^*) > 0$ implies that $\mu_{t+1}(\psi^*) > 0$. Consequently, dividing Eqn (3.7) element by element for ψ and ψ^*, we have

$$\frac{\mu_{t+1}(\psi)}{\mu_{t+1}(\psi^*)} = \frac{\psi(a_t)}{\psi^*(a_t)}\frac{\mu_t(\psi)}{\mu_t(\psi^*)}.$$

Iterating this equation from time 0 to time t and taking logs:

$$\log\left[\mu_{t+1}(\psi)\right] - \log[\mu_{t+1}(\psi^*)] - \log[\mu_0(\psi)] + \log[\mu_0(\psi^*)]$$

$$= \sum_{\tau=0}^{t}\{\log[\psi(a_\tau)] - \log[\psi^*(a_\tau)]\}.$$

It remains to show that the term on the right-hand side tends to $-\infty$. After dividing by $t + 1$, this term is equal to S_t:

$$S_t = \frac{1}{t+1}\sum_{\tau=0}^{t}\log\left[\frac{\psi(a_\tau)}{\psi^*(a_\tau)}\right].$$

We prove that S_t tends toward some strictly negative constant, yielding the desired result.

S_t is the mean of the independent and identically distributed variables $X_t = \log[\psi(a_t)/\psi^*(a_t)]$, the expectations and variances of which are finite since a_t is drawn independently from the distribution ψ^* in each period. According to the law of large numbers, S_t tends toward the mean of the distribution when t tends toward $+\infty$, that is,

$$S_t \to E_{\psi^*}\left[\log\left(\frac{\psi}{\psi^*}\right)\right] = \sum_a \log\left[\frac{\psi(a)}{\psi^*(a)}\right]\psi^*(a).$$

Since ψ is different from ψ^*, the function ψ/ψ^* is not constant. Jensen's inequality applied to the strictly concave function log yields

$$E_{\psi^*}\left[\log\left(\frac{\psi}{\psi^*}\right)\right] < \log\left[E_{\psi^*}\left(\frac{\psi}{\psi^*}\right)\right].$$

Now,

$$E_{\psi^*}\left(\frac{\psi}{\psi^*}\right) = \sum_a \frac{\psi(a)}{\psi^*(a)}\psi^*(a) = \sum_a \psi(a) = 1.$$

Thus, S_t tends almost surely toward a strictly negative value, which is what we sought. ∎

5 The Value of Information

Investors are constantly receiving information of a varied nature on securities. Their beliefs evolve according to this information. For example, in Section 4, beliefs depend on the observed securities payoffs. *In fine*, what really matters is whether investors benefit from these news. This is the question investigated here. We take the economist's view point: information has value to an individual if it allows her to make "better" decisions, that is, decisions that increase her utility.

We postulate a joint probability distribution on information (or signals) and on the states of nature. As an illustration, let us consider an investor who receives a newsletter with advance information on the business cycle $\tilde{e}$ (the "state of nature") and, by extension, on securities payoffs. This newsletter sends a signal,[12] denoted

---

12 As usual, $\tilde{s}$ denotes the random variable, and s its realization. A signal here refers to the whole variable $\tilde{s}$.

by $\tilde{s}$, which can take a finite number of values, $s = 1, \dots, S$. The joint distribution of $(\tilde{e}, \tilde{s})$ is known. In particular, after learning that $\tilde{s} = s$, investors revise the probabilities of the states according to Bayes's formula:

$$\Pr(e|s) = \frac{\Pr(e, s)}{\Pr(s)}.$$

The realized value of the signal, observed *before* the state materializes (e.g., rainfall readings prior to the harvest), influences the investment decision of the newsletter reader. Are the resulting choices better for her? Are some newsletters better than others?

A signal can convey more or less information regarding the realization of the variable of interest. If the random variable $\tilde{s}$ is independent of $\tilde{e}$, then the joint probability is the product of the marginal probabilities, and the signal is of no use for forecasting the business cycle, and *in fine* the securities payoffs. There is a natural partial ordering of signals, defined by Blackwell, which reflects their quality.

Definition 3.2   Blackwell   *The signal $\tilde{s}$, which can take S values, is more inform-ative than the $\tilde{S}'$-valued signal $\tilde{s}'$ if there exists a positive $S' \times S$ matrix M such that, for any state of nature,*

$$\Pr(\tilde{s}' = s'|e) = \sum_{s} M(s', s) \Pr(\tilde{s} = s|e), \qquad (3.8)$$

with

$$\sum_{s'} M(s', s) = 1. \qquad (3.9)$$

∎

To interpret this definition, notice that according to the last equality, $M(\cdot, s)$ defines a probability distribution on S' that is independent of the state of nature e. M is a Markov matrix. A person receiving the signal $\tilde{s}$ can thus always put herself in the same position as one receiving the signal $\tilde{s}'$. For this, it is sufficient that she draws a signal $\tilde{s}'$ under $M(\cdot, s)$. Having received s, she then "forgets" s and faces the same conditional distribution as if she had only observed $\tilde{s}'$.

Naturally, a signal $\tilde{s}$ is always at least as informative as any signal independent of the state. Indeed, if the signal $\tilde{s}'$ is independent of $\tilde{e}$, we have $\Pr(\tilde{s}' = s'|e) = \Pr(s')$.

It is sufficient to set $M(s', s) = \Pr(s')$ since then

$$\sum_s M(s', s) \Pr(\tilde{s} = s|e) = \Pr(s') \sum_s \Pr(\tilde{s} = s|e) = \Pr(s').$$

More interestingly, adding "noise" to a signal always makes it less informative.

Example 3.1 Signal $\tilde{s}'$ is a noisy signal of $\tilde{s}$ if

$$\tilde{s}' = \tilde{s} + \tilde{\varepsilon},$$

where $\tilde{\varepsilon}$ is a random variable independent of $\tilde{e}$ and $\tilde{s}$. To show that $\tilde{s}$ is more informative than $\tilde{s}'$, write

$$\Pr(\tilde{s}' = s'|e) = \sum_s \Pr(\tilde{\varepsilon} = s' - s) \Pr(\tilde{s} = s|e).$$

Setting $M(s', s) = \Pr(\tilde{\varepsilon} = s' - s)$, Eqns (3.8) and (3.9) obtain.   ■

Theorem 3.4 *The relationship "more informative than" is transitive.*   ■

This property is easy to demonstrate: It suffices to observe that the product of two Markov matrices is a Markov matrix.

The rationale for introducing the relationship "more informative than" draws on the following property. Given a choice, an economic decision maker prefers the most informative signal. To show this, let C be her choice set. If she chooses z, let $u(e, z)$ be her final utility when ultimately, the state is e. We assume that the set C is a compact, convex subset of $\mathbb{R}^K$, and the function u is continuous and concave with respect to z.

For example, consider an investor with wealth ω_0 to invest in K securities whose payoffs depend on a finite number of states: $\tilde{a}_k = a_k(e)$, $e = 1, \ldots, E$. The choice z represents the portfolio and the function u is given by

$$u(e, z) = v\left(\omega_0(1 + r) + \sum_k z_k[a_k(e) - p_k(1 + r)]\right),$$

where r is the risk-free rate.

Assume that she receives the newsletter $\tilde{s}$. When the news is s, and she uses the received information in an optimal fashion, the ensuing expected utility is $V(s)$:

$$V(s) = \max_{z \in C} \sum_e u(e, z) \Pr(e|\tilde{s} = s).$$

In the same way, we can define V' associated with another signal $\tilde{s}'$. The quality of the two signals can be compared before knowing the actual realization of the signals. This means that we compare the expected utility derived *ex ante*, $EV(\cdot)$ and $EV'(\cdot)$.

Theorem 3.5 *Consider a risk-averse investor choosing her action in a convex set C that is independent of the signal. Assume that the signal $\tilde{s}$ is more informative than the signal $\tilde{s}'$. Her ex ante expected utility upon receiving $\tilde{s}$ is at least as large as when she receives $\tilde{s}'$.* ∎

Proof of Theorem 3.5 Let $z'(s')$ be the investor's decision upon receiving the signal s'. By definition,

$$EV' = \sum_{s'} \left\{ \sum_{e} u[e, z'(s')] \Pr(e|\tilde{s}' = s') \right\} \Pr(\tilde{s}' = s').$$

Using the property

$$\Pr(\tilde{s} = s|e) \Pr(e) = \Pr(e|s) \Pr(s),$$

equality (3.8) can be rewritten as

$$\Pr(e|\tilde{s}' = s') \Pr(s') = \sum_{s} M(s', s) \Pr(e|\tilde{s} = s) \Pr(\tilde{s} = s).$$

Thus, we obtain

$$EV' = \sum_{s} \left(\sum_{e} \left\{ \sum_{s'} u[e, z'(s')]M(s', s) \right\} \Pr(e|\tilde{s} = s) \right) \Pr(\tilde{s} = s). \qquad (3.10)$$

According to condition (3.9), $M(\cdot, s)$ defines a transition probability on S' given s. The term in braces, that is, $\{\sum_{s'} u[e, z'(s')]M(s', s)\}$, yields the utility that the agent will receive in state e if $\tilde{s}'$ was drawn from this distribution, conditional on $\tilde{s} = s$. Recall that C is convex. The average decision, $z(s)$, defined by

$$z(s) = \sum_{s'} z'(s')M(s', s),$$

is thus in C. Applying Jensen's inequality, the concavity of the function u with respect to z' yields

$$\sum_{s'} u[e, z'(s')]M(s', s) \leq u[e, z(s)].$$

Hence (3.10) gives

$$EV' \leq \sum_{s} \left\{ \sum_{e} u[e, z(s)] \Pr(e|\tilde{s} = s) \right\} \Pr(\tilde{s} = s).$$

The term in braces is the agent's expected utility if she chooses the portfolio $z(s)$ when the signal $\tilde{s}$ is equal to s. By construction, this term is less than or equal to the optimal value $V(s)$. We obtain the desired result: $EV' \leq EV$. ∎

To illustrate, consider again the example of a newsletter that provides advance information on securities payoffs, or buy and sell recommendations. The value of a signal to the investor can be defined as the amount he is prepared to pay *ex ante*, before having any information, to receive it. This value yields an overall ranking of the information, that is, of the newsletters, depending on the person in question. In light of Theorem 3.5, the value of a publication increases as it is more informative.

We shall not address here the many difficulties raised by the economics of information: It is easy to imagine a market for confidential newsletters. Can several newsletters be bought? How can the newsletter be sold, rather than made freely available to all participants in the economy? Is the information liable to be manipulated?

BIBLIOGRAPHICAL NOTE

The modeling of attitudes toward risk has a long tradition that derives from the basics of probability theory. The book by von Neumann and Morgenstern (1944) laid out the axioms of expected utility. Applications were developed, especially by Rothschild and Stiglitz (1970, 1971). The book by Fishburn (1979) provides an overview of this model. Since then, the literature has diverged from the framework devised by von Neumann and Morgenstern, frequently in most imaginative fashions: Camerer's (1995) review of the literature covers a large part of the field.

The book by Hirshleifer and Riley (1992) provides a very comprehensive overview of the role played by information in choices made under uncertainty. The comparison of signals in terms of the information they contain was initiated by Blackwell (1953).

Blackwell, D. (1953). "Equivalent comparison of experiments," *Annals of Mathematics and Statistics*, **24**, 265–272.

Camerer, C. (1995). "Individual decision making." In J.H. Kagel and A.E. Roth, eds., *The handbook of experimental economics*, Princeton University Press, Princeton, NJ.

Fishburn, P. (1979). *Utility theory for decision making*, Wiley, New York.

Hirshleifer, J. and J.G. Riley (1992). *The analytics of uncertainty and information*, Cambridge University Press, Cambridge, UK.

Leland, H. (1972). "On the existence of optimal policies under uncertainty," *Journal of Economic Theory*, 4(1), 35–44.

Rothschild, M. and J. Stiglitz (1970). "Increasing risk. I: a definition," *Journal of Economic Theory*, **2**, 225–243.

Rothschild, M. and J. Stiglitz (1971). "Increasing risk. II: its economic consequences," *Journal of Economic Theory*, **3**, 66–84.

von Neumann, J. and O. Morgenstern (1944). *Theory of games and economic behavior*, Princeton University Press, Princeton, NJ.

Exercises

3.1 *Precautionary savings* Assume a consumer with wealth ω_0 today and expecting a (stochastic) wage $\tilde{\omega}$ during the next period. His preferences over consumption in the present, c_0, and in the future, $\tilde{c}$, are separable, represented by $u(c_0) + Ev(\tilde{c})$, where u and v are strictly increasing, concave, and twice differentiable functions. No borrowing is allowed and savings can be invested only at a risk-free rate r.

1 Check that current consumption c^* is optimal if it maximizes

$$u(c_0) + Ev[\tilde{\omega} + (\omega_0 - c_0)(1 + r)]$$

subject to $0 \leq c \leq \omega_0$.

2 Give the first-order conditions satisfied by the optimal consumption c^*. Are they sufficient?

3 Now assume that $0 < c^* < \omega_0$. We wish to evaluate the impact of risk in future wages on c^*.

 (a) If v is quadratic, show that c^* only depends upon the expectation of wages.

 (b) Let $\tilde{\omega} = E[\tilde{\omega}] + \sigma\tilde{\varepsilon}$, where $\tilde{\varepsilon}$ has zero mean and variance 1, and denote $c^*(\sigma)$ the optimal solution. Determine $dc^*/d\sigma$ by differentiating the first-order condition obtained in question 2. Show that $dc^*/d\sigma$ is positive if v'' is decreasing, and negative if v'' is increasing.[13] In which case can we speak of precautionary savings?

13 The following property can be used: if f is an increasing, integrable function, then the covariance of $f(\tilde{\varepsilon})$ and $\tilde{\varepsilon}$ is positive, provided it is defined.

Application: If $v(c) = c^{1-\gamma}/(1-\gamma)$, under what conditions is v concave? Do current savings increase or decrease with σ, that is, with the risk in future wages?

3.2 *Various forms of arbitrage*   The purpose of this exercise is to study some variants of the definition of arbitrage and to connect the associated notion of absence of opportunities for arbitrage with the existence of a solution to an individual's investment program.

The setting is the usual two-period model characterized by a finite number of states of nature and K securities with a payoff matrix $\tilde{a} = (a_k(e))$, $k = 1, \ldots, K$, $e = 1, \ldots, E$.

We call an arbitrage opportunity *with immediate payoff* a portfolio z such that[14]

$$z'\tilde{a} \geq 0 \quad \text{and} \quad p'z < 0.$$

We call an arbitrage opportunity *with deferred payoff* a portfolio z such that

$$p'z = 0 \quad \text{and} \quad z'\tilde{a} > 0.$$

Notice that an *opportunity for arbitrage* as defined in Chapter 2 is either with immediate or deferred benefits.

1 Provide examples (with $E = 2$ or 3 and $K = 2$) featuring only immediate, or only deferred, opportunities for arbitrage.
2 Let $\| \ \|$ be some norm on $\mathbb{R}^E$. Consider the set Z of portfolios such that $z'\tilde{a} \geq 0$ and $\|z'a\| = 1$. Now assume that there are no opportunities for arbitrage (in the sense of Chapter 2). Show that the minimum of $p'z$ on Z is strictly positive.
3 Consider an individual who invests ω_0 in the K securities. His preferences, represented by a von Neumann Morgenstern utility function v, are defined over *nonnegative* security incomes $\tilde{c}_z = z'\tilde{a}$. The function v is continuous. Assume that the feasible consumption set is not empty: there are portfolios z that satisfy the budget constraint $pz' = \omega_0$ whose payoffs are nonnegative, $\tilde{c}_z \geq 0$. Show that in the absence of arbitrage opportunities, whether with immediate or deferred payoffs, the consumer's problem has a solution.
4 In some cases, portfolios containing arbitrarily large quantities of assets can be optimal for the investor. Provide an example. Give a sufficient condition for this phenomenon not to occur. Comment.
5 Conversely, assume that there is an investor whose optimal portfolio yields positive incomes: $\tilde{c}_z(e) > 0$ for any e. Show that there are no opportunities for arbitrage, whether with immediate or deferred payoffs, when there is a risk-free asset.

14 In the case of vectors, $\geq$ denotes component-by-component inequality, $>$ component-by-component inequality with at least one strict inequality, and $\gg$ strict inequality of all components.

Portfolio choice

4

This chapter examines the portfolio choices of investors who allot a given amount of wealth to various securities. Determining how much wealth to invest is studied in the subsequent chapters. "Rational" investors select a portfolio that best suits their objectives and their needs. Their demands for financial securities are derived from preferences represented with a von Neumann Morgenstern utility criterion, as discussed in Chapter 3. We are especially interested in how the selected portfolio is related to attitudes toward risk (possibly risky), future nonfinancial incomes, and assessment on securities payoffs.

Section 1 examines a particular case, referred to as the *mean–variance analysis*, that merits a detailed examination. Under some specifications, an investor ranks portfolios solely on the basis of the expectation and variance of their returns. Thus, given his budget constraint, he selects a portfolio that is *mean–variance efficient*, meaning that the expected return cannot be increased without also increasing the variance. An examination of all mean–variance efficient portfolios provides a first approach to the notion of *risk diversification*, the basis of many widely used models in finance. When a risk-free security is available, the two "funds" theorem is obtained: Mean–variance efficient portfolios are combinations of the risk-free security and a single portfolio of risky securities, analogous to a mutual fund. The specific composition of the risky fund is independent of the investors' attitudes toward risk, as long as these investors have the same beliefs on the expectation and the variance of the securities returns. Thus, the optimal composition of the risky fund represents an ideal diversification of risky investments. Attitudes vis-à-vis risk only come into play in the determination of the respective amounts invested in the risk-free security and the fund.

No such clear cut results hold in general: Section 2 analyzes the demand for financial securities with an unrestricted von Neumann Morgenstern criterion. Finally, two specific cases, that of a quadratic utility function or of CARA and normal returns, are studied in more detail. They illustrate one of the themes underlying portfolio choice, *speculative* and *hedging* demand, and provide a link to the mean–variance analysis.

1 Mean-Variance Efficient Portfolios

This section presents the mean–variance framework. Whereas it can be linked to a von Neumann Morgenstern model (see the Section 3), this framework is used in practice for convenience. Indeed, it is simpler to work exclusively on the expectation and variance of a random variable rather than on its entire distribution.

> **The mean–variance hypothesis:** An investor ranks portfolios on the basis of the expectations and variances of their payoffs. The ranking is increasing in expectation and decreasing in variance.

Note that we do not fully specify the investor's attitude toward risk: In particular, we do not address how he arbitrates between the expectation and the variance of the payoff.

Under the mean–variance hypothesis, the investor selects a portfolio that is *mean–variance efficient*, meaning that the expected payoff cannot be increased without also increasing the variance. Of course, the expectation and the variance are evaluated by the investor, using his own beliefs.

As defined in Chapter 3, recall that a portfolio (z_*, z) with an initial value of $\omega_0 = p_* z_* + p' z$ yields a stochastic payoff in period 1:

$$\tilde{c} = z_* + \sum_{k=1}^{K} z_k \tilde{a}_k = z_* + z' \tilde{a}.$$

The expectation and the variance of the portfolio payoff are thus, respectively, given by $z_* + E z' \tilde{a}$ and $\mathrm{var}(z' \tilde{a})$. The set of mean–variance efficient portfolios is found by solving the following family of programs parameterized with a scalar M[1]:

$$\min \mathrm{var}(z' \tilde{a})$$

$$z_* + E z' \tilde{a} \geq M$$

$$p_* z_* + p' z = \omega_0.$$

---

1 The analysis conducted in this chapter is valid when the number of states of nature is infinite, provided that the variance $\mathrm{var}(\tilde{a})$ is finite.

The parameter M is interpreted as the smallest expected payoff that the investor has set as a target. The solution to this problem is the portfolio(s) with the smallest variance meeting this target.

Thus, the mean–variance efficiency criterion does not determine a unique portfolio. Indeed, to derive the demand for securities, one needs to specify the investor's attitude toward risk, which in turn dictates the trade-off between the expectation and variance of the payoff. However, any solution to the above program – any efficient portfolio – features the key property of risk *diversification*, regardless of the level of risk aversion.

We first demonstrate that the analysis can be conducted on the basis of the *return* on each dollar invested. Then we characterize efficient portfolios in two stages, starting with the situation in which no risk-free security is available.

1.1   Portfolio Composition and Returns

The set of all mean–variance efficient portfolios is homogeneous of degree 1 in wealth ω_0. Indeed, starting with a solution (z_*, z) to the program for the parameters (ω_0, M), $(\lambda z_*, \lambda z)$ solves the program for $(\lambda \omega_0, \lambda M)$ for any positive λ. This naturally leads us to work per dollar invested, as is done in finance. To this purpose, the *rate of return* of a security describes the payoff obtained from investing one dollar in the security, and the *composition* of a portfolio describes how much of each dollar is invested in each security (rather than the number of shares of each security in a portfolio). Formally, this is equivalent to a change of variables as follows:

Definition 4.1   *The gross rate of return of a security is the stochastic payoff that one dollar invested in this security today pays at time 1:*

$$\tilde{R}_k = \frac{\tilde{a}_k}{p_k}, \quad k = *, 1, \ldots, K.$$

A portfolio composition is a vector (x_*, x), such that $x* + \sum_{k=1}^{K} x_k = 1$, where x_k is the fraction of the portfolio value invested in k.   ∎

Notice that the rate of return of a risk-free security is constant, given by $R_* = (1 + r)$. Frequently, the *net returns* equal to the gross returns minus 1 are used: $\tilde{r}_k = \tilde{R}_k - 1$. We often abbreviate "rate of return" into "return."

Let us rewrite the investor's problem with these variables. The value of the portfolio (z_*, z) is $\omega_0 = p_* z_* + p'z$. If ω_0 is not nil, the portfolio composition is given by (x_*, x):

$$x_* = \frac{p_* z_*}{\omega_0}, \quad x_k = \frac{p_k z_k}{\omega_0}, \quad k = 1, \ldots, K.$$

Thus, the portfolio is characterized by its value and its composition. Moreover, the associated stochastic payoff satisfies

$$\tilde{c} = z_* + z'\tilde{a} = \omega_0 (x_* R_* + x'\tilde{R}).$$

As for a single security, the *gross return* of a portfolio is equal to its random payoff per dollar invested. According to the expression above, the gross return of a portfolio whose composition is (x_*, x) is given by

$$x_* R_* + x'\tilde{R} = x_* R_* + \sum_{k=1}^{K} x_k \tilde{R}_k,$$

or, in words,

The return of a portfolio is the linear combination of the returns of the component securities weighted by their respective shares in the portfolio composition.

Letting $\mathbf{1}_K$ represent the K-dimensional column vector consisting entirely of ones, the mean–variance efficiency can be written in terms of the just defined variables.

Definition 4.2 *The portfolio with composition (x_*, x) is mean–variance efficient if it solves:*

$$\min \mathrm{var}(x'\tilde{R}) \text{ s.t. } \begin{cases} x_* R_* + Ex'\tilde{R} \geq m \\ x_* + \mathbf{1}_K' x = 1. \end{cases}$$

for some value of m.   ∎

The parameter m is interpreted as the smallest expected return per dollar invested that the investor has set as a target, and the solution to this problem yields the portfolio(s) with the smallest variance meeting this target.

1.2 Diversification

Assume that no risk-free security is available. What is the best way to combine investments so as to minimize risks? The variance of a portfolio returns is simply expressed as a function of the variance–covariance matrix Γ of the returns of risky securities. This matrix is given by $\Gamma = (\gamma_{hk})$, where γ_{hk} is the covariance between the returns of securities h and k. The variance of the return of a portfolio of composition x is[2]

$$\operatorname{var}(x'\tilde{R}) = x'\Gamma x.$$

Consider first the "degenerate" case in which all the securities have the same expected return, $\overline{R}$. In this case, the expected returns of all portfolios are identical and equal to that value. A portfolio is thus mean–variance efficient if and only if its variance is lowest. We are seeking x, the solution to

$$\min x'\Gamma x \text{ s.t. } \mathbf{1}'_K x = 1,$$

If 2μ is the Lagrange multiplier associated with the constraint $\mathbf{1}'_K x = 1$,

$$x = \mu \Gamma^{-1} \mathbf{1}_K,$$

where μ is computed so as to satisfy the constraint.

Thus, there exists a unique optimal composition. For example, assume that all returns are independent and have the same variance: The variance–covariance matrix is proportional to the identity matrix. The optimal composition is then given by $\mathbf{1}_K/K$: The same amount, $1/K$, should be invested in each security. This is *diversification*. Otherwise, without independence or identical variance,

---

2 x is a K-dimensional column vector and Γ is a $(K \times K)$ matrix. We have

$$\gamma_{hk} = \sum_{e=1}^{E} \pi(e)[\tilde{R}_h(e) - E\tilde{R}_h][(\tilde{R}_k(e) - E\tilde{R}_k].$$

and can write

$$\Gamma = E[(\tilde{R} - E\tilde{R})(\tilde{R} - E\tilde{R})'],$$

where the $'$ denotes transposition. The variance of the return of a portfolio composed of (x_*, x) is

$$\operatorname{var}(x'\tilde{R}) = Ex'(\tilde{R} - E\tilde{R})(\tilde{R} - E\tilde{R})'x,$$

or $x'\Gamma x$. If we assume that there is no redundancy, the matrix Γ has an inverse. Otherwise, there would exist a non-nil vector x such that $x'(\tilde{R} - E\tilde{R}) = 0$, so that a portfolio of risky securities would replicate the risk-free security.

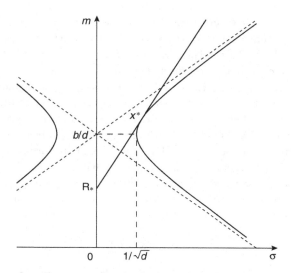

Figure 4.1 The two-fund theorem.

the optimal composition reflects differences between the variances of the security returns and their correlations.

In the general case in which expected returns differ across securities, it is necessary to arbitrate between the expectation and the variance of the return. For *a given target on expected return*, there exists a portfolio composition that minimizes risk. A graphical representation is helpful. Figure 4.1 plots the set of couples (standard error, expectation) associated with each possible portfolio in a (σ, m)-space. The couples associated with efficient compositions are on the frontier of that set, and constitute what is called the *efficiency frontier*.

1.3 The Efficiency Frontier in the Absence of a Riskless Security

Assume that there are at least two securities with different expected returns. The problem to be solved is written as

$$\min x' \Gamma x \text{ s.t.} \begin{cases} Ex'\tilde{R} = m, \\ \mathbf{1}'_K x = 1, \end{cases}$$

for some values of m in $\mathbb{R}$. In contrast to the preceding formulation, the inequality on the expected return is replaced by an equality. For each target m, a solution is a portfolio with the smallest variance whose expected return is *exactly* m. Since there are two securities with distinct expected returns, the domain defined by the two constraints is not empty, regardless of the value of m (we are using the assumption that there are no limits on short sales). Imposing an equality constraint on the expected returns simplifies the math. Extending this solution to the formulation with inequalities, which is associated with the economic problem, is trivial.

Since the function to be minimized is a convex quadratic form, bounded below by zero, and the constraints are linear, the solution exists and is characterized by the first-order necessary and sufficient conditions. Letting 2λ and 2μ, respectively, represent the multipliers for the expected return and the budget constraints, these conditions are

$$\Gamma x = \lambda E\tilde{R} + \mu \mathbf{1}_K. \tag{4.1}$$

They give, together with the two constraints, a linear system of $K + 1$ equations in the $K + 1$ unknowns (x, λ, μ). To solve this system, x can be expressed as a function of the multipliers from the first-order condition (4.1) because under the assumption of no redundancy, the matrix Γ has an inverse. Plugging this expression into the constraints gives

$$E\tilde{R}'\Gamma^{-1}E\tilde{R}\lambda + E\tilde{R}'\Gamma^{-1}\mathbf{1}_K\mu = m,$$
$$\mathbf{1}_K'\Gamma^{-1}E\tilde{R}\lambda + \mathbf{1}_K'\Gamma^{-1}\mathbf{1}_K\mu = 1.$$

This is a symmetric linear system with a strictly positive determinant. Inverting it[3] yields

$$\lambda = \frac{dm - b}{\Delta} \quad \text{and} \quad \mu = \frac{-bm + c}{\Delta}.$$

The optimal portfolio is simply obtained by using (4.1) again. We keep this calculation for later and first focus on finding the expression for the least variance as a function of m. For this, premultiply the first-order condition by x', yielding

$$\sigma^2 = \lambda m + \mu,$$

---

3 We set $d = \mathbf{1}_K'\Gamma^{-1}\mathbf{1}_K$, $b = \mathbf{1}_K'\Gamma^{-1}E\tilde{R}$, $c = E\tilde{R}'\Gamma^{-1}E\tilde{R}$, and $\Delta = dc - b^2$. It is trivial to verify that Δ is strictly positive provided there are two securities with different expected returns.

where $\sigma^2 = x'\Gamma x$ is the value of the variance of the efficient portfolio. Inserting the expressions obtained for λ and μ yields

$$\sigma^2 = \frac{dm^2 - 2bm + c}{\Delta},$$

or

$$\left(\frac{\Delta}{d}\right)\sigma^2 - \left(m - \frac{b}{d}\right)^2 = \frac{\Delta}{d^2}.$$

This is the equation for a hyperbola in the (standard error, mean) (σ, m) plane. The standard error is lowest at $m = b/d$, where its value is $1/\sqrt{d}$. In terms of the initial problem, where we sought the portfolio with the smallest variance generating an expected return of at least m (we are reverting to the formulation with inequality rather than equality), only the section of the hyperbola in which the expected return exceeds b/d is of interest. For all values of m below b/d, we wish to retain the least-variance portfolio. Any risky portfolio entails a level of risk equal to at least the minimum standard error $1/\sqrt{d}$: The nondiversifiable minimum risk. An investor who is prepared to accept a risk exceeding that minimal level can obtain a higher expected return.

1.4 Efficient Portfolios: The Case with a Risk-Free Security

Now assume that a risk-free security exists. The graphic representation of the new efficiency frontier can easily be found from its version with only risky securities. We will subsequently derive it analytically.

For one dollar to invest, x_* dollars can be put into the risk-free security (standard error $= 0$, mean $= R_*$), and $(1 - x_*) = \sum_{k=1}^{K} x_k$ dollars into some risky portfolio with standard error $\hat\sigma$ and mean $\hat m$. This operation yields a portfolio with standard error and mean given by

$$\sigma = |1 - x_*|\hat\sigma, \quad m = x_* R_* + (1 - x_*)\hat m.$$

Consider first an investment x_* in the risk-free security that is less than one, implying that the value of the risky part of the portfolio is positive. Graphically, for a given $(\hat\sigma, \hat m)$, the point (σ, m) describes the ray originating at the point representing the risk-free security $(0, R_*)$ and passing through $(\hat\sigma, \hat m)$. Now, if we consider all possible risky portfolios, $(\hat\sigma, \hat m)$ varies within a zone delimited by the hyperbola in Figure 4.1 and the set of rays describes the cone resting on the efficiency frontier.

Consider now an investment x_* greater than 1: The cone supported by the branch of the hyperbola that is symmetric with respect to the m-axis is obtained.

Mean–variance efficient combinations are located on the upper frontier of this cone: it is the ray that is tangent to the hyperbola that originates at the point representing the risk-free security. The point of tangency corresponds to a portfolio made only of risky securities x^*. This shows that all efficient portfolios are linear combinations of x^* and the risk-free security.

Theorem 4.1 The two-fund theorem *Assume there is a riskless security. For given expected returns and covariance matrix, all mean–variance efficient portfolios can be made up from two pooled investment funds: The risk-free security and a single risky fund.* ∎

These results can easily be derived analytically. Let (x_*, x) be a portfolio composition, where x is the risky component and x_* the risk-free component. Efficient compositions are solutions to

$$\min x' \Gamma x \text{ s.t.} \begin{cases} x_* R_* + E x' \tilde{R} \geq m, \\ x_* + \mathbf{1}'_K x = 1, \end{cases}$$

and the first-order conditions are written as

$$\Gamma x = \lambda E \tilde{R} + \mu \mathbf{1}_K \quad \text{and} \quad 0 = \lambda R_* + \mu, \tag{4.2}$$

whence, eliminating μ, we obtain

$$\Gamma x = \lambda (E \tilde{R} - R_* \mathbf{1}_K). \tag{4.3}$$

Assume first that λ is non-nil and that the expected return constraint is binding. We immediately see that the risky component of the portfolio is independent of the target expectation m and proportional to

$$x^* = \alpha \Gamma^{-1} (E \tilde{R} - R_* \mathbf{1}_K), \tag{4.4}$$

where α is set so as to normalize x^*. The expected return m determines the amount x_* invested in the risk-free security. Thus, the optimal portfolio consists of x_* invested in the risk-free security and $(1 - x_*)$ in portfolio x^*.

If λ is nil, then so are μ and x. We invest everything in the risk-free security, which only works if the target expectation is less than R_* – in this case, the variance is minimum, equal to zero.

Remark 4.1 In practice, the return of the riskless security, R_*, is less than b/d. This is the case pictured in Figure 4.1. All efficient portfolios contain (positive) investments in risky securities, and the amount invested in them increases with the portfolio expected return. It is theoretically possible for R_* to be greater than b/d. Then, x_* is greater than 1 for all efficient portfolios, and investors take short positions on risky securities. Here again, the greater the absolute value of the position in risky securities, the greater the expected return.

2 Portfolio Choice under the von Neumann Morgenstern Criterion

We revert to the framework introduced in Chapter 3, assuming that the investor's tastes are represented by a von Neumann Morgenstern utility function, $Ev(\tilde{c})$. The function v is increasing, concave, and twice differentiable everywhere. Since a portfolio (z_*, z) yields a stochastic payoff in period 1,

$$\tilde{c} = z_* + \sum_{k=1}^{K} z_k \tilde{a}_k = z_* + z' \tilde{a},$$

the portfolio choice is described by the following program:

An investor chooses a portfolio (z_*, z) maximizing

$$Ev(\tilde{\omega} + z_* + z'\tilde{a})$$

subject to the budget constraint,

$$p_* z_* + p'z = \omega_0.$$

It is convenient to define the "indirect" utility function, V, derived from the "primal" utility function and containing the decision variables (z_*, z):

$$V(z_*, z) \equiv Ev(\tilde{\omega} + z_* + z'\tilde{a}).$$

The investor's program is then written as

$$\max_{z_*, z} V(z_*, z), \quad \text{s.t. } p_* z_* + p'z = \omega_0. \tag{4.5}$$

In contrast to the mean–variance framework, this program is not in general homogeneous with respect to wealth. By construction, the function V inherits the properties of being increasing and concave from the function v (note, however, that the domain of portfolios over which V is defined may depend upon the matrix of incomes $\tilde{a}$). Thus, this problem has the traditional structure of a consumer's utility maximization subject to a budget constraint. There is one important difference: the domain of maximization may be unbounded because sales are allowed without restriction. Therefore, the existence of a solution is not guaranteed. When security prices offer opportunities for arbitrage, the investor benefits by taking short positions on an expensive security to finance a purchase of an inexpensive one. Without limits on trades, no optimal solution exists, as shown in Theorem 3.2.

Remark 4.2 Working directly with future contingent income, rather than using the intermediary of the portfolio, is possible. It is convenient if markets are complete and without arbitrage opportunities. The vectors of security payoffs generate the entire space of contingent incomes ($E = K+1$). As seen in Chapter 2, working directly with disposable income in each state of nature is equivalent to dealing with contingent goods whose prices are equal to the state prices. Thus, we end up with a formulation that is identical to that of the consumer in traditional microeconomic theory. Also, dropping possible redundant securities, portfolios are in a one-to-one correspondence with future incomes. When markets are incomplete, which is a possibility we do not want to preclude, the set of attainable incomes is constrained. Using future incomes as variables forces us to account for $E - K - 1$ additional constraints, and it is just as easy to work with portfolios.

The investor's program (4.5) consists of maximizing a concave function on a convex set. Thus, the first-order conditions characterize the solution. Letting λ be the multiplier associated with the budget constraint at time 0, they are written as

$$Ev'(\tilde{c}) = \lambda p_*,$$
$$Ev'(\tilde{c})\tilde{a}_k = \lambda p_k, \quad k = 1, \dots, K. \tag{4.6}$$

As expected, these conditions can be satisfied only if there are no opportunities for arbitrage. Indeed they yield the investor's "implicit" state prices.[4] To see this,

---

[4] These state prices are those for which the investor would chose the same contingent income profile if all contingent markets were to exist.

writing expectation as a sum, (4.6) gives

$$\sum_{e=1}^{E} \pi(e)v'[c(e)]a_k(e) = \lambda p_k, \quad k = *, 1, \ldots, K.$$

This shows, comparing with Theorem 2.1,

> If an optimal portfolio exists, there are no opportunities for arbitrage, and the positive vector q defined by

$$q(e) = \pi(e)v'(c_e)\lambda$$

> is a vector of state prices. It satisfies the equalities

$$\sum_{e=1}^{E} q(e)a_k(e) = p_k, \quad k = *, 1, \ldots, K.$$

If markets are complete, this last system of equations is of full rank and state prices are unique. All investors' vectors of marginal utilities for the contingent goods are thus proportional to each other.

To find a solution, note that completing the first-order conditions with the budget constraint, a system with $K + 2$ equations for solving $K + 2$ variables (z_*, z, λ) is obtained. Eliminating the multiplier λ and using the equality $p_* = 1/(1 + r)$, an optimal portfolio is thus characterized by

$$Ev'(\tilde{c})[\tilde{a}_k - (1 + r)p_k] = 0, \quad k = *, 1, \ldots, K,$$

$$p_* z_* + p'z = \omega_0. \tag{4.7}$$

3 Finance Paradigms: Quadratic and CARA Normal

In two specifications widely used in finance, quasi-explicit expressions can be derived for savings and the demands of securities. The determinants of the demand for financial securities can be easily interpreted. Furthermore, a link is established with the mean–variance criterion.

In the first specification, a quadratic utility function is assumed:

$$v(c) = c - \frac{\alpha}{2}c^2,$$

where α is sufficiently small so that the function is increasing in c in the relevant domain.

The identity $E\tilde{c}^2 = (E\tilde{c})^2 + \text{var}(\tilde{c})$ allows us to write

$$Ev(\tilde{c}) = E(\tilde{c}) - \frac{\alpha}{2}(E\tilde{c})^2 - \frac{\alpha}{2}\text{var}(\tilde{c}),$$

or

$$Ev(\tilde{c}) = v(E\tilde{c}) - \frac{\alpha}{2}\text{var}(\tilde{c}). \tag{4.8}$$

In the second specification, referred to, for short, as CARA normal, utility exhibits CARA:

$$v(c) = -\exp(-\rho c),$$

with ρ positive, and the distribution of payoffs is normal. Using the standard formula for the expectation of a log-normal variable, the expected utility of income during the second period is written as

$$Ev(\tilde{c}) = -\exp\left\{-\rho\left[E\tilde{c} - \frac{\rho}{2}\text{var}(\tilde{c})\right]\right\} = v\left[E\tilde{c} - \frac{\rho}{2}\text{var}(\tilde{c})\right]. \tag{4.9}$$

In both cases, *the agent's utility is increasing in the expectation of future income* $E\tilde{c}$ *and decreasing in its variance* $\text{var}(\tilde{c})$. It is independent of the other moments of future income.

The expectation and variance of income associated with the purchase of portfolio (z_*, z) can be easily computed, using the expression $\tilde{c} = \tilde{\omega} + z_* + z'\tilde{a}$. The linearity of the expectation and the bilinearity of the covariance give

$$E\tilde{c} = E\tilde{\omega} + z_* + z'E\tilde{a},$$

$$\text{var}(\tilde{c}) = z'\text{var}(\tilde{a})z + 2z'\text{cov}(\tilde{a}, \tilde{\omega}) + \text{var}(\tilde{\omega}).$$

In both the quadratic and CARA-normal cases, the optimal portfolio is the solution of a program:

$$\max V(z_*, z) = f[E\tilde{c}, \text{var}(\tilde{c})], \quad \text{s.t. } p_*z_* + p'z = \omega_0,$$

for some function f, where $E\tilde{c}$ and $\text{var}(\tilde{c})$ are given by their expressions in terms of (z_*, z).

The important point to note here is that the total income, not only the financial income, matters. In the presence of risky nonfinancial income, the optimal portfolio is generally not mean–variance efficient because the variance of total income, $\tilde{\omega} + z_* + z'\tilde{a}$, differs from that of financial income, $z_* + z'\tilde{a}$. However, *when* the nonfinancial income is risk-free (or uncorrelated with the securities payoffs), the quadratic and CARA-normal specifications both lead the investor to choose a mean–variance efficient portfolio.

3.1 Hedging Portfolios

Definition 4.3 *A portfolio that minimizes the variance of total income in period 1 is called a hedging portfolio.* ∎

The variance only depends on the risky securities in the portfolio, and the hedging portfolio z^h minimizes

$$\text{var}(\tilde{\omega} + z'\tilde{a}) = z' \, \text{var}(\tilde{a})z + 2z' \, \text{cov}(\tilde{a}, \tilde{\omega}) + \text{var}(\tilde{\omega}).$$

This portfolio is the one that would be chosen by an individual who is infinitely averse to variance in income (α or ρ equal to $+\infty$ in the quadratic and CARA-normal models, respectively). Thus, its value is

$$z^h = -\text{var}(\tilde{a})^{-1} \, \text{cov}(\tilde{a}, \tilde{\omega}). \tag{4.10}$$

This result has a geometric interpretation. Note that we are only interested in the variance of incomes. Thus, their expectations can be subtracted so as to work exclusively on centered incomes, that is, in the $(E - 1)$-dimensional space of variables with zero expectation. In this space, the covariance is a scalar product with associated norm as the square root of the variance, that is, the standard error. The centered incomes that are attainable with these portfolios define a subset spanned by the centered risky security payoffs, $\tilde{a}_k - (E\tilde{a}_k)$, in a K-dimensional subspace.[5] Hedging consists of choosing an income in this subspace that reduces the variance of total income to the greatest possible extent. This amounts to a projection. By definition, the projection of a vector onto a subspace is the closest vector of that subspace. Income is thus decomposed into the sum of its projection and a vector that is orthogonal to the subspace. Using the variance as the square of the distance between random variables, we can write for any centered $\tilde{x}$:

$$\tilde{x} = \text{proj}_{\tilde{a}}\tilde{x} + \tilde{x}_\perp, \quad \text{with} \; \text{proj}_{\tilde{a}}\tilde{x} = \text{cov}(\tilde{x}, \tilde{a}) \, \text{var}(\tilde{a})^{-1}(\tilde{a} - E\tilde{a}),$$

---

5 Owing to the assumption of no redundancy, the vector made of one, 1_*, is independent of the vectors $\tilde{a}_k, k = 1, \ldots, K$. Thus, by centering, the dimension of the spanned space is not reduced, and remains equal to K.

where

1 $\text{proj}_{\tilde{a}}\tilde{x}$ is a linear combination of the payoffs $\tilde{a}_k - E\tilde{a}_k$ and can thus be attained by a portfolio.

2 $\tilde{x}_\perp$ is in a subspace that is orthogonal to security payoffs (by construction, its covariance with $\tilde{a}$ is equal to 0). It is not correlated with security payoffs and consequently cannot be insured by the market.

Applying this result to nonfinancial income $\tilde{\omega} - E\tilde{\omega}$, its projection onto security payoffs is from (4.10), which is exactly the opposite of the payoffs of the hedging portfolio, that is, $-z^{h\prime}(\tilde{a} - E\tilde{a})$. Therefore, after hedging, final income is uncorrelated with security payoffs.[6] If markets are complete, $K = E - 1$, the investor can completely insure herself against nonfinancial risks: By selling the portfolio that duplicates nonfinancial income, the residual variance is nil. When markets are incomplete, some of the nonfinancial risks typically remain uninsurable on the markets.

3.2 The Demand for Risky Securities

The calculation of the demand differs slightly in the quadratic and CARA-normal cases.

Let us begin with the quadratic case. Recall the first-order conditions (4.7) for the K risky securities:

$$Ev'(\tilde{c})[\tilde{a}_k - (1 + r)p_k] = 0,$$

which can be also written as

$$Ev'(\tilde{c})E\tilde{a}_k + \text{cov}[v'(\tilde{c}), \tilde{a}_k] = (1 + r)p_k Ev'(\tilde{c}).$$

Since $v'(\tilde{c}) = 1 - \alpha\tilde{c}$, we have

$$Ev'(\tilde{c}) = v'(E\tilde{c}) \quad \text{and} \quad \text{cov}[v'(\tilde{c}), \tilde{a}_k] = -\alpha \, \text{cov}(\tilde{\omega} + z'\tilde{a}, \tilde{a}_k).$$

Stacking up these equations gives

$$v'(E\tilde{c})[E\tilde{a} - (1 + r)p] - \alpha[\text{var}(\tilde{a})z + \text{cov}(\tilde{a}, \tilde{\omega})] = 0.$$

6 This can be confirmed by calculating the following:

$$\text{cov}[\tilde{a}, \tilde{\omega} - E\tilde{\omega} - z'_h(\tilde{a} - E\tilde{a})] = \text{cov}(\tilde{a}, \tilde{\omega}) - \text{var}(\tilde{a})z_h = 0.$$

Factoring out $v'(E\tilde{c})$ yields

$$z = \text{var}(\tilde{a})^{-1}\left\{-\text{cov}(\tilde{a}, \tilde{\omega}) + \frac{v'(E\tilde{c})}{\alpha}[E\tilde{a} - (1 + r)p]\right\}$$

or, using the expression for *risk tolerance* $T(c) = v'(c)/\alpha$ (see Section 1 in Chapter 3)

$$z = \text{var}(\tilde{a})^{-1}\{-\text{cov}(\tilde{a}, \tilde{\omega}) + T(E\tilde{c})[E\tilde{a} - (1 + r)p]\}. \qquad (4.11)$$

The CARA-normal case yields the same equation, but the calculations are simpler, starting directly from the investor's problem. The investor maximizes $v\{E\tilde{c} - \rho/2[\text{var}(\tilde{c})]\}$ subject to the budget constraint. Substituting z_* from the budget constraint as a function of z, the first-order condition in z yields Eqn (4.11), using the fact that risk tolerance is equal to $1/\rho$ for CARA utility functions.

Thus, the investor's demand for securities appears as the sum of two portfolios:

1 The first is the hedging portfolio.
2 The second is proportional to $\text{var}(\tilde{a})^{-1}[E\tilde{a} - (1 + r)p]$. It is called *speculative* because it coincides with the demand of an investor with no risky nonfinancial income to hedge ($\tilde{\omega}$ constant). By intervening in the market, he is taking some risk. When security payoffs are not correlated and have the same variance, the speculative portfolio is proportional to $E\tilde{a} - (1 + r)p$, the vector of the expected security payoffs in excess of discounted prices (the discounting is necessary because prices are paid at time 0 and payoff received in the next period.) The investor buys a security if the expected payoff is larger than the discounted price and sells it if it is lower.

Thus, in the two specifications just examined, the portfolio choice responds to two goals: risk reduction and speculation. Clearly, the relative weights assigned to each of these elements depend not only on the amount of initial risk to hedge and the opportunities reflected by the securities, but also on risk tolerance: The speculative part increases with the investor's risk tolerance.

The difference with the mean–variance case merits emphasis. The two-fund theorem is only applicable to speculative demand: Speculators with the same expectations choose the same portfolios, and they behave according to the mean–variance model. Instead, the composition of the hedging portfolio depends on individual nonfinancial incomes and usually varies from one investor to the other. Overall, in this model, any difference in portfolio composition must be attributable to variations in hedging requirements or to heterogeneous beliefs on the securities payoffs.

Remark 4.3

1 The expression (4.11) for the optimal portfolio is not entirely explicit in the quadratic case, since risk tolerance depends on total expected income, and thus on the investment on the risk-free security and ultimately on the interest rate.
2 When we move beyond these two simple specifications, the first-order conditions in (4.6) are no longer linear in z and the demand for securities simultaneously reflects hedging needs and a desire for profitable investments – though it is usually not feasible to distinguish between these two elements.

BIBLIOGRAPHICAL NOTE

Mean–variance analysis, founded by Markowitz (1952), is very popular in finance. The presentation here is similar to that in Ingersoll (1987). The volume edited by Diamond and Rothschild (1978) contains applications and critical insights on the von Neumann Morgenstern theory.

Diamond, P. and M. Rothschild (1978). *Uncertainty in economics*, Academic Press, Boston, MA.
Ingersoll, J.E. Jr. (1987). *Theory of financial decision making*, Rowman and Littlefield, New York.
Markowitz, H. (1952). "Portfolio selection," *Journal of Finance*, 7, 77–91.

Exercises

4.1 *The mean-variance criterion*   Consider a stock market with two risky securities ($k = 1, 2$). Their returns (per dollar invested) are denoted by $\tilde{R}_k, k = 1, 2$, with mathematical expectation and standard deviation m_k and σ_k, respectively. Let ρ be the correlation coefficient between $\tilde{R}_1$ and $\tilde{R}_2$, that is, $\rho = \text{cov}(\tilde{R}_1, \tilde{R}_2)/(\sigma_1 \sigma_2)$. There is also a riskless security ($k = *$) that yields $R_* = (1 + r)$ per dollar invested.

Let $\tilde{R}$ be the return of a portfolio of composition x, that is,

$$\tilde{R} = x_* R_* + x_1 \tilde{R}_1 + x_2 \tilde{R}_2,$$

in which x_k represents the fraction invested in k ($k = *, 1, 2$):

$$x_* + x_1 + x_2 = 1.$$

There is no condition on the sign of the x_k, implying that short selling of any security is allowed. Finally, denote the mathematical expectation and the standard deviation of $\tilde{R}$ by m and σ, respectively.

1 Show that all portfolios that consist exclusively of risky securities define a curve in the plane (σ, m). Represent this curve by assuming $m_1 = 2, m_2 = 1, \sigma_1 = 2, \sigma_2 = 1$, in the cases $\rho = 1, \rho = 1/2, \rho = 0$, and $\rho = -1$. Identify the part of the curve that can be reached when short sales are not allowed. Comment.

2 Assume that $\rho = 1/2$ and $m_* = 1/2$. Find the equation of the efficiency frontier. What is the composition of the mutual fund of risky securities chosen by any investor? Comment.

3 Characterize the demand of securities of an investor with preferences represented by a utility function $U(m, \sigma) = m - \alpha \sigma^2, \alpha > 0$.

4.2 Maximizing utility and the mean–variance criterion Under some circumstances, the quadratic utility function leads to the choice of mean–variance efficient portfolios. However, it has two drawbacks: First, the possible values for income must be restricted to the domain on which the function is increasing (recall that a concave quadratic function is surely decreasing for sufficiently high values of its argument). But most of all, absolute risk aversion increases with the level of wealth in the case of the quadratic function, which violates current observations.

An alternative rationale for mean–variance analysis makes use of assumptions that are not on the form of the utility function, but rather on the distribution of portfolio returns.

I *The normal case*

An investor invests wealth ω_0 to acquire a portfolio z comprised of K securities. With the usual notations, $p'z = \omega_0$, and the portfolio yields a random financial income of $z'\tilde{a} = \sum_{k=1}^{K} z_k \tilde{a}_k$ at time 1.

The investors' preferences over financial incomes are represented by a von Neumann Morgenstern utility index $v: \mathbb{R} \to \mathbb{R}$ – a strictly increasing, strictly concave, and twice continuously differentiable function.

Let g denote the probability density function of the standard normal distribution:

$$g(x) = \frac{1}{\sqrt{2\pi}} \exp\left(-\frac{x^2}{2}\right).$$

To ensure that the integrals are well defined, we assume that there exists a number M such that, for all m and σ, the functions $f(x) = v(x), v'(x)$ or $v''(x)$ satisfy

$$\lim_{x \to \pm\infty} |x^2 f(m + \sigma x) g(x)| \leq M.$$

1 Check that the choice of a portfolio only depends on the mean and variance of its payoffs. Denoting by (m, σ) the couple (mean, standard error) associated with the portfolio z, define

$$V(m, \sigma) = Ev(z'\tilde{a}).$$

Show that

$$\frac{\partial V}{\partial m} = Ev'(z'\tilde{a}) \quad \text{and} \quad \frac{\partial V}{\partial \sigma} = \sigma Ev''(z'\tilde{a}).$$

Demonstrate that the function V is concave in (m, σ). What is the form of the indifference curves of V in the (σ, m) plane?

2 Compute the optimal portfolio for a utility function with CARA $\rho > 0$:

$$v(x) = -\exp(-\rho x).$$

Assume that there exists a risk-free security. How do investor's choices vary with their risk aversions?

II Non-normal distributions

The preceding analysis relies on two properties: (1) Normal distributions are characterized by two parameters, and (2) any linear combination of the components of a jointly normal vector has a normal distribution.

The mean–variance analysis extends to families of random variables whose distributions depend on two parameters and that are stable by linear combination. There are many such families besides the multivariate normal distribution: They are called elliptical distributions. We examine here an example. Let $(\tilde{\alpha}, \tilde{\beta})$

be a couple of real random variables with density function $h(\alpha, \beta)$, where $\tilde{\beta}$ is strictly positive with probability 1.

1 Consider the family of random variables $\tilde{a}$, whose conditional distribution given (α, β) is a normal distribution with mean αM and variance $\beta \Sigma^2$, for a couple (M, Σ) of $\mathbb{R} \times \mathbb{R}_+$.
   (a) Demonstrate that the family is stable by linear combination.
   (b) Compute the unconditional expectation and variance of $\tilde{a}$. Show that, if $E\tilde{\alpha} \neq 0$, the unconditional expectation and variance characterize the distribution within the family studied. Does this property extend to the multivariate case?

2 Consider an investor with CARA ρ. In the specific case in which $\alpha = 1$ and $\tilde{\beta}$ has an exponential distribution with parameter μ,

$$h(\beta) = \mu \exp(-\mu\beta),$$

compute the indirect utility function $V(m, \sigma)$, where (m, σ) represent the unconditional mean and standard error of a portfolio payoff. Specify the domain over which it is defined. Derive the portfolio demand. Compare it with the normal case above.

4.3 *Speculative and hedging demands*   Let a security be priced p at time $t = 0$ with an expected payoff at $t = 1$ (future price + dividend) denoted by $\tilde{a}$. The risk-free interest rate between $t = 0$ and $t = 1$ is r. We consider an investor whose preferences are represented by a strictly concave von Neumann Morgenstern criterion v on income at date 1.

1 The investor's initial wealth is composed of w_0 units of money. If she purchases z shares of the security at $t = 1$, her expected wealth at $t = 1$ is

$$\tilde{w} = (1 + r)w_0 + (\tilde{a} - (1 + r)p)z.$$

   Write the first-order conditions characterizing the demand of security. Show that the demand is
   (a) nil if $(1 + r)p = E\tilde{a}$;
   (b) positive if $(1 + r)p < E\tilde{a}$;
   (c) negative if $(1 + r)p > E\tilde{a}$.

2 Now assume that the investor initially has w_0 units of money and z_0 of the security. Using 1, decompose her demand into a speculative and a hedging component.

Optimal risk sharing and insurance

5

How can risky future resources be best shared when agents have differing attitudes toward risk? Traditionally, this question has been broached in two manners: A normative approach and an institutional approach. What are the features of an optimal allocation of risk? What types of markets or institutions allow such an optimum to be achieved, and under what conditions?

Characterizing the optimal allocation of risky resources among economic agents leads us to make a distinction between individual idiosyncratic risks (car accidents, fires, noncontagious diseases, etc.) and macroeconomic risks (business cycles, storms, natural disasters, epidemics, etc.). Individual idiosyncratic risks, by definition, have no impact on the aggregate resources in the economy. The optimal allocation of individual risks then implies *mutualization*, as shown in Section 1: The idiosyncratic risks are pooled, so that *ex post* there is no microeconomic risk left.

The implementation of optimal allocations in a decentralized way is examined in Section 2. It is again bringing to the forefront the issue of markets completeness. Indeed, if trades are unconstrained, an optimal risk-sharing allocation can result from the decentralized operation of a complete system of contingent markets (or Arrow–Debreu markets). In the absence of complete markets, optimality can nevertheless be achieved with a set of well-designed markets. Both *primary* securities based on individuals risky resources and *options* on aggregate wealth should be available. This property provides one possible explanation for the impressive proliferation of derivatives in recent years.

However, markets do not establish themselves! Their smooth functioning may be impaired due to incentives problems (unemployment insurance may reduce recipients' job search effort) and to privileged information by one of the contracting parties (a used car seller is better informed than the potential buyers on the car; alife insurance purchaser has some information on his health status; a financial market expert knows how to interpret firms data, etc.). Market failures are briefly described in Section 3, the final section.

1 The Optimal Allocation of Risk

Risk disappears as soon as the outcome of the anticipated event materializes and is known. Thus, risk sharing is only meaningful before the observation of the actual occurrence. An insurance contract illustrates this type of risk sharing. It specifies how much will be paid out as a function of whether an accident occurs and the level of damages. Similarly, trading an option induces a specific allocation of risk between the buyer and the seller that is linked to the evolution of the price of the underlying security.

For this type of a contract, which is contingent on the occurrence of a specific event, to be operational, it is essential that the event be observable with no possibility of contestation and that it be beyond manipulation by any of the parties to the contract. As before, we shall conduct the analysis by representing the contingencies with *states of nature*. These states are assumed exogenous, hence not manipulable, and perfectly observable by all parties. An allocation of risk specifies the amounts allotted to each of the parties in every possible state: It is said to be *contingent* on the states of nature. Once the state has been realized, the transfers specified in the contract are implemented with no possibility of default.

1.1 The Model

There is a single good and two dates: Today, $t = 0$, when the contingent exchange contracts are signed, and tomorrow, $t = 1$, when they are settled. In this section, as well as throughout this chapter, the focus is on allocating risky resources; hence, to simplify, individuals do not consume today.

The data are

1 the set $\mathcal{E}$ of possible states of nature at $t = 1$, assumed to be finite for simplicity:
$$\mathcal{E} = \{1, \ldots, e, \ldots, E\};$$

2 the probability distribution on $\mathcal{E}$, denoted by π; $\mathcal{E}$ can always be chosen such that $\pi(e) > 0$, for all e. All economic agents have the same beliefs: The probability π is known to all. This assumption specifically precludes certain actors having access to insider information;

3 global resources available in each state: $\omega(e)$ if e occurs, $\omega(e) > 0$;

4 agents, indexed by i, $i = 1, \ldots, I$. They value income and are risk averse or risk neutral. Their preferences are represented by a von Neumann Morgenstern utility function, v^i for agent i, where v^i is concave and strictly increasing.

Definition 5.1

1 *An allocation $(\tilde{c}^i)_{i=1,\ldots,I}$ specifies the consumption $\tilde{c}^i = c^i(e) \geq 0$ of each individual i in each state e.*

2 *It is feasible if it satisfies the scarcity constraints:*

$$\sum_{i=1}^{I} c^i(e) = \omega(e) \ \forall e. \tag{5.1}$$

3 *It is optimal if it is feasible and there is no other feasible allocation $(\tilde{c}'^i)_{i=1,\ldots,I}$ that provides greater utility to one agent without reducing that of any other:*

$$E[v^i(\tilde{c}'^i)] \geq E[v^i(\tilde{c}^i)] \ \forall i,$$

$$E[v^i(\tilde{c}'i)] > E[v^i(\tilde{c}^i)] \ for \ some \ i,$$

$$\Rightarrow \sum_{i=1}^{I} c'^i(e) > \omega(e) \ for \ at \ least \ one \ state \ e. \qquad \blacksquare$$

This notion of optimality is viewed *ex ante* because the utility levels are evaluated before the realized state is known. As explained previously, *ex ante* optimality is the relevant notion in insurance. In contrast, *ex post* optimality evaluates welfare in each state after it is known. When there is only a single good, as in the current case, this concept is irrelevant: Once the state is known, any allocation of the total available resources is optimal. In other words, any waste-free allocation is optimal *ex post*.

1.2 Insuring Individual Idiosyncratic Risks

If individuals are strictly risk averse, an optimal allocation satisfies a very specific property, known as the mutuality principle (it was first obtained by Borch (1960) in the early 1960s). This principle asserts that individuals' incomes are identical across states with identical aggregate resources. Therefore, individuals bear risks only when unavoidable.

Theorem 5.1 Mutuality principle *Assume that beliefs are identical and individuals are strictly risk averse. An optimal allocation* $(\tilde{c}^i)_{i=1,...,I}$ *satisfies*

$$\omega(e) = \omega(e') \Rightarrow c^i(e) = c^i(e') \; \forall i. \qquad \blacksquare$$

Proof of Theorem 5.1 Let $(\tilde{c}^i)$ be an optimal allocation. First, to develop the intuition, consider the case in which the aggregate resource is not risky: $\omega(e) = \omega$, for all e. If the consumption of some individuals is risky, consider an alternative allocation in which, in every state, everyone receives the expectation of consumption levels in the reference situation: $c'^i(e) = E(\tilde{c}^i)$, for all i and all e. This allocation is feasible. Since $(\tilde{c}^i)$ is feasible, condition (5.1) holds: $\sum_{i=1}^{I} c^i(e) = \omega$, for all e. Thus, taking expectations, $\sum_{i=1}^{I} \tilde{c}'(e) = \omega$ is satisfied. Furthermore, each individual whose allocation was risky is made better off because she obtains the same expected consumption as before, but without risk. This contradicts the optimality of the initial allocation $(\tilde{c}^i)$.

The argument extends to the case in which the aggregate resource varies across states. For a given possible value of ω, let $\mathcal{E}'$ denote the (not empty) set of states in which aggregate resources equal ω. If some individual's consumption is not constant in $\mathcal{E}'$, we can modify the allocation in $\mathcal{E}'$ by giving everyone the expectation of her consumption in $\mathcal{E}'$:

$$c'^i(e) = E[\tilde{c}^i|\omega(e) = \omega] \; \forall e \in \mathcal{E}'.$$

The new allocation is feasible, and

$$E[v^i(\tilde{c}'^i)|\omega(e) = \omega] = v^i[E(\tilde{c}^i|\omega(e) = \omega)].$$

By applying Jensen's inequality to the strictly concave functions v^i, we have

$$E[v^i(\tilde{c}'^i)|\omega(e) = \omega] = v^i\{E[\tilde{c}^i|\omega(e) = \omega]\} > E[v^i(\tilde{c}^i)|\omega(e) = \omega],$$

for individuals whose consumption is not constant in $\mathcal{E}'$. Since the allocation over states not in $\mathcal{E}'$ remains unaltered, their level of utility has strictly increased.

Nothing has changed for the other individuals. Therefore the initial allocation was not optimal. ∎

This result provides the rationale for insuring idiosyncratic risks. Assume, for example, that there is always the same proportion of ill people within a population.[1] If the productivity of all healthy individuals is equal, the per capita wealth remains constant regardless of the identity of the ill. According to the mutuality principle, each person's consumption must be constant and, in particular, independent of his health status. This type of risk sharing is exactly what a mutual company seeks to achieve.

As the demonstration makes clear, the mutuality principle is only valid when everybody shares the same beliefs. To illustrate this point, let us look at an example with two individuals and two states. Consider the extreme case in which the first individual assigns a zero probability to the second state, and conversely for the second individual. Even if the amount to be shared is identical in the two states, an optimal arrangement will allot all of the resource to the first individual in state 1 and all to the second in state 2. The existence of bets is often associated with differences in beliefs, as at races for example. A bet can be interpreted as a contingent contract on a random outcome. The betters' total resources remain constant: There is no macroeconomic risk. If two individuals have different beliefs, say, on the physical condition of horses, they may both believe that it is in their interest to take an additional risk when entering into a bet (on top of any simple pleasure in gaming).

1.3 Optimality: Characterization

If individuals are risk averse, thanks to the mutuality principle, optimal income levels depend on the state only though the available aggregate resources in that state. They are described by some functions, say C^i for each i: $c^i(e) = C^i(\omega(e))$. These functions determine how the *macroeconomic* fluctuations affect individual incomes. They are often called *sharing rules*. This section determines some properties of these rules. We first characterize optimal allocations with possibly risk neutral individuals.

The set of feasible allocations is convex and utilities are concave. Thus, as in traditional microeconomic theory, the set of optima can be described by

1 This assumption is approximately true for a large population subject to independent health risks.

assigning weights to individuals and maximizing the weighted sum of their utilities under the feasibility constraint. If all consumption levels are strictly positive,[2] the first-order conditions are necessary and sufficient. Whence:

Theorem 5.2 *Let* $(\tilde{c}^i)_{i=1,\ldots,I}$ *be a feasible allocation, with* $c^i(e) > 0$ *for all i and all e. It is optimal if, and only if, there exist weights* $(\lambda^i)_{i=1,\ldots,I}$, $\mu(e)$, $e \in \mathcal{E}$, *all of which are positive, such that*

$$\lambda^i v'^i[c^i(e)] = \mu(e) \ \forall i, e. \tag{5.2}$$

or, equivalently, if

$$\frac{v'^i[c^i(e)]}{v'^i[c^i(e')]} \text{ is independent of } i \ \forall e, e'. \tag{5.3}$$

∎

Proof of Theorem 5.2 At an optimum, it is impossible to increase the utility level of one individual, for example, agent 1, without lowering that of others. Thus, an optimal allocation solves:

$$\max E[v^1(\tilde{c}'^1)], \text{ s.t.} \begin{cases} \displaystyle\sum_{i=1}^{I} c'^i(e) = \omega(e) & \forall e, \\ E[v^i(\tilde{c}'^i)] \geq \bar{v}^i & \forall i \geq 2. \end{cases}$$

Letting λ^i represent the multipliers associated with the individuals constraints i, $i \geq 2$, and $\lambda_1 = 1$, the allocation solves

$$\max \sum_{i=1}^{I} \lambda^i E[v^i(\tilde{c}'^i)], \text{ s.t.} \sum_{i=1}^{I} c'^i(e) = \omega(e) \ \forall e.$$

In other words, it maximizes a weighted sum of utility levels under the scarcity constraints. Conversely, it is clear that any solution to such a program is an

---

2 A utility function v^i satisfies the Inada condition if $\lim_{c \to 0} v'^i(c) = \infty$. Under this condition, for all investors, a "corner" solution is precluded at an optimum and the analysis can be restricted to strictly positive c^i in all states.

If a utility function is not defined on $\mathbb{R}_+$, it is sufficient to replace the condition "$c^i(e) > 0$" by the condition "$c^i(e)$ belongs to the interior of the consumption domain."

optimum. Letting $\mu(e)\pi(e)$ denote the multiplier associated with the resource constraint in state e, the necessary first-order conditions are

$$\lambda^i v'^i[c^i(e)] = \mu(e) \ \forall i, e.$$

They are sufficient because the program is convex. ∎

This theorem indicates how, given the preferences of all individuals, the individual consumptions should vary with the state, that is, with the fluctuations in aggregate resources, in order to reach optimality. Two examples first serve as an illustration.

Example 5.1 *Risk neutrality* The optimality conditions (5.2) obtain when individuals are risk averse or risk neutral (but recall that the mutuality principle only holds when they are all strictly risk averse). Assume that agent 1 is risk neutral: $u^1(c) = c$, for all c positive or not. The optimality conditions applied to agent 1, $\lambda^1 = \mu(e)$, for all e, imply that $\mu(e)$ is state independent. Thus, for the remaining individuals, $v'^i[c^i(e)]$ is also constant. If they are risk averse, their marginal utility v'^i is strictly decreasing in consumption. Therefore, their consumption is constant across the different states. This means that individual 1 insures the others. The set of optima is thus easy to describe: Any optimum can be reached by allotting a sure level of consumption to each agent other than agent 1, who receives whatever is left over. ∎

Example 5.2 *CARA* Let all agents have CARA: $v^i(c) = -\exp(-\rho^i c)/\rho^i$, for all i. Let ρ be the harmonic mean of the ρ^i's:

$$\frac{1}{\rho} = \sum_i \frac{1}{\rho^i}.$$

For reasons that will become clear, the index ρ is called a measure of *aggregate risk aversion*. The optimality conditions are written as

$$\lambda^i \exp[-\rho^i c^i(e)] = \mu(e) \ \forall i.$$

Or, taking logs,

$$\log \lambda^i - \rho^i c^i(e) = \log[\mu(e)] \ \forall i. \tag{5.4}$$

Dividing by ρ^i and summing over i while accounting for the scarcity constraint, $\mu(e)$ is expressed as a function of aggregate wealth:

$$\sum_i \frac{\log \lambda^i}{\rho^i} - \omega(e) = \frac{1}{\rho} \log[\mu(e)].$$

Plugging this expression into (5.4) gives

$$c^i(e) = \frac{\log \lambda^i}{\rho^i} + \frac{\rho}{\rho^i} \left[\omega(e) - \sum_i \frac{\log \lambda^i}{\rho^i} \right] \ \forall i.$$

Taking expectation gives that $\log \lambda^i/\rho^i = E(\tilde{c}^i)$, which finally allows us to write the following:

If all individuals are characterized by CARA, optimal allocations have the following form:

$$c^i(e) = E(\tilde{c}^i) + \frac{\rho}{\rho^i}[\omega(e) - E(\tilde{\omega})] \ \forall i, \ e,$$

$$\sum_i E(\tilde{c}^i) = E(\tilde{\omega}).$$

At the optimum, the risks associated with the fluctuations in available resources thus are allocated independently of the relative weights assigned to agents in the social welfare index: Each individual receives a share of the variation of $\omega(e)$ around the mean, share that is proportional to his risk tolerance.[3] The sharing rule is linear: $C^i(\omega) = E(\tilde{c}^i) + \rho/\rho^i[\omega - E(\tilde{\omega})]$. The set of all optima is described by letting the distribution of $E\tilde{\omega}$ among agents, that is, the $E(\tilde{c}^i)$, vary. This separability between the distribution of the fluctuations and that of the expectation of the resources is specific to the situation where risk aversion is independent of the income level. ∎

What can be generalized?

Property 5.1 *Assume that all agents are strictly risk averse. At any optimal allocation, individual consumption levels increase with aggregate resources: The sharing rules, C^i for i, are all increasing.* ∎

This property states that all agents participate both in aggregate gains and in aggregate losses. The precise shape of the sharing rules depends on the preferences of all individuals, and one cannot hope for more general properties.

3 Other utility functions also give rise to linear sharing rules, as characterized by Wilson (1968).

Proof of Property 5.1 The marginal utilities v'^i are all strictly decreasing. Thus, according to condition (5.2), we have

$$\mu(e) < \mu(e') \Leftrightarrow c^i(e) > c^i(e') \ \forall i, \qquad (5.5)$$

and similarly replacing inequalities by equalities everywhere. This implies that for any two states e and e', consumption levels in state e are all either greater than, less than, or equal to those in state e'. Now the scarcity constraints hold. Thus, if $\omega(e) > \omega(e')$, we are necessarily in the first case, and we obtain

$$\mu(e) < \mu(e') \Leftrightarrow \omega(e) > \omega(e'), \qquad (5.6)$$

and similarly by replacing inequalities by equalities. Owing to (5.5) again, this gives the result. ∎

2 Decentralization

How can an optimum be reached? In many situations, individuals have a claim on a share of risky aggregate resources. It is unlikely that this initial allocation be optimal. We investigate here which kind of decentralized institutions allow optimality to be reached.

2.1 Complete Markets

Initially each individual i is entitled to $\omega^i(e)$ if state e materializes. Thus, the aggregate resources available in state e are equal to $\omega(e) = \sum_i \omega^i(e)$.

Let there be a complete set of contingent (Arrow–Debreu) markets: One for each state of nature. These markets are open *ex ante*, before the state is known. Recall that, by definition, one unit of a security contingent on e provides its owner with a claim to one unit of money if e materializes and nothing otherwise. Its price, denoted $q(e)$, is the *state price*, already seen in the study of valuation by arbitrage. Investor i's budget constraint at time 0 is written as

$$\sum_e q(e)z^i(e) = 0,$$

where $z^i(e)$ is the number of contracts contingent on state e purchased. Consequently, i's consumption in state e is $c^i(e) = \omega^i(e) + z^i(e)$. The definition of a competitive equilibrium in Arrow–Debreu markets is defined as in classical microeconomics.

Definition 5.2 *The price vector $q = (q(e))$ and individuals' portfolios $(z^i)_{i=1,\ldots,I}$ constitute an equilibrium if*

1 for all i, $z^i = (z^i(e))$ is a portfolio demanded by i given the prevailing prices:

$$z^i \text{ maximizes } \sum_e \pi(e) v^i(\omega^i(e) + z^i(e)) \text{ subject to the budget constraint,}$$

$$\sum_e q(e) z^i(e) = 0;$$

2 demand is equal to supply:

$$\sum_i z^i(e) = 0 \ \forall e. \qquad \blacksquare$$

Formally, this equilibrium is the standard Walrasian equilibrium in which contingent goods rather than physical goods are exchanged. An application of general results ensures that

1 there exists an equilibrium associated with the initial income distribution $(\tilde{\omega}^i)_{i=1,\ldots,I}$;
2 every equilibrium allocation is optimal.

The analysis is easily transposed to a complete markets structure, without necessarily requiring the existence of Arrow–Debreu securities. The link between state prices and the value of any security is given by arbitrage:

$$p_k = \sum_e a_k(e) q(e), \qquad (5.7)$$

in which as usual $a_k(e)$ is the payoff of one unit of security k in state e.

Note that state prices are defined up to a multiplicative constant. They can be normalized by

$$\sum_e q(e) = 1.$$

As seen in Chapter 2, the normalized state price vector can be interpreted as a *risk-adjusted probability distribution* and the price of any asset is equal to the mathematical expectation of its payoffs, computed with this probability.

2.2 State Prices, Objective Probability, and Aggregate Wealth

Equilibrium state prices, or equivalently the risk-adjusted probability, of course, depend on the true probability distribution but other factors play a role. We analyze here more closely the relationship between the risk-adjusted probability and the objective probability. For this, it is convenient to write the first-order condition associated with agent i's maximization problem:

$$\pi(e)v'^{i}[c^{i}(e)] = v^{i}q(e), \tag{5.8}$$

with v^{i} the multiplier associated with i's budget constraint. Thus, the conditions (5.2) that characterize optimality are satisfied, which is not surprising since an equilibrium allocation is optimal. Furthermore, comparing (5.8) and (5.2) shows that the multipliers $\mu(\cdot)$ (up to a multiplicative constant) associated with the scarcity constraints and the risk-adjusted probability are related by

$$q(e) = \pi(e)\mu(e).$$

Recall that with strictly risk averse individuals, by (5.6), the multipliers $\mu(e)$ are a function of the available aggregate resource $\omega(e)$ in state e, a function that is decreasing. Thus, according to the above formula, a state price depends both on the probability of occurrence of that state and on the available aggregate resource. Since the multiplier μ decreases with wealth:

> If individuals are strictly risk averse and aggregate wealth is uncertain, then state prices are not proportional to the objective probability, or equivalently the risk-adjusted probability differs from the objective probability: It is corrected by a factor that puts more weight on states with less wealth.

This correcting factor depends on the agents' level of risk aversion. When markets are complete, state prices both reflect the probability of occurrence of the states and the relative scarcity of resources across them.

2.3 The Role of Options

The decentralization of an optimum through Arrow–Debreu markets remains somewhat abstract. An optimal allocation can also be reached as an equilibrium in a more realistic market structure. This is the case if agents are able to exchange *options* on aggregate wealth alongside *primary* assets linked to each individual's risky income.

To show this property we start with two results that are interesting in their own right. The first makes explicit the role that options can effectively play as a truly new instrument for sharing risks. The second result pertains to the decentralization of an optimum under a *spanning* condition.

By truly new instrument, we mean that the option cannot be replicated by a portfolio made of preexisting securities. Therefore, it generates new opportunities for trade. This is not the case whenever the option can be valued by arbitrage. Then, because the option can be replicated, its use can only be explained as a matter of convenience, say in a dynamic context, and by a possible reduction in transaction costs. In contrast, the following theorem shows that, in a market that is incomplete a priori, options can "complete" the markets.

Theorem 5.3 *Consider a security yielding a payoff $\tilde{a}$ taking L values: $a^1 > a^2 > \cdots > a^L > 0$, $a^L \neq 0$. Let there exist $L - 1$ call options with strike prices $a^2, \ldots, a^L$, respectively. Then any random income $\tilde{c}$ contingent on the security payoff $\tilde{a}$ can be replicated by a portfolio comprising the security and the $L - 1$ options: There exists $z = (z_1, \ldots, z_L)$ such that*

$$\tilde{c} = z_1 \tilde{a} + \sum_{\ell=2,\ldots,L} z_\ell (\tilde{a} - a^\ell)^+. \tag{5.9}$$

∎

This theorem can be understood as follows. The only relevant events are the possible values of the security payoff. In other words, there are L relevant states, one for each value a_ℓ of $\tilde{a}$. The theorem states that any income contingent on these states can be obtained from a portfolio comprising the security and the $L - 1$ options: The $L - 1$ options complete the markets.

Proof of Theorem 5.3   It is sufficient to demonstrate that the options and the security generate complete markets. Since there are L states and L securities, we only need to show that the payoffs are linearly independent. Putting first the options, with exercise prices in decreasing order, and last the security, the matrix of asset payoffs is

$$\begin{pmatrix} a^1 - a^2 & 0 & \cdots & \cdots & 0 \\ a^1 - a^3 & a^2 - a^3 & \cdots & \cdots & 0 \\ \cdot & \cdot & \cdot & & \cdot \\ a^1 - a^L & a^2 - a^L & \cdot & \cdot & 0 \\ a^1 & a^2 & \cdot & \cdot & a^L \end{pmatrix},$$

which is upper diagonal. Since none of the terms in the diagonal is nil, this matrix has an inverse.[4] This proves that the assets payoffs are linearly independent. ∎

To state our second result, we need to define an equilibrium at date 0 in an arbitrary market structure. Let us as usual describe the securities by their payoffs, $(\tilde{a}_1, \ldots, \tilde{a}_K)$. Given prices $p = (p_k)$, investor i's budget constraint at time 0 is written as $\sum p_k z_k = 0$. If individual i buys portfolio z, he obtains consumption

$$c(e) = \omega^i(e) + \sum_k z_k a_k(e),$$

in state e.

A competitive equilibrium at prices p is defined as in classical microeconomics, by requiring that each investor demands a portfolio z^i that maximizes his utility subject to his budget constraint, and that markets are balanced:

$$\sum_i z^i = 0.$$

Theorem 5.4 Spanning *Given $\mathcal{E}$ and an initial income distribution $(\tilde{\omega}^i)_{i=1,\ldots,I}$, let $(\tilde{c}^{*i})_{i=1,\ldots,I}$ be an equilibrium allocation associated with complete markets. Consider a set of K securities with payoffs $\tilde{a}$ spanning this allocation, that is, for which,*

For all i there exists a portfolio z^i such that $\tilde{c}^{*i} = \omega^i + z^{i'}\tilde{a}$.

Then $(\tilde{c}^{*i})$ is also an equilibrium allocation in an economy in which only the K securities $\tilde{a}$ are exchanged. ∎

Proof of Theorem 5.4   Let $(q(e))$ be the equilibrium state prices associated with the allocation $(\tilde{c}^{*i})_{i=1,\ldots,I}$. By arbitrage, the security prices are, by (5.7),

$$p_k = \sum_e a_k(e)q(e) \ \forall k.$$

Consider now the economy with the K securities at prices equal to p. Individual i can buy any portfolio z that satisfies the budget constraint $\sum_k p_k z_k = 0$. Swapping the summation signs, this budget constraint can be written as

$$\sum_e q(e)\left[\sum_k z_k a_k(e)\right] = 0.$$

---

4 In the case where a_L is equal to zero, a similar property holds, provided the last call option is chosen with exercise price $a_L - 1$, instead of a_L.

By buying portfolio z, agent i gets consumption:

$$c(e) = \omega^i(e) + \sum_k z_k a_k(e),$$

in state e. Thus, the consumption levels that agent i can attain by trading the K securities *necessarily* satisfy the budget constraint of the economy with complete markets:

$$\sum_e q(e)[c(e) - \omega^i(e)] = 0. \qquad (5.10)$$

Conversely, any consumption bundle satisfying this equation and spanned by the securities is attainable in the K securities economy.

Now, since $(\tilde{c}^{*i})_{i=1,\dots,I}$ is an equilibrium allocation in complete markets, $\tilde{c}^{*i}$ is i's preferred consumption among those satisfying Eqn (5.10). Since $\tilde{c}^{*i}$ is spanned by the K securities payoffs $(\tilde{a})$, it is surely i's preferred choice when only these K securities are exchanged. Therefore, agent i demands any portfolio z^{*i} that yields $\tilde{c}^{*i}$. Furthermore, the feasibility condition, $\sum_i \tilde{c}^{*i} - \tilde{\omega}^i = 0$, ensures that $\sum_i z^{*i} = 0$. It follows that the price p together with the portfolios $(z^{*i})_{i=1,\dots,I}$ form an equilibrium for the economy with market structure $(\tilde{a})$. ∎

The condition that the agents' net trades $\tilde{c}^i - \tilde{\omega}^i$ belong to the vector space spanned by security payoffs is called the *spanning condition* . If there are as many linearly independent securities as there are states of nature, this condition is always satisfied regardless of the initial distribution of wealth or the allocation considered. Markets are complete, and the result is trivial. Theorem 5.4 is of interest when there are fewer securities than states of nature.

We can now state the final result. Let us call a security representing agents' risky wealth a *primary security* – for example, one that provides a claim to the profits $\tilde{\omega}^i$ of a firm created by entrepreneur i.

Theorem 5.5 *Assume that the traded securities include the primary securities $\tilde{\omega}^i$ for each i and options on aggregate resources, and that individuals are risk averse. Then any equilibrium allocation obtained with complete markets is also an equilibrium for this system of markets.* ∎

Proof of Theorem 5.5 An equilibrium allocation $(\tilde{c}^{*i})_{i=1,\dots,I}$ in complete markets is optimal. Therefore, individuals' consumptions are a function of aggregate wealth: $\tilde{c}^{*i} = C^i(\tilde{\omega})$. According to Theorem 5.4, it is sufficient to show that, for any i, the net trade $C^i(\tilde{\omega}) - \tilde{\omega}^i$ belongs to the vector space spanned by the securities payoffs. This is true since the securities exchanged include the primary securities $\tilde{\omega}^i$, and the function of aggregate wealth $C^i(\tilde{\omega})$ is spanned by the options according to Theorem 5.3. ∎

The availability of the primary securities and of the options on the aggregate resources ensures that an equilibrium allocation with complete markets is spanned *whatever* the preferences. For some specific preferences profiles, such as those with constant risk aversion, the optimal sharing rules are linear in the aggregate resource (see Example 5.2). In this case, trading the primary securities suffices to satisfy the spanning condition.

3   Market Failures

Is it realistic to assume the existence of a system of complete competitive markets? In the case of individual risks, obviously not, since there would only be a single seller per market! However, we have seen how mutualization allows this problem to be partly solved. As to collective risks, the essential question is to establish whether markets can function properly. Now, differences (or asymmetries) in the availability of information that plague situations of uncertainty cast doubt on the applicability of traditional competitive mechanisms. We present some illustrative examples here.

Information and Insurance Contracts

Let us return to the framework of individual risks that can, theoretically, be insured by a mutual company. Issues related to information actually prove quite serious. A priori, individuals are not identical. Some feature a higher probability than others of having an automobile accident or falling sick. This probability depends on numerous factors but, all in all, can be separated into an "innate" component that is beyond anyone's control (I have slow reflexes, I have a genetic predisposition to diabetes, etc.) and another component reflecting efforts made to avoid the injury (I stick to the speed limit, I don't eat too much sugar, etc.).

The relative importance of these two components varies with the situation, but it is rare that both do not play some role. The latter component, called *moral hazard*, makes full insurance suboptimal. The former leads to *adverse selection* and complicates the analysis of competition.

An insurance company seeks to identify the needs of its clientele as nearly as possible and to offer contracts by class of risk. It may draw on statistical data. The variable of interest, the likelihood of an accident, is unobservable but frequently correlated with observable characteristics (age, sex, profession) on which the contracts are made contingent. If an insurer does not attempt to select, another one will do so, and lure away some of the customer base. For example, assume that a car insurer offers an undifferentiated insurance that returns the "mean" of benefits paid out if the clientele is representative of the population mean. Another insurer can offer a contract with a lower premium but a higher deductible, and thus draw away the "better" drivers (this is called a *market skimming* strategy). The first insurer will only be able to attract the worst drivers and in consequence will lose money. Thus, by offering a sufficiently broad range of contracts, insurers provide an incentive to individuals to self-select by revealing some of their own characteristics. It can be demonstrated that under this type of competition, an equilibrium may fail to exist. This suggests instability, and may provide a rationale for regulation making it possible for everyone to obtain insurance.

The Hirshleifer Effect

This effect, named after the author who first formulated it, describes the negative impact that the premature release of information may have on the allocation of risks. Consider the case of an entrepreneur who contemplates a potential investment. A group of investors interested in this project may benefit from participating in the firm. Indeed, if these investors are risk neutral, the entrepreneur can sell them the firm for a price equal to the mathematical expectation of the anticipated revenues.

Now assume that everyone in the economy, the entrepreneur and investors, learn how much revenue will be generated *before* settling the contract. An exchange now is necessarily settled at the known value. From an *ex ante* point of view, the entrepreneur is no longer insured: He is worse off while investors are not better off. Advanced information here is detrimental.

The Market for Lemons (Akerlof)

A more puzzling phenomenon even occurs if only the entrepreneur knows how much revenue will be generated – in contrast to the investors who are aware, however, that she has this inside information. Consequently, the entrepreneur will wish to keep the firm if the price she can receive for it is below the expected sure revenue. Thus, the investors know that any price that is accepted (or proposed) by the entrepreneur exceeds that revenue, and consequently they no longer have an interest in investing. Even if a formal market were to exist, it would not function. This mechanism may explain why some reputable but insufficiently transparent stock exchanges have been abandoned. It is also one of the arguments put forward to promote laws against insider trading.

For markets to fulfill their roles, it is necessary to organize the dissemination of available information so that eventual differences in knowledge do not create an unfair advantage to insiders and discourage investors. This is the basis for regulations that describe the information that must be provided to stockholders. This also explains the existence of bodies that gather and release information on firms that use markets. These bodies are called rating agencies[5] since they "rate" the risk attached to bonds issued by firms.

The market failure just described has been first illustrated with "the market for lemons," explaining the decline in interindividual sales of used cars to the benefit of institutions that guarantee the sales.

Further problems linked with information are investigated in Chapter 7.

BIBLIOGRAPHICAL NOTE

Arrow (1964) was the first to show that, if agents' expectations are correct, it is sufficient in an economy with several goods that a limited number of contingent tradable assets be available on spot markets open in every period to support the optimum. Borch introduced the mutuality principle in a seminal article published in 1960. His book (1992) examines insurance in many areas (reinsurance, life insurance, etc.). Wilson (1968) derives some properties for the sharing rules and examines the validity of the mutuality principle in more general contexts. The previously quoted book by Diamond and Rothschild (1978) groups basic articles on uncertainty, covering issues ranging from modeling preferences to market failure when agents possess private information.

The role of options in mitigating the absence of some markets is broached by Ross (1976). The presentation here follows Demange and Laroque (1999), who study some extensions. The problems created by market incompleteness are legion.

5 The three most well known are Fitch, Moody's, and Standard and Poor's.

Arrow, K.J. (1964). "The role of securities in the optimal allocation of risk-bearing," *The Review of Economic Studies*, **31**, 91–96.

Borch, K. (1960). "The safety loading of reinsurance premiums," *Skandinavrsk Aktuarieskrift*, 153–184.

Borch, K. (1992). *Economics of insurance*, Advanced Textbooks in Economics, North-Holland, Amsterdam.

Demange, G. and G. Laroque (1999). "Efficiency and options on the market index," *Economic Theory*, **14**(1), 227–236.

Diamond, P. and M. Rothschild (1978). *Uncertainty in economics*, Academic Press, Boston, MA.

Ross, S. (1976). "Options and efficiency," *The Quarterly Journal of Economics*, **90**, 75–89.

Wilson, R. (1968). "The theory of syndicates," *Econometrica*, **36**(1), 113–132.

Exercises

5.1 *Reinsurance contracts*   Consider two insurance companies $i = 1, 2$. Company i's reserves are equal to R^i at $t = 0$. It will reimburse a (stochastic) level of claims $\tilde{x}^i$ at $t = 1$. The interest rate is assumed to be nil. Hence, company i's future revenues at $t = 1$ are $\tilde{\omega}^i = R^i - \tilde{x}^i$.

Company i's utility is measured by a von Neumann Morgenstern utility function v^i. Thus, without reinsurance, company i's utility level is equal to $E[v^i(\tilde{\omega}^i)]$.

1 Assume that $\tilde{x}^1$ and $\tilde{x}^2$ are independent. At $t = 0$, the companies agree to sign a reinsurance contract along the following terms: If the claims payable at $t = 1$ are x^1 and x^2, respectively, firm 1 will pay $y(x^1, x^2)$ and firm 2 $(x^1 + x^2) - y(x^1, x^2)$, where y is a function remaining to be defined.
   (a) Define an optimal contract y and provide the first-order conditions.
   (b) Verify that y only depends on (x^1, x^2) through the sum $x^1 + x^2$. What is this property called?
   (c) What can you say about the monotonicity properties of these two companies' revenues with respect to the total level of damages $(x^1 + x^2)$?
2 If $v^i(c) = ac - b(c^2/2)$, for $i = 1, 2$, show that the optimal contracts are linear. Interpret the form of the optimal contracts as being composed of a fixed transfer and the repurchase of a fraction of the damages.

5.2 *Exchange rate risk*   Consider an economy consisting of a single entrepreneur and a consumer/speculator, respectively, indexed by i and s. There is a single risky good, available at times 0 and 1. Agents' tastes bear on their final wealth in terms of the good at time 1.

The consumer/speculator is risk neutral: He maximizes the mathematical expectation of his wealth $\tilde{c}^s$. Initially, at time 0, he owns a quantity ω^s, $\omega^s > 1$, of the good. This good can be stored at no cost from one period to the next (the quantity stored S is nonnegative).

The entrepreneur has no wealth at $t = 0$ and is risk averse. He has a von Neumann Morgenstern $v^i(c^i)$ utility function, concave, increasing, twice continuously differentiable, and defined on $\mathbb{R}$. He has access to a production technology: An investment of x, $x > 0$, in period 0 yields a quantity $g(x)$ in period 1, with g increasing, concave, and twice differentiable on $\mathbb{R}_{++}$. We assume that $g'(1) < 1$, $g(0) = 0$, and $\lim_{x \to 0} g'(x) = \infty$. The good is produced for export and sold for foreign currency, at an exchange rate, $\tilde{\tau}$, that may be stochastic. The income, in terms of domestic goods, of producing $g(x)$ for the foreign market is thus $\tilde{\tau} g(x)$.

1 Borrowing and lending is unlimited between times 0 and 1. Let r be the associated interest rate; z^i represent borrowing by i and z^s lending by s. Write and solve the two agents' programs in terms of the interest rate.

2 Assume that the exchange rate is fixed at $\tau = 1$. Show that the equilibrium interest rate is equal to zero and describe the allocation of resources.

3 From now on, the exchange rate is stochastic: $\tilde{\tau}$ takes the values $\frac{1}{2}$ and $\frac{3}{2}$ with equal probability.

Show that, for all r, the entrepreneur's production and utility levels are lower than under a fixed exchange rate regime.[6] What is the equilibrium interest rate?

4 Assume now that a forward market for currency has been created. At time 0, a contract can be bought or sold, one unit of which provides a claim to τ units of the domestic good at time 1.

Denote p^f the price of this contract, and z^{if} and z^{sf} the demands of domestic agents on this market. Write out the two agents programs. Describe an equilibrium on the credit and forward markets. Compute the equilibrium. Comment.

5 The production is in fact risky: An input x yields the random quantity $g(x)\tilde{\varepsilon}$, where $\tilde{\varepsilon}$ is positive with mean 1.

---

6 The following property is useful: If f is an increasing, integrable function, then the covariance of $f(\tilde{\tau})$ and $\tilde{\tau}$, provided it is defined, is positive.

Assume that the interest rate is nil, that p^f equals 1, and that the entrepreneur's utility is represented by a mean–variance criterion:

$$v^i(\tilde{c}^i) = E\tilde{c}^i - \frac{\rho^i}{2}\text{var}(\tilde{c}^i).$$

Compute the entrepreneur's supply of foreign currency on the forward market for a given level of input x as a function of the variance of the exchange rate and the covariance between this rate and sales. Can this be interpreted as the sum of a hedging and a speculative supply?

6 To spread the risks associated with production, a market is created for a new security. One unit of this security procures a claim to $\tilde{\varepsilon}$ at date 1. What is the equilibrium price of this asset? Write out the entrepreneur's program in this institutional setting and the corresponding first-order conditions. Why do the financial market and the forward currency market not constitute a complete set of markets (to simplify, assume that $\tilde{\varepsilon}$ can take a finite number of values, n). What is required to complete these markets? In your opinion, would this make it possible to raise investment levels to those observed in the fixed exchange-rate regime of question 2?

5.3 Incomplete markets and stock exchanges Consider an economy with a single consumption good. There are two periods, $t = 0, 1$, and, at time 1, two states of nature, $e = 1, 2$.

There are two consumers in this economy, $i = 1, 2$. The initial resources of individual 1 are constant over time and independent of the state of nature: He receives 1 at period 0 and 1 at period 1 in each state. Individual 2, a farmer, owns 1 at period 0. The value of his crop is only positive if climatic conditions are propitious, in state 2: At date 1, he has nothing in state 1, and 2 in state 2.

The agents' tastes are represented by a von Neumann Morgenstern utility function that remains invariant over time. For agent 1, $u^1(x) = v^1(x) = x$, and for agent 2, $u^2(y) = v^2(y) = \log y$. Furthermore, agents have a preference for the present: At time 0, they discount the future with the factor $\delta, 0 < \delta < 1$.

Finally, the probability that state 1 occurs is π, and that of state 2 is $1 - \pi$. These probabilities are known to the agents.

1 Write the consumers' utility functions. Compute the risk aversion indices and comment on the shape of the functions.

2 Determine the Pareto optima (to simplify, assume that the sign on individual 1's consumption is unrestricted: Negative consumption corresponds to a provision

of services). Compute the associated system of contingent prices, using good 0 as the numeraire.

3 Now assume that a single security is available. It is riskless: One unit of the security procures an unconditional claim on one unit of the good at time 1.

Define the competitive equilibrium. Without calculation, determine the price of the security at time 0 in terms of good 0.

Compute the equilibrium allocation for $\pi = \frac{1}{2}, \delta = \frac{1}{3}$.

Is this a Pareto optimum?

4 The farmer, individual 2, decides that his business is too risky and chooses to go public. When the corporation is established, he swaps his right to receive two units of the good in state 2 for the entirety of the stock. The shares of the company are negotiable on the exchange at time 0.

Define and compute the competitive equilibrium. Why is it Pareto optimal?

Equilibrium on the stock exchange and risk sharing

What is the purpose of a stock exchange? The answer to this question depends on whom you ask. To some, it's a way for those who already have enough money to get more; to others, it's a way for companies to raise fresh capital to finance their activities; to yet others, it is a tool with which capitalists settle their accounts or reorganize their control of the productive system, and so on. All of these answers have an element of truth, but they neglect what economists would probably consider the essential function of stock exchanges. *Stock exchanges allow the risks associated with productive activities to be spread among investors. In this way, they guide firms into taking risks that are most in keeping with the desires of market participants.*

Stock exchanges underlie the institution of incorporated companies, allowing large risks to be distributed among many contributors of funds. The market allows the initial providers of funds to divest themselves of the firm by reselling their shares at any time. It provides liquidity by giving a public market for stocks. On this basis it facilitates investment. But it also severs the link between the stockholder, who can resell her share and may thus have a short investment horizon, and the manager of the firm who, at least initially, is reliant on the long-term viability of his labors.

Our goal in this chapter is to formalize and examine the risk distribution role that stock exchanges fulfill. This is done in the extremely simple framework of an exchange economy without production, with only one time period, and under *symmetric information*. By symmetric information, we mean that all investors are equally (or symmetrically) informed: Not only do they all share the same representation of states of the world and of the incomes accruing in these states, just like in models of arbitrage, but they also attribute the same probability to the occurrence of these states.

We first describe how the prices of risky securities are formed on competitive stock exchanges in which all investors hold mean–variance efficient portfolios.

This is known as the CAPM. It yields well-known relationships between the expected returns of risky assets and their "beta" in equilibrium. Mean–variance efficiency is a strong assumption that is subsequently put into perspective.

The final section uses a full description of the economy: agents' attitudes toward risk, uncertainty over the available primary resources, and preference for the present. Current consumption, portfolio choice, and the prices of all securities, risky and risk-free are jointly determined at equilibrium. This is known as the CCAPM. Not only are some relationships between risk premia derived as in the CAPM, but also their level. Finally, special attention is given to the determination of the risk-free rate, and its relation with the fluctuations in the economy. This study will be developed in Chapter 8.

1 The Amounts at Stake

The main features of the US households balance sheet accounts at the end of the year 2003 are described in Table 6.1.

To make sense of these large numbers, it is useful to recall that the US Gross Domestic Product, a measure of the overall production of the year, was equal to 11 trillion dollars in 2003. The net worth of the households is approximately equal to 4 years of production.

Of this total net worth, tangible assets – homes and durable goods, 18.4 trillions – represent slightly less than a half, in fact, less than a quarter if we deduct from their gross value the credits – mortgages and consumer credits, 9.3 trillions – that were contracted when acquiring them.

A large fraction of the wealth, approximately three-quarters, is therefore held in financial assets. Of these, a third, pension fund reserves and equity in noncorporate businesses, is illiquid. The remainder is made of money, credit instruments (treasury bonds, municipal securities, corporate, and foreign bonds issued by institutions and firms to finance their activities), and corporate equities. The last two categories are liquid when they are listed on an exchange market.

Most of the young, small companies are not listed on a stock exchange. Their shares cannot be traded by the public at large. A firm seeking outside equity capital and a public market for its stock holds an initial public offering (IPO), which is the first sale of stock to the public. The IPOs represented on the three main US stock exchanges (Nasdaq, Nyse, and Amex) a total of 105 billions dollars in 1999, 113 in 2000, and 44 in 2001, respectively (source: CommScan EquiDesk). The sharp

Table 6.1   Households balance sheet accounts in the United States amounts outstanding at the end of 2003 (in trillions of dollars)

	Assets	Liabilities
Assets	52.8	9.6
Tangible assets	18.4	
Real estate	15.0	
Consumer durable goods	3.4	
Financial assets	34.5	9.6
Deposits	5.2	
Mortgages	0.1	6.7
Other credit market instruments	2.1	2.6
Life insurance reserves	1.0	
Pension fund reserves	8.8	
Corporate equities	6.4	
Mutual fund shares	3.0	
Equity in noncorporate businesses	5.9	
Others	1.9	0.3
Net worth		43.2

Source: http://www.federalreserve.gov/releases/Z1/Current/

decrease is linked to the telecommunications crash. Investors purchasing stocks in IPOs generally accept considerable risks for the possibility of large gains.

The world market capitalization of US listed companies in 2003 was 31.3 trillions. These include capitalization abroad, for example, 2.4 on the London Stock exchange, 3.0 on the Tokyo Stock Exchange, and only 14.1 on one the three main US stock exchanges. Finally, the average daily dollar value of trading in 2003 was 38.5 billions (source: NYSE).

All these data reflect the importance of stock exchanges.

2   The Stock Exchange

The description of the stock exchange resembles that in the previous chapters (see Section 2.1 of Chapter 3). The market is open at time $t = 0$ (today), and the future is compressed into a single period, $t = 1$. Risk is represented by a finite set of states of nature, indexed by e, $e = 1, \ldots, E$.

2.1 The Securities

There are K risky securities, indexed with k, $k = 1, \ldots, K$. One unit of the security is defined by the payoff to which it yields a claim in the future in the different states: $\tilde{a}_k = (a_k(e))_{e=1,\ldots,E}$. The $(K \times E)$ matrix of payoffs from the risky securities is denoted by $\tilde{a}$. These payoffs are *exogenous*. They do not depend on currently established prices on the stock exchange, and are fixed prior to and independently of the equilibrium determination.

There is also a risk-free security, indexed by $*$, that allows investors to lend or borrow without risk. The risk-free security is defined by $a_*(e) = 1$, for all e. Recall that from Chapter 3 securities can be taken to be not *redundant*.

Trade is unconstrained: transaction costs are nil, short sales are allowed, and there are no limits on buys or sales.

2.2 Investors

There are I investors, $i = 1, \ldots, I$, who participate in the market. Each investor owns an initial portfolio of securities, $(z_*^i(0), z^i(0))$, and income ω_0^i at time 0 (income at date 0 includes both nonfinancial income and dividends paid by the initial securities holdings). Furthermore, at time 1, agent i receives a stochastic nonfinancial income flow that is completely described by the states of nature: $\tilde{\omega}^i = \omega^i(e)$, $e = 1, \ldots, E$. This income may come from activities external to financial markets, from labor, or from an unlisted private company. Like the revenues yielded by securities, non financial income is exogenous.

Let the prices of the risk-free and risky securities at time $t = 0$ be $p_* = 1/(1+r)$ and p_k, $k = 1, \ldots, K$, respectively. Investor i's portfolio, (z_*^i, z^i), together with the initial expenditure (or consumption) c_0^i at time 0, satisfies the budget constraint

$$c_0^i + p_* z_*^i + p'z^i = \omega_0^i + p_* z_*^i(0) + p'z^i(0), \tag{6.1}$$

and leads to an expenditure plan $\tilde{c}^i = c^i(e)$, $e = 1, \ldots, E$, in state e at time 1:

$$c^i(e) = \omega^i(e) + z_*^i + \sum_{k=1}^{K} a_k(e) z_k^i. \tag{6.2}$$

Investors' portfolio choices depend on their beliefs. We assume here that these beliefs are identical (or homogeneous), which is usually referred to as the assumption of symmetric information.

Hypothesis 6.1   Symmetric information   *Agents share identical beliefs: They all attribute the same probability $\pi(e)$ to the occurrence of state $e, e = 1, \ldots, E$.*

By definition, $\sum_{e=1}^{E} \pi(e) = 1$ and, without loss of generality $\pi(e) > 0$, for all e (one can drop the states that would have a zero probability of occurrence).

The tastes of the typical investor are represented by a von Neumann Morgenstern utility function that is separable between expenditures during the two periods:

$$U^i(c_0^i, \tilde{c}^i) = u^i(c_0^i) + \delta E[v^i(\tilde{c}^i)].$$

The mathematical expectation is computed using the probability distribution π. The functions u^i and v^i are increasing, concave, and twice continuously differentiable. v^i is the instantaneous von Neumann Morgenstern utility index for incomes at time 1.

2.3   Equilibrium

A competitive equilibrium on the stock market is defined in a standard way, by requiring that the aggregate demand of all securities is equal to the aggregate supply. The aggregate quantity of risk-free security is denoted by z_*:

$$z_* = \sum_{i=1}^{I} z_*^i(0).$$

The portfolio that comprises all risky securities listed on the exchange is called the *market portfolio*. It will play an important role in the analysis. It is denoted by z^m, indexed by the superscript m, defined by

$$z_k^m = \sum_{i=1}^{I} z_k^i(0), \quad k = 1, \ldots, K. \tag{6.3}$$

Definition 6.1   *A competitive equilibrium on the security (stock) market is given by a set of portfolios $(z_*^i, z^i)_{i=1,\ldots,I}$, an interest rate r, and a price vector p in $\mathbb{R}^K$, such that*

1 For all $i, i = 1, \ldots, I$, (z_*^i, z^i) is agent i's optimal portfolio, that is, the portfolio that maximizes his utility under the constraints (6.1) and (6.2), when the rate r, and prices p, are treated as given;

2 The demand of securities is equal to the available supply:

$$\sum_{i=1}^{I} z_*^i = z_*, \quad \sum_{i=1}^{I} z^i = \sum_{i=1}^{I} z^i(0) = z^m. \tag{6.4}$$

∎

Note that by construction of the investors programs, aggregate expenditure at date 1 is equal to the aggregate (financial and nonfinancial) incomes:

$$\sum_{I} \tilde{c}^i = \sum_{i} \tilde{\omega}^i + z_* + z^{m\prime}\tilde{a}.$$

It is easy to see that the definition of an equilibrium implies that aggregate consumption is equal to aggregate income[1] at $t = 0$:

$$\sum_{i} c_0^i = \sum_{i} \omega_0^i.$$

Just like in general equilibrium models, there is typically no analytical solution for equilibrium prices. In the quadratic or CARA-normal frameworks, the prices of risky securities have a quasi-explicit expression as a function of the fundamentals and of the equilibrium interest rate. This allows us in turn to examine the determination of the interest rate and the distribution of risks. We begin with the even simpler case in which agents' nonfinancial incomes are riskless.

3 The CAPM

In this section, all investors choose a mean–variance efficient portfolio. If risk aversion and preference for the present are not specified, equilibrium cannot be completely described. We nonetheless obtain relationships between the returns of the various securities at equilibrium – these are called the CAPM relationships. A complete determination of equilibrium, including the risk-free interest rate, is left for the following section.

---

1 This follows from Walras's law. There are $K + 2$ goods traded at time 0, the consumption good and the $K + 1$ securities. We normalize prices using the consumption good as the numeraire. The prices of the $K + 1$ securities are expressed in terms of the good at time 0. When the budget constraints at time 0 are identically satisfied, the equality of the demands for the $K + 1$ securities to their supply (condition 2 of Definition 6.1) implies the equality of aggregate income to aggregate expenditure at date 0.

3.1 Returns

The equilibrium prices of securities, or equivalently their returns, possess very unique features. Indeed, since investors have the same beliefs and there exists a risk-free asset, the risky part of their portfolios all have the same composition according to the two-fund theorem (Chapter 4). Consequently, at equilibrium, this composition is necessarily that of the portfolio comprising all risky securities listed on the exchange – the market portfolio. This observation allows a simple description of the fundamental relationships of the CAPM on the returns of risky securities.

Let x^m denote the composition of the market portfolio and $\tilde{R}^m$ its return. The share of security k in the portfolio is the ratio of its capitalization to total capitalization:

$$x_k^m = \frac{p_k z_k^m}{p'z^m}.$$

The return to the market portfolio is the ratio of the payoff to which it provides a claim to its "price," total market capitalization:

$$\tilde{R}^m = \frac{z^{m'}\tilde{a}}{p'z^m} = \sum_{k=1}^{K} \frac{p_k z_k^m}{p'z^m} \tilde{R}_k.$$

It is equal to a weighted sum of the returns of individual securities, the weights being the shares of the securities in total market capitalization.

Theorem 6.1   CAPM relationships   *Assume that all investors have the same probability distribution on the securities payoffs and choose a mean–variance efficient portfolio. If the net return to the risk-free asset is r, the equilibrium returns satisfy*

$$E(\tilde{R}_k) - (1 + r) = \beta_k\{E[\tilde{R}^m] - (1 + r)\}, \quad k = 1, ..., K, \tag{6.5}$$

where

$$\beta_k = \frac{\mathrm{cov}(\tilde{R}_k, \tilde{R}^m)}{\mathrm{var}\,\tilde{R}^m}. \qquad\blacksquare$$

The *risk premium* associated with the ownership of one dollar in security k is defined as the difference between its expected return and the risk-free return. In the CAPM, according to (6.5) the risk premium is the product of the security's *beta* with the risk premium on the market portfolio. Note that the risk premium of the market portfolio is not determined by the CAPM. Both from the empirical and theoretical points of view, the premium can be assumed to be positive (as we shall see later on). The β captures all the security specific characteristics that play a role in determining its risk premium, in relation to the market risk premium. The formula implies that any "idiosyncratic"risk that is uncorrelated with the return of the market portfolio does not modify the β. If the correlation between the returns of a security and of the market portfolio is nil, the expectation of the return of this security is equal to the risk-free return, however great the return variance. The beta is negative for a security payoff that varies against the market. Such a security allows the market risk to be hedged, which explains why the security return is lower than $1 + r$.

Indeed, the risk premium of the market portfolio can be interpreted as the price of risk, and any security risk is valued by multiplying this price by the quantity of market risk as measured by the beta it contains. This partly explains the popularity of this model. A priori, under the mean–variance hypothesis, the description of the model includes the covariances of the returns of all securities, that is, $K \times (K + 1)/2$ parameters. If the equilibrium relationship is approximately satisfied, then all that is required to determine the expectation of the equilibrium returns of the securities is the price of risk and the K values of the betas – a much smaller number of parameters.

The relationship in (6.5) is often represented graphically in the (beta, expected return) space. Under the assumptions of Theorem 6.1, points (β_k, ER_k), associated with the different securities, are aligned on the *market line*, of intercept $(1 + r)$ and slope $E(\tilde{R}^m) - (1 + r)$. Many empirical studies have sought to test this prediction of the model. One of the difficulties is that it is based on the mathematical expectation of returns, which in turn derive from investors' unobservable beliefs on payoffs. Thus, it is necessary to make assumptions on beliefs, which makes interpretation of the results difficult (cf. Copeland and Weston 1983). Another difficulty relates to the definition of the market portfolio. Should all securities, domestic and international, be included? More generally, the CAPM assumes that all investors' risky incomes can be exchanged on the market, a very strong assumption. We shall relax it in the next section.

In financial practice, this model is often used as an indicator of the (temporary?) under- or overvaluation of securities. The procedure is as follows. Betas are considered more stable than expected returns. They are estimated from past empirical covariances. Current mathematical expectations of returns are estimated on the basis of various pieces of information, for example, regarding future payouts. Then a linear regression is performed, which provides the market line. The position of the (β_k, ER_k) of a specific asset k "above" the estimated market line suggests an underevaluation: compared with other securities with a similar amount of risk that cannot be diversified (i.e., same β), the expected return of the security is larger. Similarly, a position "below" the estimated market line suggests an overevaluation of asset k.

Proof of Theorem 6.1 If beliefs are identical, all investors choose the same composition for the risky shares in their portfolios, which satisfies the equation (Section 2.2, Chapter 3):

$$\Gamma x = \lambda[E(\tilde{R}) - (1 + r)\mathbf{1}_K]. \tag{6.6}$$

At equilibrium, it must coincide with that of the market portfolio. Whence

$$\Gamma x^m = \lambda[E(\tilde{R}) - (1 + r)\mathbf{1}_K].$$

Recall that Γx^m is the vector the kth element of which is the covariance of the return of security k with that of the market portfolio x^m, or $\mathrm{cov}(\tilde{R}_k, \tilde{R}^m)$. Row k of the equation is written as $\mathrm{cov}(\tilde{R}_k, \tilde{R}^m) = \lambda[E(\tilde{R}_k) - (1 + r)]$.

To eliminate λ, we premultiply the expression above by the transposition of x^m which, using the equality $x^{m'}\mathbf{1}_K = 1$, yields

$$\mathrm{var}(\tilde{R}^m) = \lambda[E(\tilde{R}^m) - (1 + r)].$$

Carrying λ, we obtain the fundamental equation of the CAPM.   ■

3.2 Equilibrium Prices

The CAPM relationships, which are in terms of returns, can easily be rewritten in terms of prices. This is more in keeping with the practice in economics: Agents (investors) are active on markets and derive utility from goods (stochastic future incomes from securities). They base their demand on prices that adjust to balance the markets. To study general equilibrium and the determination of the risk-free rate, it will, in fact, be necessary to look at prices. Thus, to compare more easily with the next section, it is worthwhile to state the CAPM relationships with prices. The market portfolio distributes all risky financial incomes and its price equals total capitalization, or

$$\tilde{R}^m = \frac{\tilde{a}^m}{p^m} \quad \text{with } \tilde{a}^m = z^{m'}\tilde{a} \text{ and } p^m = p'z^m.$$

Using this expression and the definition of the return, $\tilde{R}^k = \tilde{a}^k/p^k$, we substitute into Eqn (6.5) of the CAPM and rearrange to obtain:

$$p_k = \frac{E(\tilde{a}_k)}{1+r} - \frac{\text{cov}(\tilde{a}_k, \tilde{a}^m)}{\text{var}(\tilde{a}^m)} \left[\frac{E(\tilde{a}^m)}{1+r} - p^m \right], \quad k = 1, \ldots, K. \qquad (6.7)$$

The price of a risky security is equal to the discounted expectation of its revenues minus a term, the *risk premium*, is analogous to that in the previous section. Given the premium on the market portfolio, $E(\tilde{a}^m)/(1+r) - p^m$, and the risk-free rate r, mean–variance analysis allows prices (or risk premiums) to be determined for individual securities. The complete equilibrium model will allow us to better understand the determinants of the risk premium on the market portfolio and of the risk-free rate, including the extent of the risks to be shared, the investors' risk aversions, and the preferences for the present.

4 The General Equilibrium Model and Price Determination

Let us return to the model in Section 2. We want to jointly determine current consumption, portfolio choice, and the prices of all securities, risky and risk-free, at equilibrium. The paradigms of finance introduced in Chapter 4 will allow us to do that.

It is useful to recall the problem that investors solve. They choose a portfolio (z_*^i, z^i) that maximizes their utility:

$$U^i(c_0^i, \tilde{c}^i) = u^i(c_0^i) + \delta E[v^i(\tilde{c}^i)],$$

under the budget constraint

$$c_0^i + \frac{z_*^i}{1+r} + p'z^i = \omega_0^i + p_* z_*^i(0) + p'z^i(0),$$

in the knowledge that their future income will be

$$\tilde{c}^i = \tilde{\omega}^i + z_*^i + z^{i\prime}\tilde{a}.$$

The model is one of the paradigms of finance: either individuals utility in period 1, v^i, are all quadratic or they are all CARA and the vectors $(\tilde{a}, \tilde{\omega}^i)$ are normally distributed. In both cases, the first-order conditions associated with the demand for securities lead to Eqn (4.11) from Chapter 4:

$$\text{var}(\tilde{a})z^i = -\text{cov}(\tilde{a}, \tilde{\omega}^i) + T^i[E(\tilde{c}^i)][E(\tilde{a}) - (1+r)p]. \tag{6.8}$$

4.1 Prices of Risky Securities

Owing to the shape of the demands, the prices of risky securities can easily be expressed as a function of the risk-free interest rate. Inspecting (6.8) reveals that the sum of the individual demands is equal to that of a single investors whose future income would be the sum of individual incomes and whose risk tolerance is the sum of individuals' risk tolerances. It is then sufficient to write that at the equilibrium price this aggregate (or representative) investor demands the market portfolio. More precisely, define the *economy risk tolerance* by

$$T(c) = \sum_{i=1}^{I} T^i(c^i).$$

In the quadratic case, $v^i(c) = c - \alpha^i c^2/2$, this expression is a function of aggregate demand:

$$T^i(c^i) = -\frac{v'^i(c^i)}{v''^i(c^i)} = \frac{1}{\alpha^i} - c^i,$$

and

$$T(c) = \frac{1}{\alpha} - c, \quad \text{where } c = \sum_{i} c^i \text{ and } \frac{1}{\alpha} = \sum_{i=1}^{I} \frac{1}{\alpha^i}. \tag{6.9}$$

In the CARA case, $v^i(c^i) = -\exp(-\rho^i c^i)$ and the economy risk tolerance is

$$\frac{1}{\rho} = \sum_{i=1}^{I} \frac{1}{\rho^i}.$$

Summing over individual demands for risky securities, we have

$$\text{var}(\tilde{a}) \sum_{i=1}^{I} z_i = \sum_{i=1}^{I} \{T^i[E(\tilde{c}^i)][E(\tilde{a}) - (1+r)p] - \text{cov}(\tilde{a}, \tilde{\omega}^i)\}.$$

As previously stated, we obtain the expression for the demand of an investor whose utility function is quadratic or CARA (with coefficient α or ρ)

and whose nonfinancial income equals total nonfinancial individual incomes $\tilde{\omega} = \sum_{i=1}^{I} \tilde{\omega}^i$:

$$\text{var}(\tilde{a})z = T[E(\tilde{c})][E(\tilde{a}) - (1+r)p] - \text{cov}(\tilde{a}, \tilde{\omega}),$$

where variables with no index represent quantities for the whole economy.

The equilibrium condition on securities imposes that, at time 1, consumption is equal to the whole available resources in each state, including financial and nonfinancial incomes, so that

$$\tilde{c}^m = \sum_{i=1}^{i} \tilde{c}^i = \tilde{\omega} + z_* + z^{m\prime}\tilde{a}. \tag{6.10}$$

Observing that $\text{cov}(\tilde{a}, \tilde{c}^m) = \text{var}(\tilde{a})z^m + \text{cov}(\tilde{a}, \tilde{\omega})$ gives the following theorem.

Theorem 6.2 *In the paradigmatic cases of finance, when utility functions are quadratic or CARA with normally distributed risks, the equilibrium prices of risky securities are given by*

$$p_k = \frac{E\tilde{a}_k}{1+r} - \frac{\text{cov}(\tilde{a}_k, \tilde{c}^m)}{(1+r)T(E\tilde{c}^m)}, \quad k = 1, \ldots, K, \tag{6.11}$$

where c^m and $T(E\tilde{c}^m)$ are the economy aggregate consumption and risk tolerance, respectively. ∎

This model is called the CCAPM. In comparison with the CAPM, it constitutes an important advance for analysis.

First, instead of providing mere relationships between the prices of various securities, the model links these prices to (more fundamental) underlying movements in consumptions and incomes. The price of risk is determined based on the fundamental characteristics of the economy, represented here by macroeconomic fluctuations in consumption. Indeed, the price of a risky security is equal to the discounted expectation of the dividends to which it provides a claim, minus a *risk premium* that is proportional to the correlation between the security payoff and aggregate risk in the economy as represented by domestic consumption $\tilde{c}^m$.

Second, it applies to a more general situation, in which the fluctuation in future resources are not all attributable to financial incomes: as made clear by (6.10), aggregate consumption also includes nonfinancial incomes. The risk premium on the market portfolio, which can be computed from (6.11), depends on these nonfinancial incomes:

$$\frac{E\tilde{a}_m}{1+r} - p^m = \frac{\mathrm{cov}(\tilde{a}^m, \tilde{c}^m)}{(1+r)T(E\tilde{c}^m)},$$

This explains why the risk premium can be assumed positive since the overall resources and the financial ones are likely to be positively correlated. This is true of course in the special case of the CAPM where fluctuations are all due to financial incomes since then $\tilde{c}^m = \tilde{a}^m$.

Buyers of a security benefit from the risk premium to compensate them for assuming the risk. It is greatest for securities that are perfectly correlated with aggregate risk, and nil when these risks are orthogonal. When a security's dividends are negatively correlated with aggregate risk it can be used to hedge against macroeconomic risk, and its price exceeds the discounted value of the dividends associated with it. The risk premium is lower to the extent that there are agents in the economy who are very risk tolerant. In particular, if there is a risk neutral agent with a linear von Neumann Morgenstern utility function, then $T[E(\tilde{c})]$ is infinite and the prices of all securities are equal to the discounted value of the mathematical expectation of their dividends.

4.2 The Allocation of Risks

Now that we have derived the prices of the risky securities, it remains to evaluate the allocation of risks, and to determine the interest rate.

We start by computing the agents' portfolios of risky securities and future risky incomes at equilibrium. By a simple substitution of the price into i's demand (6.8):

$$z^i = \mathrm{var}(\tilde{a})^{-1} \left\{ \frac{T^i[E(\tilde{c}^i)]}{T[E(\tilde{c})]} \mathrm{cov}(\tilde{a}, \tilde{c}^m) - \mathrm{cov}(\tilde{a}, \tilde{\omega}^i) \right\}. \tag{6.12}$$

To focus on the distribution of risks, it is sufficient to consider the difference of incomes from their means, as in Chapter 4 when we were examining the hedging portfolio. This allows us to eliminate z_*^i, which is still unknown at this point.

This yields[2]:

$$\tilde{c}^i - E(\tilde{c}^i) = \tilde{\omega}^i - E(\tilde{\omega}^i) - \text{cov}(\tilde{\omega}^i, \tilde{a})\text{var}(\tilde{a})^{-1}(\tilde{a}) - E(\tilde{a})]$$

$$+ \frac{T^i[E(\tilde{c}^i)]}{T[E(\tilde{c})]}\text{cov}(\tilde{c}^m, \tilde{a}) \, \text{var}(\tilde{a})^{-1}[\tilde{a} - E(\tilde{a})]. \tag{6.13}$$

As before, this equation is interpreted using the projection associated with the variance. Recall that, if $\tilde{x}$ is normalized, we can write

$$\tilde{x} = \text{proj}_{\tilde{a}}\tilde{x} + \tilde{x}_\perp, \quad \text{with proj}_{\tilde{a}}\tilde{x} = \text{cov}(\tilde{x}, \tilde{a})\text{var}(\tilde{a})^{-1}[\tilde{a} - E(\tilde{a})].$$

And Eqn (6.13) can be rewritten as

$$\tilde{c}^i - E(\tilde{c}^i) = [(\tilde{\omega}^i - E(\tilde{\omega}^i)]_\perp + \frac{T^i[E(\tilde{c}^i)]}{T[E(\tilde{c})]}\text{proj}_{\tilde{a}}[\tilde{c}^m - E(\tilde{c}^m)]. \tag{6.14}$$

The distribution of risks at equilibrium can then easily be interpreted:

1 The first term, $[\tilde{\omega}^i - E(\tilde{\omega}^i)]_\perp$, is the risk associated with fluctuations in non-financial incomes that is not insurable on the market and that the agent must assume.
2 The second term is proportional to the risk affecting total income in period 1 and which, through the securities, is tradable. This risk is split among market participants in proportion to their risk tolerance.

4.3 Determination of the Interest Rate

While many of the qualitative properties of the distribution of risks at equilibrium derive from the equations given above, the allocation of resources is not fully determined: We still need to determine the risk-free interest rate (or equivalently the price of the risk-free security) and the level of the individual investments in the risk-free security. This yields consumption at time 0 and expected consumption at time 1 for all agents. Indeed, in the quadratic case, it is only when the values of the expectations $E(\tilde{c}^i)$ are known that we can derive risk tolerances and the distribution of market capitalization in the economy. In the CARA-normal case, where this tolerance is constant, the interest rate is required for determining the level of security prices.

2 Recall that $\text{cov}(\tilde{a}, \tilde{b}) = \text{cov}(\tilde{b}, \tilde{a})'$.

The complete solution of the model and the missing risk-free interest rate can be obtained through the demand for the risk-free security, which is characterized by the first-order condition:

$$u'^i(c_0^i) = (1 + r)\delta E[v'^i(\tilde{c}^i)],\tag{6.15}$$

and the equilibrium condition:

$$\sum_i z_*^i = z_*.\tag{6.16}$$

In the general case, there is no explicit analytical solution. However, the CARA-normal case allows for a quasi-explicit solution. This particular case is simpler because there is no interaction between the allocation of risks at equilibrium and the determination of the interest rate. Indeed, the undiscounted prices of the risky securities, $p(1 + r)$, agents' risky portfolios, and the allocation of risks are all independent of the equilibrium on the risk-free market (in Eqs (6.11), (6.12), and (6.13), risk tolerances are independent of agents' mean consumption). Thus, knowing the allocation of risks, we can compute the risk-free interest rate using the demand and supply equation for the risk-free security.

Note that, according to Walras's law, the equilibrium condition (6.16) on the risk-free market (under equilibrium for risky securities) is equivalent to the income–expenditure equality at time 0

$$\sum_i c_0^i = \sum_i \omega_0^i = \omega_0.$$

For all i, we assume that

$$u^i(c^i) = v^i(c^i) = -\exp(-\rho^i c).$$

Then, the logarithm of the first-order condition (6.15) can be written as

$$c_0^i = -\frac{1}{\rho^i}\log[\delta(1 + r)] + E(\tilde{c}^i) - \frac{\rho^i}{2}\text{var}(\tilde{c}^i).$$

The value of the variance of future consumption depends directly on the existing market structure, which follows from (6.14). Using the same notation:

$$\text{var}(\tilde{c}^i) = \text{var}(\tilde{\omega}_\perp^i) + \left(\frac{\rho}{\rho^i}\right)^2 \text{var}(\text{proj}_a \tilde{c}^m).$$

Summing over the is and rearranging the terms, the equilibrium condition $\sum_i c_0^i = \omega_0$ yields

$$\log(1 + r) = -\log(\delta) + \rho \left[E(\tilde{c}^m) - \omega_0 - \sum_i \frac{\rho^i}{2} \text{var}(\tilde{\omega}_\perp^i) - \frac{\rho}{2} \text{var}(\text{proj}_{\tilde{a}} \tilde{c}^m) \right],$$

which provides the value of the equilibrium interest rate.

This rate depends on the difference between the mathematical expectation of total incomes in the two periods, agents' preferences for the present and levels of risk aversion, and on how risks are distributed. In the particular case under consideration, the effects attributable to the mathematical expectation of incomes are separable from those attributable to their variance: The impact of the income differential is analyzed like in the certainty case.

In the absence of risks, the interest rate equals the psychological discount rate if incomes are identical in both periods; it is greater if expected future incomes are greater (otherwise, individuals would wish to borrow). As to risks, the interest rate decreases with the variance of future nonfinancial incomes, measured as the sum of the variance of agents' future nonfinancial incomes weighted by their risk aversions. This is brought on by precautionary savings. Ceteris paribus, a rise in future risks entails excess savings, and the rate must fall to balance the market.[3] This effect depends on the possibilities for diversification of risks and on the degree of completeness of markets. It is at its greatest when there is no market. Here, creating a new security that allows for a better distribution of risks increases the interest rate.[4]

According to Eqn (6.11), the price of a risky security depends on the interest rate, the correlation between its return and macroeconomic consumption, and the economy-wide risk tolerance (which is constant and equal to $1/\rho$ here): It does not directly depend on the number and the nature of the securities exchanged. Thus, in this model, the impact of the degree of completeness on prices operates exclusively through the risk-free interest rate.

BIBLIOGRAPHICAL NOTE

The CAPM was developed by Sharpe (1964) and Lintner (1965). Copeland and Weston (1983) present a review of several empirical studies. The existence of

3 This property is closely linked to the form of the utility function, as we shall see when examining the spot curve in Chapter 8.
4 The demonstration of this property is a little convoluted, so it is given in an appendix to this chapter.

equilibrium does not follow from application of traditional equilibrium models: At least in the CARA-normal case, portfolios are not constrained to yield positive returns, so that the restriction to a bounded set of portfolios is not a simple matter. The interested reader may refer to the article by Nielsen (1990). Ross (1978) was the first to question the assumption that investors' future income is fully tradable on the market. The general theory of incomplete markets is laid down in the book of Magill and Quinzii (1996).

Copeland, T. and J.F. Weston (1983). *Financial theory and corporate policy*, Addison Wesley Publishing Company, Boston.

Lintner, J. (1965). "The valuation of risky assets and the selection of risky investments in stock portfolios and capital budgets," *The Review of Economics and Statistics*, **47**(1), 13–37.

Magill, M. and M. Quinzii (1996). *Theory of Incomplete Markets*, MIT Press, Cambridge, MA.

Nielsen, L. (1990). "Existence of equilibrium in CAPM," *Journal of Economic Theory*, **52**(1), 223–231.

Ross, S.A. (1978). "The current status of the capital asset pricing model," *Journal of Finance*, **33**, 885–901.

Sharpe, W.F. (1964). "Capital asset prices: a theory of market equilibrium under conditions of risk," *Journal of Finance*, **19**(3), 425–442.

Exercises

6.1 *Financial markets and normal incomes* Consider, at $t = 0$, the market for a security yielding a (stochastic) income $\tilde{a}$ at $t = 1$. There are two kinds of investors (also called traders):

1. I "rational" traders: individual $i, i = 1, \ldots, I$, demands z^i units so as to maximize $E[u^i(\tilde{c}^i)]$, where u^i is a von Neumann Morgenstern utility function and $\tilde{c}^i = \tilde{w}^i + (\tilde{a} - p)z^i$ (thus, there are no initial holdings of securities).
2. "noise" traders who satisfy occasional liquidity or investment needs. Their demand is assumed independent of the price and denoted by $\tilde{x}$.

We make the following assumptions:

(a) $(\tilde{w}_1, \ldots, \tilde{w}_n, \tilde{a}, \tilde{x})$ is normal,
(b) $\tilde{x}$ is independent of the other variables and its expectation is nil,

Chapter 6

(c) $u^i(c) = -\exp(-\rho^i c)$, where $\rho^i > 0$. We denote aggregate risk aversion by ρ. It is given by

$$\frac{1}{\rho} = \sum_{i=1,\ldots,n} \frac{1}{\rho^i}.$$

1 Recall why, under these assumptions, individual i maximizes

$$v^i(\tilde{c}^i) = E(\tilde{c}^i) - \frac{\rho^i}{2}\mathrm{var}(\tilde{c}^i).$$

Compute his security demand $z^i(p)$. Verify that his utility gain,

$$v^i(\tilde{c}^i) - v^i(\tilde{w}^i),$$

is equal to

$$\frac{\rho^i}{2}\mathrm{var}[z^i(p)\tilde{a})],$$

and that[5]

$$E[u^i(\tilde{c}^i)] = E[u^i(\tilde{w}^i)]\exp[-(\rho^i z^i(p))^2\mathrm{var}(\tilde{a})/2].$$

2 Assume that there are no noise traders: $\tilde{x} = 0$. Compute the equilibrium price. Show that

$$v^i(\tilde{c}^i) = v^i(\tilde{w}^i) + \frac{\rho^i}{2}\mathrm{var}\left[E\left(\frac{\rho}{\rho^i}\tilde{w} - \tilde{w}^i|\tilde{a}\right)\right],$$

where $\tilde{c}^i$ is his consumption at equilibrium. Recall that, if $(\tilde{\eta}, \tilde{\varepsilon})$ is normal, then

$$E(\tilde{\eta}|\tilde{\varepsilon}) = E(\tilde{\eta}) + \frac{\mathrm{cov}(\tilde{\eta}, \tilde{\varepsilon})}{\mathrm{var}(\tilde{\varepsilon})}[\tilde{\varepsilon} - E(\tilde{\varepsilon}))].$$

3 If $\tilde{x}$ is not nil, then the price becomes a stochastic variable, $\tilde{p}$, that depends on the realization of $\tilde{x}$. It is defined by

$$\sum_{i=1,\ldots,n} z^i(\tilde{p}) + \tilde{x} = 0.$$

Calculate $\tilde{p}$.

4 Let initial endowments be sure: $\tilde{w}^i, i = 1, \ldots, n$, are not random. What is the sign of $\tilde{p} - E(\tilde{a})$? Compute the expectation of $E[u^i(\tilde{c}^i)]$ for agent i (the expectation being taken *ex ante* before the realization of $\tilde{x}$). Does he benefit from the activities of noise traders? Why?

[5] Be careful to distinguish between u and v.

5 Compute the level of $E[u^i(\tilde{c}^i)]$ when $\tilde{w}^i$ is risky. What new effect created by $\tilde{x}$ appears? Explain your results.

Note: For questions 4 and 5, use the following equation (the Rao equation). If $\tilde{\varepsilon}$ is normally distributed, then,

$$E[\exp(-\tilde{\varepsilon}^2)] = \frac{1}{\sqrt{1 + 2\mathrm{var}(\tilde{\varepsilon})}} \exp\left\{-\frac{[E(\tilde{\varepsilon})]^2}{1 + 2\,\mathrm{var}(\tilde{\varepsilon})}\right\}.$$

6.2 Risk sharing, the CAPM, and complete markets   Consider an economy with two investors indexed by A and B. There is a single risky good, and agents' tastes concerning their final wealth $\tilde{c}$ are represented by von Neumann Morgenstern utility functions:

$$u^A(c) = c - ac^2/2,$$
$$u^B(c) = c,$$

where a is a small positive number.

There are two risky securities in this economy. These two assets, 1 and 2, each yield 1 dollar with probability $\frac{1}{2}$ and nil with probability $\frac{1}{2}$. The events that determine the yields of these two securities are independent. Initially, agent A has two units of asset 1 in her portfolio, while agent B has one unit of asset 2.

1 Write the utilities of the two agents as a function of their portfolio (z_1, z_2).
2 Determine the competitive equilibrium price that will be established when a market is opened on which security 1 can be traded for security 2. Compute the portfolios and the distribution of risks at equilibrium.
3 Now, instead of opening a market for only the two securities 1 and 2, imagine that the market is for three items, these two securities plus a risk-free asset 3 yielding one unit of good in all states of nature. Determine the characteristics of the competitive equilibrium. Compute the βs associated with assets 1 and 2.
4 Are markets complete in questions 2 and 3? In what sense can the equilibrium be considered optimal?

6.3 CAPM and differences in beliefs

1 At $t = 0$, a security yielding a stochastic revenue $\tilde{a}$ at $t = 1$ is put up for sale. The total number issued is normalized at 1. There are n investors active in this market (the issuer no longer participates). They each dispose of an initial wealth ω, part of which they can also invest at the risk-free rate r. Their preferences over wealth $\tilde{c}$ at time 1 are represented by a mean–variance function:

$$E(\tilde{c}) - \frac{\rho}{2}\mathrm{var}(\tilde{c}), \tag{6.17}$$

where the parameter ρ is the same for everyone. They all estimate the standard error of $\tilde{a}$ as σ_a, but differ in their beliefs on its mathematical expectation. n_1 investors expect $E\tilde{a}$ to be equal to $\bar{a}_1$, the n_2 others believe it to be equal to $\bar{a}_2$. This is known by all, but nothing motivates them to revise their estimates.

1 Let p be the security price. Define and compute the equilibrium.
2 Now assume that it is group 1 whose beliefs are correct. Verify that their utility level exceeds that of the agents in group 2.

II Now consider an infinite time horizon, $t = 0, 1, \ldots$:

1 the risky security has an infinite life span and, at the beginning of the period t, pays out a dividend $\tilde{d}_t$ for each unit held,
2 the dividends are independent and identically distributed,
3 at each time t, n new investors arrive on the market. Their preferences are given by (6.17) and they possess wealth ω, that they can invest in the risky asset and a risk-free asset yielding r. During the subsequent period, $t + 1$, they receive dividends and interest on their portfolio, sell it, and leave the market.

1 Now assume that all investors anticipate the same mathematical expectation $\bar{d}$ and the same standard error σ_d for the dividend. Show that there exists an equilibrium price that is constant at all times.
2 Now assume that at each time t the n new investors are divided into two groups.
   (a) the n_1 in group 1 correctly evaluates the mathematical expectation of $\tilde{d}$ as $\bar{d}$,
   (b) the $n_2 = n - n_1$ in group 2 evaluates it at $\bar{d} + \varepsilon_t$, where ε_t is the realization of a stochastic variable $\tilde{\varepsilon}_t$ at time t.
      The variables $\tilde{\varepsilon}_t$ are independent and identically distributed over time with mean $\bar{\varepsilon}$ and standard error σ_ε. They are also independent of the dividends $\tilde{d}_t$. At time t, the realization ε_t is known by all, but the future values $\tilde{\varepsilon}_\tau$, $\tau > t$, are not.

- How do you interpret the cases $\bar{\varepsilon} = 0, \bar{\varepsilon} > 0, \bar{\varepsilon} < 0$?
- Show that the price at t necessarily depends on ε_t.
- We seek an equilibrium in which the price p_t at t is a function of the realization of ε_t: $p_t = P(\varepsilon_t)$, where the function P is independent of time. We denote the expectation and the standard error of $P(\tilde{\varepsilon})$ by $\bar{p}$ and σ_p, respectively.

Define and characterize the equilibrium.
If $\bar{\varepsilon} = 0$, what is the impact on the mathematical expectation and the standard error of the price of the beliefs of individuals in group 2?

Appendix

Without loss of generality, it is sufficient to show that

$$- \sum_i \rho^i \mathrm{var}(\tilde{\omega}_\perp^i) \leq -\rho \, \mathrm{var}\left(\sum_i \tilde{\omega}_\perp^i \right),$$

which implies that, when the $\tilde{\omega}_\perp^i$ are orthogonal to the space spanned by the incomes from securities (left-hand side), the interest rate is lower than when $\tilde{\omega}_\perp^i$ belongs to that space. We seek to verify this inequality for all correlation structures of the $\tilde{\omega}_\perp^i$ and for all values of ρ^i, with

$$\frac{1}{\rho} = \sum_i \frac{1}{\rho^i}.$$

In light of the homogeneity in (ρ^i), we can fix ρ at 1. Thus, we wish to show that the quantity

$$A = \sum_i \rho^i \mathrm{var}(\tilde{\omega}_\perp^i) - \mathrm{var}\left(\sum_i \tilde{\omega}_\perp^i \right)$$

is positive or nil. The first-order condition for a minimum of A in (ρ^i), subject to the constraint $1 = \sum_i 1/\rho^i$ (multiplier λ) is

$$\mathrm{var}(\tilde{\omega}_\perp^i) = \frac{\lambda}{(\rho^i)^2}.$$

Whence,

$$\rho^i = \sqrt{\frac{\lambda}{\mathrm{var}(\tilde{\omega}_\perp^i)}}, \quad \lambda = \left[\sum_i \sqrt{\mathrm{var}(\tilde{\omega}_\perp^i)} \right]^2,$$

and, for the values of (ρ^i) minimizing A,

$$A^* = \left[\sum_i \sqrt{\mathrm{var}(\tilde{\omega}_\perp^i)} \right]^2 - \mathrm{var}\left(\sum_i \tilde{\omega}_\perp^i \right).$$

This can also be written as

$$A^* = \sum_{i,j} \left[\sqrt{\mathrm{var}(\tilde{\omega}_\perp^i)} \sqrt{\mathrm{var}(\tilde{\omega}_\perp^j)} - \mathrm{cov}(\tilde{\omega}_\perp^i, \tilde{\omega}_\perp^j) \right],$$

which is always positive and only cancels when all the $\tilde{\omega}_\perp^i$ are collinear, with correlation equal to $+1$.

Trade and information / 7

In previous chapters, economic agents all shared the same view of the uncertain prospects confronting them. Their beliefs on the future payoffs yielded by the securities were all identical, represented by the same probability distribution. While the assumption of identical beliefs is plausible enough when risks are clearly identified and the understanding of the environment is objective, it fails to capture many situations. This chapter analyzes trades between individuals who may have distinct assessments of future events. These differences arise for instance because of inside information.

Section 1 examines how the theories developed so far, arbitrage and equilibrium, can be adapted to the case in which agents have *differing beliefs*. As a result, no equilibrium exists if these beliefs are too divergent (in a sense to be made precise). The analysis pertains to the short term, in which individuals infer nothing from observations on prices or trades: Their beliefs are fixed.

Beliefs are, however, likely to change over time. Subsequent sections examine the impact of the arrival of new information – be it information provided by newsletters, by the observation of payoffs, or prices – on the evolution of beliefs and on trades. The analysis differs depending on whether the information is public or *private* to the agents (in which case the information is called *asymmetric*).

We start by studying the impact of an early public disclosure of information. It comes through two basic channels. On the one hand, information may improve production decisions and, therefore, increase the resources available in the economy. On the other hand, playing in the opposite direction, information revealed before the opening of insurance markets may impair risk sharing. Section 2 describes these mechanisms, starting with the benchmark situation in which information has no impact (the no-trade result).

When information is private, the analysis becomes particularly involved because prices may convey part of this private information. The mechanism at work can be described as follows. A trader receiving private information on the future value of a security before trade adjusts his demand accordingly. As a result, aggregate demand, and hence the market clearing price, depend on the various news received by traders. Thus, price has some informational content that can be used by the market participants who are aware of this. Under the *rational expectations* hypothesis, traders make the best use of all relevant information. Section 3 introduces the general concepts and addresses the fundamental question of whether prices reveal all private relevant information under the rational expectations hypothesis. Section 4 illustrates the argument in the CARA-normal model. Equilibria can be computed, the transmission of private signals through prices be analyzed, and the impact of insiders assessed.

Most of the previous analysis is conducted in a setup where securities payoffs, and the associated risks, are *exogenous*. In many situations, uncertain variables not only depend partly on exogenous events but also on the decisions of economic agents. For example, savings and investment change the distribution of securities payoffs in the future, but expectations on these payoffs also affect savings and investment. The last section relaxes the assumption that the distribution of risks is exogenously given. This is the framework in which the notion of rational expectations was introduced by Muth (1961). An example illustrates the interactions between information, investment in risky activities, and the functioning of markets.

1 Short-Term Equilibrium

The following setup resembles those in the preceding chapters with one notable difference: Homogeneous expectations are not assumed. Agents can have differing perceptions of the distribution of securities payoffs.[1] Beliefs that are too far apart, in a sense yet to be defined, preclude the existence of an equilibrium: Different investors, all of them certain of their convictions, may want to assume diametrically opposed and inconsistent positions. The characterization of well-defined optimal portfolios through the absence of arbitrage opportunities presented in Chapter 3 proves very useful for clarifying this point. This analysis is short term, in the sense that participants do not revise their beliefs as a function of their observations on prices or exchanged quantities.

To simplify, in this section, as well as throughout this chapter, the focus is on portfolio choices: Investors do not consume today.

---

1 The beliefs of the various agents are fixed here, unlike in the following sections.

1.1 Investors

Consider an investor i. His wealth today consists of an initial portfolio $z^i(0)$ of K risky securities and he will receive a risk-free, nonfinancial income ω^i at date 1. Thus, all uncertainty is associated with the securities payoffs $(\tilde{a}_k)$.

The financial market is competitive. As usual, the prices of the K risky securities are denoted by $p = (p_k)$, and the return on the risk-free security is r. The final portfolio after trade, (z^i_*, z^i), satisfies the budget constraint at time 0:

$$z^i_*/(1+r) + p'z^i = p'z^i(0),$$

and yields consumption at time 1:

$$\tilde{c}^i = \omega^i + z^i_* + \sum_{k=1}^{K} \tilde{a}_k z^i_k.$$

Plugging the value of z^i_* from the initial budget equation into future income gives

$$\tilde{c}^i = \omega^i + (1+r)p'z^i(0) + \sum_{k=1}^{K} [\tilde{a}_k - p_k(1+r)]z^i_k.$$

For now, the model is standard. However, assume that *expectations on the revenue yielded by securities $(\tilde{a}_k)$ are specific to each investor: Formally investor i's expectations are represented by a probability distribution ψ^i on $\mathbb{R}^K$.*

Investor i's preferences on income in period 1 are represented by a von Neumann Morgenstern utility index, v^i. Thus, investor i demands a portfolio $z^i = (z^i_k)$ of risky securities maximizing

$$E_i v^i \left(\omega^i + (1+r)p'z^i(0) + \sum_{k=1}^{K} [\tilde{a}_k - p_k(1+r)]z^i_k \right),$$

where E_i denotes the mathematical expectation computed with the probability measure corresponding to investor i's expectations.

Let us assume that, for all i, $i = 1, \ldots, I$:

1 the utility function, v^i is continuously differentiable, strictly increasing, and strictly concave from $\mathbb{R}_+$ into $\mathbb{R}$;
2 $\omega^i + z^{i'}(0)\tilde{a}$ is strictly positive with probability 1;
3 the support of the probability distribution ψ^i is bounded in $\mathbb{R}^K$. Furthermore, it is not reduced to a single point.

According to condition 1, utility is only defined for a positive income: The investor has to choose a portfolio that ensures a positive income. Thanks to condition 2, the investor can simply retain his initial portfolio. This condition is satisfied provided that the investor owns positive quantities of the securities and the securities payoffs are nonnegative, which is the case with stocks for instance. Condition 3 requires that the individual is not too overconfident: He is not sure that the payoffs will take a given specific value. This assumption is quite natural. An individual who is sure about the future payoffs value is willing to take infinitely large positions whenever securities prices differ from his expected (discounted) payoff, which is not realistic.

1.2 Equilibrium

A natural definition of equilibrium is as follows:

Definition 7.1 *A competitive equilibrium on the securities market is given by a set of portfolios* $(z^i)_{i=1,...,I}$, *an interest rate* r, *and a price vector* p *in* $\mathbb{R}^K$, *such that*

1 *for each* i, z^i *is demanded by agent* i *at price* p *and rate* r;
2 *demand is equal to supply:*

$$\sum_{i=1}^{I} z^i = \sum_{i=1}^{I} z^i(0).$$

∎

The first equilibrium condition requires that each investor's problem has a solution. From Section 3 of Chapter 3, the existence of such a solution is linked to (subjective) arbitrage opportunities. A portfolio z is an *arbitrage opportunity* for investor i if, *under the distribution* ψ^i, its income is nonnegative and strictly positive with positive probability, that is,

$$\sum_{k=1}^{K} [\tilde{a}_k - p_k(1 + r)]z_k \geq 0,$$

with positive probability of strict inequality under ψ^i.

If the price of a security, discounted at time 1, is expected to be below its payoff (at time 1) with probability 1, then it is in the investor's interest to borrow without limits in the risk-free security to buy the former, regardless of his utility function. Conversely, if the price is higher, the investor will profit with probability 1 from short selling the risky security and investing the yield of that sale in the sure security. The argument extends to any portfolio: An investor i who has an arbitrage opportunity, has no "optimal" portfolio. As shown in Chapter 3, more can be said.

For simplicity, let us assume from now on that each investor thinks possible only a finite set of circumstances, that is, the support of ψ^i has a finite number of points for every i. Let Δ^i be the set of convex combinations with strictly positive weights of the payoffs in the support of beliefs ψ^i. Then, according to Theorem 3.2, the three following properties are equivalent:

1 Investor i has no arbitrage opportunities;
2 Investor i has an optimal portfolio;
3 The price vector discounted at time 1, $(1 + r)p$, belongs to[2] Δ^i.

Since at equilibrium, each investor has an optimal portfolio, an equilibrium may exist only if agents' expectations demonstrate a high degree of consistency: The equilibrium price must be such that agents concur on the absence of profitable arbitrage at that price. It turns out that this is sufficient.

Theorem 7.1 *Let the support of ψ^i be finite for each i, but not reduced to a single point. Then a necessary and sufficient condition for the existence of equilibrium on financial markets is that there is at least one price p for which no investor has an opportunity of arbitrage: The intersection of the Δ^i is nonempty.* ∎

Proof of Theorem 7.1 As just said, the condition is necessary by Theorem 3.2. We show that it is sufficient in the simple case of a single risky security.

Take the intersection of the convex envelopes of the supports of the expectations of agents present in the economy. Each support is an interval, so that this intersection, which by assumption is nonempty, is also an interval, denoted $[\underline{a}_1, \bar{a}_1]$, with $\underline{a}_1 < \bar{a}_1$.

Note that the aggregate demand for the security is defined and continuous at all discounted prices $p_1(1 + r)$ in $(\underline{a}_1, \bar{a}_1)$. It is thus sufficient to show that it tends toward $+\infty$ when the price tends toward its lower bound, and toward $-\infty$ when the price tends toward its upper bound.

To see this, consider a sequence $p_1^n(1 + r^n)$ converging to $\underline{a}_1$ and let us examine the corresponding sequence of security demands z_1^n for an agent whose lower bound of the expectation support equals $\underline{a}_1$. By construction, there is at least one

---

2 Without finite support, the property is that the vector $(1 + r)p$ belongs to the relative interior of the convex envelope of the support of the beliefs.

such agent. His demand satisfies (dropping the individual's index)

$$E(v\{\omega + [\tilde{a}_1 - p_1^n(1 + r^n)]z_1^n\}) \geq E(v\{\omega + [\tilde{a}_1 - p_1^n(1 + r^n)]z\}),$$

for any admissible z. We claim that the sequence (z_1^n) is not bounded. By contradiction, if it is bounded, it has a finite accumulation point $\bar{z}$. Then, by continuity, the aforementioned inequality is satisfied at $\bar{z}$ for $p_1(1 + r) = \underline{a}_1$. Thus, $\bar{z}$ is the asset demand at price p_1, which contradicts Theorem 3.2. Thus, the sequence has no accumulation point. Since it is bounded from below, it tends toward $+\infty$. Now the demand of agents whose expectations supports include an element less than $\underline{a}_1$ is bounded. Therefore aggregate demand tends toward $+\infty$ when the price tends toward its lower bound. A similar argument applies when the price tends toward the upper bound $\bar{a}_1$. ∎

The existence of an equilibrium presupposes that the agents' beliefs, more precisely, the supports of their beliefs, are compatible. This condition is satisfied for instance when the investors' forecasts are very fuzzy or when the set of securities payoffs that they deem possible is large, such as when all the supports contain an interval $[0, \bar{a}]$, for large $\bar{a}$. The existence condition only involves the supports: As to the probability distributions, they can widely differ as long as the convex envelopes of the supports are compatible. Then prices reflect differences of opinion between investors.

In the previous discussion, the payoffs yielded by the risky securities are *exogenous* and independent of the prices at which the securities are traded. There are many instances in which future payoffs may be influenced by today's price. The preceding analysis can be easily extended when the dependence of expectations on prices is given exogenously. Then the probability distribution of payoffs depends on the current price. The demand for the security is well defined for prices, evaluated at time 1, that belong to the interior of the convex envelope of the support of future payoffs (which itself is a function of said prices). In order to ensure that the security demand remains a continuous function of prices, expectations have to be assumed to vary continuously with prices. This type of assumption is very natural: If a price movement today would create a quantum shift in the prospects of the security yield, it is highly unlikely that the demand would be a continuous function of the price.

Why would the market participants have persistently different expectations? A typical case involves some having inside information on the prospects of a firm. The market price may reveal more or less information, depending on the behavior of informed agents – which may be the reason why expectations depend on the current price. The remainder of this chapter touches on all these themes.

2 Public Information and Markets

The information that continually arrives on markets influences investors' beliefs and changes the equilibrium price and the allocation of risks in the economy. Its impact greatly depends on when it becomes available and whether it is private or public in nature.

Section 3 addresses the situation in which information is private, diffuse, and dispersed among various stakeholders. Here instead, information is public – known to all. More precisely, all participants are assumed to have identical beliefs, both before and after the realization of the signal: They assign the same a priori probabilities of occurrence to security payoffs, they observe the same signals and revise their beliefs in the same fashion upon observing the signals. To sum up, information is symmetric at every stage, and this fact is known to all.

As in Chapter 3, the arrival of information is modeled with a signal. The information does *not* come as a surprise to the participants in the market: Indeed, according to the definition of the states of nature, the existence of the signal and the values that it may take are all incorporated in the states of nature. Figure 7.1 illustrates the framework: There are three states of nature at $t = 1$, designated with two letters, either u for "up" or d for "down," and an "up" in the first subperiod is necessarily followed by another "up." At $t = \frac{1}{2}$, *interim*, the first letter is determined. This may be hidden until $t = 1$, or the information may be revealed, with the announcement of $\tilde{s}$ at the interim date. Is this type of public signal liable to modify and improve the allocation of resources throughout the economy?

New information typically changes the distribution of perceived risks. Also, and perhaps more importantly, information enlarges the decision space by allowing the economic agents to take actions based on the value taken by the signal at the interim date. We start by examining, as a benchmark, a situation in which information is not socially beneficial. According to a general result known as the "No-Trade Theorem," if complete markets are opened before the information is revealed and if the information does not modify the available aggregate resources in the economy in each state of nature, participants have no incentive to exchange: The absence of trade is an equilibrium. Although the setup is specific,

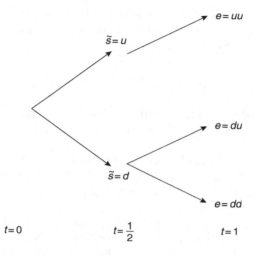

Figure 7.1 Information: The signal $\tilde{s}$ is announced at $t = \frac{1}{2}$.

it is instructive to understand the argument, which is described in Section 2.1. Next, some examples illustrate how the two effects of information – change in the perception of risks and change in the decision space – interact.

2.1 *Ex ante* Complete Markets and Public Information in an Exchange Economy

Consider the situation as studied in Section 1 of Chapter 5, in which a risky aggregate resource, $\tilde{\omega}$, is to be shared among I individuals. At $t = 0$, contingent contracts are signed, and at $t = 1$, the state is observed and resources are distributed according to the contracts. In addition, some information arrives between the two dates. Formally,

1 at time 0, *ex ante*, all agents assign the same probability distribution to states. The initial contingent allocation ($\tilde{c}^i = c^i(e)$) is optimal.
2 at time $\frac{1}{2}$, *interim*, a public signal, which is the realization of a random variable $\tilde{s}$, is observed (e.g., the level of rainfall before a harvest). Can risk sharing be improved upon in light of this signal before the state materializes?

The joint distribution of $(\tilde{e}, \tilde{s})$ is known to all. After observing the realization s of $\tilde{s}$, individuals revise the probabilities of the states according to the Bayesian formula (using the obvious notation):

$$\pi(e|s) = \frac{\Pr(e, s)}{\Pr(s)}.$$

A fundamental result is that, starting with an *ex ante* optimal allocation, new information does not create mutually beneficial exchanges.

Theorem 7.2 *Consider an allocation of a risky resource that is Pareto optimal* ex ante. *Let $\tilde{s}$ be a signal the realization of which is announced publicly interim at time $\frac{1}{2}$. Whatever the value of the signal, there are no trades that benefit everyone.* ∎

Proof[3] *of Theorem 7.2* The proof proceeds by contradiction. Let $(\tilde{c}^i)_{i=1,\dots,I}$ be the initial Pareto optimal allocation. Assume that, when the value of the signal is s_0, there exist trades that are beneficial to all. Let $\Delta c^i(e, s_0)$ be agent i's trade when the signal is s_0. For all i,

$$E[v^i(\tilde{c}^i + \Delta c^i(\tilde{e}, s_0))|s_0] \geq E[v^i(\tilde{c}^i)|s_0],$$

with at least one strict inequality.

Consider the allocation contingent on both e and the signal s, denoted by $(\tilde{c}^i + \tilde{\Delta} c^i)$ in which, in addition to $(\tilde{c}^i)$, the beneficial trades $\Delta c^i(e, s_0)$ are implemented after s_0, and nothing is changed after a signal distinct from s_0: $\Delta c^i(e, s) = 0$, for all i if $s \neq s_0$. Expected utility conditional on s_0 is increased while utility conditional on s, $s \neq s_0$, is unchanged. Thus, taking expectations *ex ante*

$$E[v^i(\tilde{c}^i + \tilde{\Delta} c^i)] \geq E[v^i(\tilde{c}^i)] \quad \forall i, \tag{7.1}$$

with at least one strict inequality.

Define the allocation $(\tilde{c}^{i\prime})$ contingent on state e by

$$c^{i\prime}(e) = E[c^i(e) + \Delta c^i(e, \tilde{s})|e] \quad \forall i, e.$$

It is feasible. In addition, according to Jensen's inequality

$$v^i[c^{i\prime}(e)] = v^i\{E[c^i(e) + \Delta c^i(e, \tilde{s})|e]\} \geq E[v^i[c^i(e) + \Delta c^i(e, \tilde{s})]|e].$$

---

3 The following demonstration deals with the primal allocation of incomes. We could also use the price system as sketched below after Corollary 7. 1.

Ex ante, we take the mathematical expectation of these inequalities. By composition of the conditional expectations,

$$E[v^i(\tilde{c}^{i\prime})] \geq E[v^i(\tilde{c}^i + \tilde{\Delta}c^i)],$$

whence, using (7.1),

$$E[v^i(\tilde{c}^{i\prime})] \geq E[v^i(\tilde{c}^i)],$$

with at least one strict inequality. This yields the desired contradiction, since the allocation $(\tilde{c}^i)$ is Pareto optimal. ∎

If all individuals are strictly risk averse, a stronger property obtains. Not only are there no trades that benefit all, but every trade harms at least one individual.

The previous result can be straightforwardly applied to examine the effect of information on the equilibrium allocation in an exchange economy *with complete markets*. As in the study of the decentralization of a Pareto optimal allocation of Section 5.2 of Chapter 5, consider a private ownership economy, where trader i owns a claim $\tilde{\omega}^i$ on date 1 resources. All the traders share the same beliefs. Markets are opened at time 0. Prior to the outcomes of operations and the resolution of uncertainty at $t = 1$, information on final securities payoffs is revealed at time $\frac{1}{2}$. Does the arrival of information induce trade at time $\frac{1}{2}$?

Since markets are complete, there is no loss of generality in considering a complete set of Arrow–Debreu securities.[4] The formal description of the model is as follows:

1. At time 0, there are competitive markets for the Arrow–Debreu securities. All individuals share the same beliefs π where $\pi(e)$ designates the *ex ante* probability of state e occurring. Investor i with initial endowment $(\omega^i(e))$ maximizes his expected utility $\sum_e \pi(e)v^i(\omega^i(e) + z^i(e))$ subject to the budget constraint $\sum_e q(e)z^i(e) = 0$. An equilibrium is a price system $q = (q(e))$ such that the demand for securities is equal to zero.
2. Information arrives at time $\frac{1}{2}$, represented, as before, by a signal, and markets are reopened.

Now, since markets are complete, risk sharing after the trades at time $t = 0$ is Pareto optimal. The following is then a direct consequence of Theorem 7.2.

Corollary 7.1 *"No-Trade" Theorem* *Consider an equilibrium obtained at time 0 with a complete system of markets. Let $\tilde{s}$ be a signal the realization of which is announced*

---

4 The result extends easily to the case where the traders have nonzero initial portfolios.

publicly at time $\frac{1}{2}$. The absence of trades, whatever the realization of the signal, is an equilibrium at time $\frac{1}{2}$. ∎

While there is no trade when the information is revealed, prices do change![5] Indeed, let $(\tilde{c}^i)$ be the contingent allocation that is in equilibrium both at time 0 and at time $\frac{1}{2}$. Marginal utilities are proportional to equilibrium state prices $(q(e))$. At time 0, for all i, there exists $\lambda_i > 0$, such that

$$q(e) = \lambda_i v^{i\prime}[c^i(e)]\pi(e) \ \forall e,$$

where $\pi(e)$ designates the *ex ante* probability of state e occurring. Similarly, at time $\frac{1}{2}$, the marginal utility of an Arrow–Debreu security satisfies:

$$Q(s)(e) = \lambda_i v^{i\prime}[c^i(e)]\pi(e|si),$$

in which $\pi(e|s)$ is the probability of occurrence of state e conditional on the received public signal. Therefore, the state price is multiplied by the ratio $\pi(e|s)/\pi(e)$:

$$Q(s)(e) = \frac{q(e)\pi(e|s)}{\pi(e)}. \tag{7.2}$$

The fundamental reason for this result is that initial *complete* markets induce a Pareto optimal distribution of risky resources. The new information makes certain events known earlier. But, it does not allow total resource availability to be altered (in an exchange economy), nor does it offer the possibility of relevant new contingent contracts between agents since, markets being complete, they were optimal as of time 0. As we saw in Theorem 7.2, whatever the value of the signal, there are no trades that benefit everyone. If agents again exchange at an equilibrium at time $\frac{1}{2}$, then no one must lose from these trades.

2.2 The Impact of Information: Production and Incomplete Markets

Two crucial aspects of an early disclosure of information are missing from the previous analysis: First, as examined in Chapter 3, more information enables investors to make better decisions, thereby possibly increasing the resources available in the

---

5 It is paradoxical to discuss prices when there is no trade! In fact, instead of prices, one should talk of marginal rates of substitution.

economy; second, playing in the opposite direction, information revealed before the opening of insurance markets may impair risk sharing.

An early arrival of information is usually associated with the possibility of taking better informed decisions. For instance, looking at Figure 7.1, suppose that an irreversible physical investment has to be decided *interim*. In the absence of information, this decision is based on the initial knowledge: It cannot depend on the (unknown) value of the signal. Instead, in the presence of information, different decisions can be made when the signal u or d is revealed in the first subperiod. If u means a larger return on the investment than d in the second subperiod, then a larger investment will be carried out in the u than in the d case. Since the decision under ignorance is always possible, in a large number of models with production and irreversible investments, the early arrival of information *enlarges the set of feasible productions*. Thus, any optimum of the economy without information is Pareto dominated by an optimum of the economy with information. When markets are *ex ante* complete, information is likely to be profitable.[6]

We have already pointed out the *Hirshleifer effect*, according to which premature revelation of information is detrimental to risk sharing, when markets are incomplete. Consider the case of the owner of a business with uncertain revenues. In the absence of information, she can share the risk with a group of investors who are interested in the project by issuing shares on the stock exchange. For example, if these investors are risk neutral, the entrepreneur can sell them the firm for a price equal to the mathematical expectation of the anticipated revenues. If the uncertainty is resolved before going to market, there is no longer any risk to share. The sales price is equal to the *ex post* value of the firm, and the initial owner reaps all the rewards in the event of success and bears all the losses in the event of failure.

Therefore, in general, it is essential to know whether the information induces a *change in the resources* available in the economy, by a better targeting of investments for example, or whether the economic interplay causes a redistribution of fixed resources whose level is inalterable as of the moment at which the signal is known, as in an exchange economy. It is also crucial to specify whether the signal arrives *before* or *after* the opening of markets.

---

6 The comparison is valid for the optima but not necessarily for the equilibria because the arrival of information may change the distribution of wealth. As in a standard economy, it is not sure that the (any) equilibrium of the economy with information Pareto dominates an equilibrium of the economy without information.

To illustrate this point, let us reexamine and expand the example described by Hirshleifer a little.

An entrepreneur must determine production y at $t = 0$ before knowing the output's selling price, $\tilde{a}$. Production costs are $c(y)$, where c is an increasing and convex function. The profit is $ay - c(y)$ if the realized price is a. The individual entrepreneur who is the sole proprietor of the firm chooses a value of y so as to maximize $E[u(\tilde{a}y - c(y))]$. Recall that, according to Theorem 3.5, a signal $\tilde{s}$ on $\tilde{a}$, prior to the choice of y, is always beneficial. There is a frictionless market for lending and borrowing; to simplify, the risk-free interest rate is assumed to be nil.

The firm is listed on a stock exchange at time $t = 0$. If the market is risk neutral, the value of the firm is equal to the expected profit, or $qy - c(y)$, where $q = E(\tilde{a})$. In the absence of information, since the entrepreneur can costlessly cover all bases, it is optimal for her to sell the firm off entirely and choose the output level y_0 so as to maximize

$$qy - c(y).$$

Now assume that there exists a public signal concerning $\tilde{a}$, and denote

$$q(s) = E[\tilde{a}|s].$$

Production levels, trade, and the entrepreneur's utility are derived in three situations that differ according to the date at which the entrepreneur receives the signal.

1 Information arrives after production decisions and trades. In this case, the distribution of risks is optimal before reception of the signal, and everyone's utility level remains unchanged. The entrepreneur has already sold all of her firm and received $qy - c(y)$, the value of the firm adjusts to $q(s)y - c(y)$. Production equals y_0.

2 Information arrives after the entrepreneur has committed the production, y, but before the trades. The value of the firm is given by $q(s)y - c(y)$. The entrepreneur still wishes to sell off the firm completely, since she can costlessly hedge against residual risk. However, unlike in the previous case, she assumes the risk associated with variability in the price $q(s)$ as a function of the signal. The information is detrimental to her. In fact, for all y fixed, the concavity of v implies

$$E[v(q(s)y - c(y))] \leq v(E[q(s)y - c(y)]) \leq v[qy - c(y)].$$

The production level y_1 is chosen *ex ante* to maximize

$$E[v(q(s)y - c(y))].$$

It is below[7] y_0. The poorer performance of markets in the allocation of risks causes production to be lower.

3 The signal arrives before the production decision and trades. Like before, the entrepreneur sells the firm in full. If the signal is s, she chooses production $y(s)$ to maximize $v(q(s)y - c(y))$, yielding the utility level: $V(s) = v(q(s)y(s) - c[y(s)])$.

Two effects are operating here. The entrepreneur now bears a risk related to fluctuations in the stock exchange, but can eventually increase output to benefit from higher prices, at least if production is sufficiently flexible. To understand this mechanism, consider two extremes. If production is inflexible, $y = y_0$, and only the Hirshleifer effect is operational. The entrepreneur is penalized by the information that undermines her hedging opportunities. Conversely, according to Theorem 3.5, if the entrepreneur is risk neutral and production is flexible, the stock market serves no purpose for her, while the information allows her to better adjust production to the sales price. We have, for all values of s,

$$E[qy - c(y)|s] \le \max_y E[qy - c(y)|s] = \max_y q(s)y - c(y)$$

and, taking expectations *ex ante*, if $y(s)$ represents optimal investment when the signal is s,

$$E[qy - c(y)] \le E[q(s)y(s) - c[y(s)]].$$

This is true for all y, in particular, for the optimal investment in the absence of information.

Overall, early revelation of public information may allow irreversible investments to be better allocated, make production more efficient, and increase overall resources in the economy. This positive effect juxtaposes with the poorer

---

7 To prove this property, note that y_1 solves the first-order condition:

$$F(y) = E[q(s) - c'(y)]v'[q(s)y - c(y)] = 0.$$

The concavity of v and the convexity of c imply that F is decreasing in y. Thus, it is sufficient to demonstrate that $F(y_0) < 0$. Now, y_0 is characterized by $Eq(s) = q = c'(y_0)$. Thus,

$$F(y_0) = E[q(s) - q]v'[q(s)y_0 - c(y_0)].$$

The negativity of $F(y_0)$ follows because v' is positive decreasing.

allocation of risks when markets are initially incomplete and the arrival of information shuts down interim markets (the Hirshleifer effect). The balance is an empirical matter, which is to be identified on a case-by-case basis.

3 Private Information

And what if the information is not public, but rather private? Can an agent receiving insider information benefit from it? To examine this question, it is first necessary to adapt the notion of equilibrium to situations in which stakeholders possess private information.

The structure of information considered in this section is specified as follows:

1 At time 0, *ex ante*, investors have beliefs that are identical across states of nature, given by π.
2 At time $\frac{1}{2}$, individual i observes the realization s_i of a signal $\tilde{s}_i$. This signal is called *private* because it is not seen by other investors.

Crucially, most of the analysis is carried out under the *common knowledge* assumption[8]: Whereas i does not observe the signal received by another investor j, he knows that j receives a signal $\tilde{s}_j$, and even knows the full distribution of the whole vector $(\tilde{e}, \tilde{s}_1, \tilde{s}_2, \ldots, \tilde{s}_I)$.

The signal received by an investor may give information on the securities payoffs. Signals received by different investors may be correlated, even containing identical components. Hence, the observation of the signal s_i may provide i with information, not only on the future payoffs or the future state of the economy, but also on the private signals received by others.

In this setup, each individual is likely to seek which information others have. An important question is whether trades, and more precisely, prices convey such information. It is instructive to start with the extreme case of naïve investors.

3.1 Equilibrium with Naïve Traders

This section assumes informed investors to be *naïve* in the sense that they modify their forecasts of securities payoffs *exclusively* in light of their private information.

---

8 This assumption has to be satisfied by every "rational" investor (except for noise traders in the last section, and possibly for naïve traders).

This leads to the simplest definition of an equilibrium in a situation with private information[9]: This is the short-term equilibrium, as described in Section 1 of this chapter, when the beliefs of each agent are updated by the signal he has received. More precisely, when individual i observes the realization s_i of a private signal $\tilde{s}_i$, his belief, ψ^i, is given by the conditional distribution $\pi(e|s_i)$.

To illustrate this, consider a complete market equilibrium at time 0, as in Section 2.1. The equilibrium allocation is thus optimal *ex ante* and the marginal utilities are proportional to the state prices. For all i, there exists $\lambda_i > 0$ such that

$$q(e) = \lambda_i v^{i\prime}[c_0^i(e)]\pi(e).$$

At time $\frac{1}{2}$, the investor's belief typically is revised in light of the realization of his private information, resulting in a change in security demand. More precisely, the *naïve* agent i's willingness to pay for the contingent securities, in light of s_i, becomes proportional to $v^{i\prime}[c_0^i(e)]\pi(e|s_i)$, that is, proportional to

$$q(e)\frac{\pi(e|s_i)}{\pi(e)}.$$

At the initial allocation, *given only the difference in agents' private information*, their willingness to pay for securities at time $\frac{1}{2}$ is no longer proportional to each other's if their a posteriori probabilities differ. Private information creates incentives to trade and results in a new allocation (as in the equilibrium computed in the following section).

Thus, even if the initial allocation is optimal *ex ante*, trades will occur on the market at time $\frac{1}{2}$ because agents choose a portfolio during the intermediate period in consideration only of their private information s_i. According to Theorem 7.2, some individuals will surely lose in these exchanges.

The equilibrium with *naïve* traders is not retained by most analysts today. It neglects the fact that the price is a source of information, and that rational investors will seek to use this public information to build their forecasts and choose their portfolios. Let us again look at Hirshleifer's example, in which an entrepreneur (e.g., agent 1) is the only one to have information on the only traded risky security. Assume that, unlike all other investors, she knows exactly how much the security will payoff. What will happen? *If all investors know that the entrepreneur*

9 The equilibrium is sometimes qualified as Walrasian since prices are only used to define the terms of trade and not for their informational content.

has this insider information and make full use of their knowledge, everything will transpire as if the information were public. Indeed, the entrepreneur will wish to keep the firm if the price she can receive for it is below the revenue anticipated with certainty. Thus, investors deduce that any price that is accepted (or proposed) by the entrepreneur exceeds that revenue, and consequently they no longer have an interest in investing. That is how the price reveals private information. However, this scenario is somewhat spurious: The insider has full information and is the only one who does – and everyone else knows this. This should motivate more strategic behavior in order to hide some of the information and is outside the scope of this book. In the next section, the transmission of information through prices is examined in a framework in which competitive behavior is plausible: Information is disseminated and participants each receive a private signal.

3.2 Private Information and Rational Expectations

How can one describe the information conveyed by prices? As in Section 1 of this chapter, one could directly assume that agents' beliefs ψ^i depend on the price system observed on the market. However, what is at stake is precisely to provide a basis for this dependence, in particular to determine how investors should modify their beliefs in response to prices. One must begin upstream. The revision of beliefs must be derived from a model of the information each agent is liable to receive, and of how this information modifies demand and, by extension, equilibrium prices. This introspection implies recurrence: How I revise my own beliefs depends on how other market participants expect me to modify them along with my demand, and so on. The generally accepted hypothesis, which also underlies the *rational expectations* equilibrium, is a fixed point in the introspection process.

   We first give a definition and then discuss its interpretation. The stock exchange is described as usual by the securities payoffs. We are interested in the exchanges at the time when individuals receive their private signals. The total number of securities in circulation is denoted by $z^m = \sum_i z^i(0)$. *The crucial point is that investors know how prices react to the set of received signals*: The trading price is a function, $p = P(s)$, of the vector of all signals, $s = (s_1, \ldots, s_I)$, and individuals know the form of the function P. Investors are said to be "rational" because, when forming their demand, they account for their private signal and the information revealed by the observation of the asset prices $p = P(s)$.

Definition 7.2 *A rational expectations equilibrium specifies a price function of the private signals, $P(s)$, that satisfies for each I-tuple of signals $s = (s_1, \ldots, s_I)$:*

1 *Investor i chooses portfolio $z^i(p, s_i)$ maximizing his expected utility, conditional on the value assumed by the signal s_i and the realization of the price $P(\tilde{s}) = p$:*

$$E[v^i(c^i)|p = P(s), \tilde{s}_i = s_i],$$

subject to the budget constraint;

2 *Trades are balanced:*

$$\sum_i z^i(p, s_i) = z^m \text{ at the price } p = P(s). \qquad \blacksquare$$

The price plays two roles: It not only defines the budget constraint but also carries information. This type of equilibrium requires much more sophistication from traders than the naïve equilibrium. According to the definition, a minimal requirement is a precise initial knowledge of the impact of the signals on prices: Investors must know the price function P at least. How is such a knowledge acquired? Before discussing this point, let us raise another difficulty.

By which process do prices simultaneously transmit information and reach their equilibrium value? In an exchange economy, following Walras, one often invokes an imaginary auctioneer who calls out a price, receives supplies and demands for the given price, and revises it until equilibrium is reached. The auctioneer knows nothing about the signals received by private agents: Thus, there is no reason for agents to infer any information from the price called out by the auctioneer, especially during the first round, and even subsequently any inference seems extremely complicated whatever the state. This problem is alleviated if one assumes that the process is not interactive, but rather occurs in one step. In this scenario, each investor submits a *demand function* in terms of prices to the auctioneer, who then sets a price that eliminates excess demand.

This is similar to the functioning of stock exchanges at the opening and closing of the trading day. Investors can submit different types of orders: Market orders (these specify what quantity to buy or sell regardless of the price), limit orders (buy (sell) transactions for a certain quantity that are executed only when the price reaches a given maximum (minimum)), and stop orders (transactions for a certain quantity that are triggered as soon as the price falls below a floor or rises above a ceiling). Investors can submit any combination of these orders that they choose, allowing a general demand function to be approximated in keeping with the theory.

It remains to describe how investors come to know the price function P.

A first justification is to assume that all participants know the structure of the economy (the theoretical model in our case), that is, the value of initial resources, the form of the utility functions, and the nature of the information each agent is liable to receive (but not the values taken but the signals). Moreover, this knowledge is *shared*: Everyone knows that everyone knows ... that everyone has the same initial knowledge of the model. And, finally, from this knowledge, they are able to compute the demand and the equilibrium price. This is clearly a particularly demanding level of knowledge and of rationality in the reasoning process, especially in light of the uncertainty concerning the behavior of other investors that exists in reality.

A second traditional justification for equilibrium is a learning process in a context of repetition. It can be applied if private information becomes public after the conclusion of operations, but it is particularly difficult to identify and correct one's errors in this context.

To conclude, when prices reveal private information, the rational expectations equilibrium is the most fragile notion of equilibrium we have encountered in this book.

3.3 Revelation of Information by Prices

The revelation of information by prices is a major theme in finance. Markets are said to be *strongly efficient*[10] if they reveal all available relevant information.

As a benchmark, we consider here an exchange economy, in which an optimal allocation of risky resources has been contracted at time 0, as in Section 2.1. Private signals are received interim, at time $\frac{1}{2}$ before the realization of the state. We know that with public information no exchange would take place, in contrast to the naïve equilibrium. The no-trade theorem (Corollary 7.1) extends to the case of private information under rational expectations: There is an equilibrium in which all relevant information is revealed by prices if individuals receive private information at time $\frac{1}{2}$. In other words, it is as if the information was public and no trades occur on the intermediary date.

The crucial point is to define *all relevant information*. The value assumed by the signal s has no intrinsic value other than the information it contains concerning

---

10 This concept of efficiency should not be confused with Pareto efficiency.

the states. *All relevant information* is the probability of the states conditional on the set of all private signals s.

Let us examine the information contributed by prices when markets are complete. We can revert to a complete system of Arrow–Debreu securities. If all information is revealed, that is, if s is public information, then the equilibrium state prices satisfy (7.2):

$$Q(s)(e) = \frac{q(e)\pi(e|s)}{\pi(e)}.$$

They are in a one-to-one correspondence with the states conditional on s. Consequently, if all agents know the model, they will be able to infer the a posteriori probability of the states from (7.2) by simply observing the state prices, $Q(s)(e)$, and will not wish to trade. This shows the following result.

Theorem 7.3 *Consider an equilibrium at time 0 with complete markets. At time $\frac{1}{2}$, agent $i, i = 1, \ldots, I$, receives the private signal $\tilde{s}_i$, and markets open.*

The absence of trade at time $\frac{1}{2}$ is a rational expectations equilibrium associated with prices that are completely revealing.[11] ∎

To what extent is this result robust? As we have seen, the relevant information is the probability distribution of the states of nature. The price system is perfectly revealing if, and only if, the function P linking the equilibrium price system to the state probabilities is one to one. If there are a finite number of securities, K, the vector of state prices, which is defined up to a constant, provides $K - 1$ signals (formally, the normalized vector of state prices is a point in the simplex of $\mathbb{R}^K$). Individuals observe these prices. If the dimension of the state prices is less than the number of securities, there must be an equilibrium in which prices are perfectly revealing. Conversely, if the dimension of the state space is greater than or equal to the number of securities, prices can never be perfectly revealing and the preceding theorem is inapplicable. We shall see that, in practice, when modeling the interaction between prices and information on financial markets, some noise is frequently introduced so that prices only reveal part of the information.

---

11 The attentive reader will notice a difficulty interpreting this result. Economic agents are purported to observe prices at equilibrium, and yet there are no trades at equilibrium. We will pick up on this issue in the following section.

176

4 Information: The Normal Model

When markets are complete and the initial allocation is Pareto optimal, new information will not induce trades, as we have just seen. To study the more interesting case in which the initial allocation is not Pareto optimal, the CARA-normal framework is routinely used in finance. Normal variables have a simple property that is useful for the analysis of information. If the couple $(\tilde{a}, \tilde{s})$, with values in $\mathbb{R}^K \times \mathbb{R}^I$, is normally distributed, then the distribution of $\tilde{a}$, conditional on $\tilde{s} = s$, is also normal, with expectation and variance given by

$$E(\tilde{a}|s) = E(\tilde{a}) + \text{cov}(\tilde{a}, \tilde{s})[\text{var}(\tilde{s})]^{-1}[s - E(\tilde{s})],$$

$$\text{var}(\tilde{a}|s) = \text{var}(\tilde{a}) - \text{cov}(\tilde{a}, \tilde{s})[\text{var}(\tilde{s})]^{-1}\text{cov}(\tilde{s}, \tilde{a}). \qquad (7.3)$$

The conditional variance does not depend on the realization of the variable $\tilde{s}$. The preceding definitions of equilibrium can easily be applied to this context.

Consider an economy with a risk-free security with a fixed interest rate[12] r and a single risky security paying $\tilde{a}$ in the future and for which investors receive private signals, $\tilde{s}_i$ for individual i. To simplify, take $r = 0$. Formally, we take the CARA-normal assumptions:

1 The risk aversion of agent $i, i = 1, \ldots, I$, is constant and equal to ρ^i, and his initial endowment in the risky asset is $z^i(0)$. Let ρ denote aggregate risk aversion, defined by $1/\rho = \sum_i 1/\rho^i$;
2 The variables $(\tilde{a}, \tilde{s}_1, \ldots, \tilde{s}_I)$, in which $\tilde{s}_i$ denotes i's signal, have a joint normal distribution.

In this framework, equilibria can be computed and the transmission of information be analyzed. It is useful to start with naïve traders.

Naïve traders. The sale of the initial asset and the repurchase of z allow agent i to consume $pz^i(0) + z(\tilde{a} - p)$ in period 1. Naïve behavior consists of choosing z to maximize

$$E\{v^i[pz^i(0) + z(\tilde{a} - p)]|\tilde{s}_i = s_i\}.$$

---

12 This analysis is in *partial* equilibrium: The price of the risk-free security is fixed, independent of the price determination of the risky security.

Let $z_n^i(p, s_i)$ be naïve demand. According to (4.11), its form is

$$z_n^i(p, s_i) = \frac{E(\tilde{a}|s_i) - p}{\rho^i \operatorname{var}(\tilde{a}|s_i)}.$$

If all participants are naïve, the equilibrium price is such that

$$\sum_i z_n^i(p, s_i) = z^m.$$

The price p depends on the signals, and thus at least partially reveals them. In the special case of only one participant receiving a signal (as in the Hirshleifer example), the equilibrium price is a function of that signal and, if the relationship is one to one, reveals it completely. Here,

$$\frac{E(\tilde{a}|s_1) - p}{\rho^1 \operatorname{var}(\tilde{a}|s_1)} + \sum_{i=2,\ldots,I} \frac{E(\tilde{a}) - p}{\rho^i \operatorname{var}(\tilde{a})} - z^m = 0 \qquad (7.4)$$

and the price is a linear function (thus one to one) of s_1. Other participants should infer the value of the signal from observing the price and change their demand as a result, which would undercut equilibrium.

4.1 Rational Expectations and the Aggregation of Information

Recall that the price system is called *strongly efficient* if it reveals all relevant information, public and private. In the event of strong efficiency, the price is identical to what would be observed if all signals $s = (s_1, \ldots, s_I)$ were public. This seems excessively demanding. However, an economy satisfying the CARA-normal assumptions has a rational expectations equilibrium that is strongly efficient, in which all relevant private information is revealed by the price system. This equilibrium is identical to the one that would be established if private signals were publicly announced. Note that, unlike in the previous section, markets are not complete.[13]

---

13 To establish a link with the material in the previous section, the states of nature can be identified with the values that $\tilde{a}$ may assume, or $\mathbb{R}$ here. There are an infinite number of states and the signals are in $\mathbb{R}^I$. Since there is only one security, markets are not complete. Nonetheless, the distribution of states conditional on $\tilde{s}$ is normal and only depends on the value assumed by the information through the conditional expectation, $E(\tilde{a}|s)$. The variance, $\operatorname{var}(\tilde{a}|\tilde{s} = s)$, is independent of the value of the signal.

If all signals are public, a simple adaptation of (7.4) reveals that the form of the equilibrium is

$$P(s) = E(\tilde{a}|s) - \rho z^m \operatorname{var}(\tilde{a}|s). \tag{7.5}$$

We wish to show that this price function is a rational expectations equilibrium. At a rational expectations equilibrium, individual i's demand depends, a priori, on the information revealed by his signal $\tilde{s}_i$ and by the price $P(s) = p$:

$$z^i = \frac{E[\tilde{a}|s_i, P(s) = p] - p}{\rho^i \operatorname{var}[\tilde{a}|s_i, P(s) = p]}. \tag{7.6}$$

The key point is as follows: If it is common knowledge that the price is given by (7.5), then observation of $p = P(s)$ reveals $E(\tilde{a}|s)$ since, by assumption, under normality the conditional variance $\operatorname{var}(\tilde{a}|\tilde{s})$ is constant and independent of the realization of the signal s and of common knowledge. $E(\tilde{a}|s)$ is the best possible information about the distribution of $\tilde{a}$, and the signal s_i does not reveal any more than the price:

$$E[\tilde{a}|s_i, P(s) = p] = E[\tilde{a}|P(s) = p] = E(\tilde{a}|s).$$

$E(\tilde{a}|s)$ is called a sufficient statistics. Conditional on the observation of the equilibrium price, investor i knows that $\tilde{a}$ is normally distributed with mean $E(\tilde{a}|s)$ and variance $\operatorname{var}(\tilde{a}|s)$, and consequently demands quantity

$$z^i = \frac{E[\tilde{a}|P(s) = p] - p}{\rho^i \operatorname{var}(\tilde{a}|s)}. \tag{7.7}$$

This demand coincides with what it would be if $(s_1, \ldots, s_I)$ was public information, despite the fact that he is not able to observe the private signals received by each market participant from observations on the price. Thus, we have shown that the equilibrium price in an economy in which all information is public is the same as a rational expectations equilibrium price in an economy with private information.

We can identify the information contained in the price more precisely. Assume that the signal can be written as $\tilde{s}_i = \tilde{a} + \tilde{\varepsilon}_i$, where $\tilde{\varepsilon}_i$ is independent of $\tilde{a}$, with expected value zero.[14] Thus, it can be interpreted as a noisy estimate of the security's future value, with the term $\tilde{\varepsilon}_i$ representing the error. It is useful to introduce h_i, the reciprocal of the variance of $\tilde{\varepsilon}_i$, which is called the *precision* of the signal. Similarly, h is the reciprocal of the variance of $\tilde{a}$. If the errors of the various signals are mutually independent, applying (7.3) yields

$$E(\tilde{a}|s) = \frac{h}{h + \sum_i h_i} E(\tilde{a}) + \sum_i \frac{h_i}{h + \sum_i h_i} s_i, \tag{7.8}$$

which is a convex combination of the a priori expectation of $\tilde{a}$ and the signals, weighted by the measures of their precisions.

The property of the efficient transmission of information by prices is satisfied in a number of models. These models present a paradox: If investors do not use their private information s_i, but only the price, to formulate their demand, we formally arrive at the same equilibrium. However, if investors do not use their private information when formulating their demands, how can it become incorporated into the price? Even more to the point, if prices costlessly reveal all relevant information, then there is no reason to undertake costly information gathering activities. One way to interpret these equilibria and resolve the paradox is to consider this allocation as the limiting case in a long process during which investors gather information that is transmitted by the prices after a certain lag. For example, a lag between the execution of purchase or sell orders and the public disclosure of the transaction, in particular of its price, may allow informed agents to benefit from their informational edge, and to thus recuperate their outlays on information. The *microstructure of financial markets* examines how private information is disseminated by trades depending on the precise rules that govern the operations of the markets.

Section 4.2 presents another approach that has also been the subject of a voluminous literature. It is based on models in which prices do not have the property of strong efficiency. It consists of introducing *noise* into the system – *noise traders* prevent perfect transmission of private information.

---

14 This formulation is without loss of generality, up to an affine transformation of the signal – which obviously does not change the information it contains – as long as it actually conveys information on $\tilde{a}$. Let

$$\tilde{s}_i = \alpha \tilde{a} + \beta + \tilde{v}_i$$

be the regression equation of the signal on $\tilde{a}$. If α differs from 0, it suffices to transform the signal into $(\tilde{s}_i - \beta)/\alpha$. If α is nil, the signal does not contribute any information. The formulation in the text thus is not restrictive if the noise $\tilde{\varepsilon}_i$ is allowed to have an infinite variance.

4.2 Noise and the Transmission of Information by Prices

In the previous model, only security yields were uncertain. In practice, the world is full of other sources of uncertainty, which may be related to nonfinancial income, the presence or absence of a specific type of participant based on the state of his health, and so on. If the information bears both on the security payoffs and on other random elements, the price reflects all the available information and does not, in general, allow the part affecting the security payoff to be distinguished from the remainder. It does not perfectly reveal the signal, and is not strongly efficient.

To formalize this idea, assume that investors are joined on the market by agents, called *noise traders*, who purchase and sell for reasons that are not related to the security payoff, for example, because of liquidity needs subsequent to exogenous occurrences known only to themselves (such as a death and the liquidation of an estate). Their demand is denoted by $\tilde{n}$. Assume that the distribution of $(\tilde{a}, \tilde{s}, \tilde{n})$ is normal and that $\tilde{n}$ is independent of all other variables. As before, the model structure (including the distribution of the random variables) is known by all investors and public knowledge.

The equilibrium price is a function of $\tilde{n}$ and of the signals $\tilde{s}$. Price formation is described by slightly adapting the general principles described above.

Definition 7.3 *In the presence of demand shocks $\tilde{n}$, a rational expectations equilibrium is a price function $P(s_1, \ldots, s_I, n)$, such that for each $(s, n) = (s_1, \ldots, s_I, n)$:*

1 *investor i chooses a portfolio $z^i(p, s_i)$ so as to maximize utility, conditional on the value assumed by the signal s_i and the realization of the price $P(\tilde{s}, \tilde{n}) = p$;*
2 *Trades are balanced: For all (s, n)*

$$\sum_{i=1}^{I} z^i(p, s_i) + n = z^m \ \text{at } p = P(s, n).$$ ∎

To simplify the calculation of the equilibrium, assume furthermore a particular structure for the information. Let there be two categories of rational investors. All the first receive the same signal $\tilde{s}$, and the others do not. In the CARA-normal framework, the demand of several individuals possessing the same information can be aggregated. It is that of a single investor whose risk tolerance is the sum of individuals' tolerances and whose wealth is their aggregate wealth. The model can thus be reduced to one with only two investors, each being representative of all agents receiving the same information:

There are two *rational* investors:

1 An informed investor (or insider), receiving the signal $\tilde{s}$, whose risk aversion is ρ^1 and whose initial portfolio is $z^1(0)$.
2 An uninformed investor whose risk aversion is ρ^2 with initial portfolio $z^2(0)$.
3 The vector $(\tilde{a}, \tilde{s}, \tilde{n})$ is normal, the expectation of $\tilde{n}$ is zero, and $\mathrm{var}(\tilde{a}|s) > 0$.

Theorem 7.4 *Under the above assumptions, there exists a rational expectations equilibrium in which the price is an affine function of*

$$\gamma = E(\tilde{a}|s) + \rho^1 \, \mathrm{var}(\tilde{a}|s)n. \tag{7.9}$$

The equilibrium price is given by

$$P(s, n) = E(\tilde{a}|\gamma) + \frac{\rho_*}{\rho_*^1}[\gamma - E(\tilde{a}|\gamma)] - \rho_* z^m \, \mathrm{var}(\tilde{a}), \tag{7.10}$$

where

$$\frac{1}{\rho_*} = \frac{1}{\rho_*^1} + \frac{1}{\rho_*^2}, \quad \rho_*^1 = \rho^1 \frac{\mathrm{var}(\tilde{a}|s)}{\mathrm{var}(\tilde{a})}, \quad \rho_*^2 = \rho^2 \frac{\mathrm{var}(\tilde{a}|\gamma)}{\mathrm{var}(\tilde{a})}. \tag{7.11}$$

∎

The information known to the public, that is, by the rational operators who observe prices, is γ – a noisy version of the insider information. The price varies with the insiders' demand, a function of their information, and with liquidity shocks. The relative weight of these two terms determines the precision of the information contained in the prices. The transmission of information is all the more effective that informed investors react to their private signals, that is, that they are not very risk averse or they possess very precise information (formally, $\rho^1 \, \mathrm{var}(\tilde{a}|\tilde{s})$ is small).

From the perspective of the uninformed investor, the price of the security differs from the expectation of its payoff by two terms:

1 $-\rho_* z^m \, \mathrm{var}(\tilde{a})$ is the traditional risk premium;
2 $\rho_*[\gamma - E(\tilde{a}|\gamma)]/\rho_*^1$ is directly connected to the asymmetry of information. This term is interpreted as a risk premium associated with the difference in information between the informed investor and the others. Indeed, we can write

$$\gamma - E(\tilde{a}|\gamma) = E(\tilde{a}|s) - E(\tilde{a}|\gamma) - \rho^1 \, \mathrm{var}(\tilde{a}|s)n.$$

$\gamma - E(\tilde{a}|\gamma)$ is an unbiased estimate of the information differential $E(\tilde{a}|s) - E(\tilde{a}|\gamma)$ between informed and uninformed rational investors. It is as if the market accounts for this risk and requires compensation for it.

Proof of Theorem 7.4   Note that the price does not bring information on $\tilde{a}$ to the informed investor. Given a realization of $\tilde{s}$ and of $\tilde{n}$, the equation for equilibrium is

$$\frac{E(\tilde{a}|s) - p}{\rho^1 \operatorname{var}(\tilde{a}|s)} + \frac{E(\tilde{a}|p) - p}{\rho^2 \operatorname{var}(\tilde{a}|p)} + n - z^m = 0. \qquad (7.12)$$

All realizations of $(\tilde{s}, \tilde{n})$ that give the same value to $n + E(\tilde{a}|s)/\rho^1 \operatorname{var}(\tilde{a}|s)$, (i.e., to γ) are associated to the same price p. Thus, it is natural to look for an equilibrium that is an affine function of γ. Linearity implies that normality is preserved and it is sufficient to replace $E(\tilde{a}|p)$ with $E(\tilde{a}|\gamma)$, and $\operatorname{var}(\tilde{a}|p)$ with $\operatorname{var}(\tilde{a}|\gamma)$, in Eqn (7.12). Using the expressions for ρ_*^i, we obtain

$$\frac{\gamma}{\rho_*^1 \operatorname{var}(\tilde{a})} + \frac{E(\tilde{a}|\gamma)}{\rho_*^2 \operatorname{var}(\tilde{a})} - \frac{p}{\rho_* \operatorname{var}(\tilde{a})} - z^m = 0,$$

yielding (7.10).   ∎

This class of model, with noisy information, is very widely used to represent the evolution of stock prices and their reactions to new information – and more generally to address issues related to asymmetric information in the functioning of financial markets.

4.3 Insiders

Consider an individual entrepreneur who knows more than anyone else about the value of her firm, and decides whether to go public. This raises the issue of regulating insider trading: Would it be better to have an institutional structure that minimizes our entrepreneur's opportunities to use her insider information on the market, or to simply opt for an uncompromising laissez-faire approach that will allow the (partial) transmission of the information to all agents in the economy through stock price movements?

The entrepreneur, agent 1, initially has full ownership of the firm (normalized as one unit of the security $z^1(0) = 1$) and then puts it up for sale on the stock exchange. The buyers, agent 2, do not possess any securities initially, $z^2(0) = 0$. At the time of the exchanges, the entrepreneur has insider information, $\tilde{s}$, on the firm's earnings. Can she capitalize on this information?

To simplify the calculations, assume that the market is risk neutral ($\rho^2 = 0$) and denote the entrepreneur's risk aversion $\rho = \rho^1$. Three institutional arrangements are considered in turn and compared from the point of view of the entrepreneur. This allows us to identify the strengths and weaknesses of the stock exchange and the role of regulation.

1 In the *absence of a stock exchange*, the entrepreneur's *ex ante* utility is generated by the payoffs $\tilde{a}$ generated by the firm. It is equal to

$$U_0 = -E[\exp(-\rho\tilde{a})] = -\exp\left[-\rho E(\tilde{a}) + \frac{(\rho)^2}{2}\mathrm{var}(\tilde{a})\right].$$

2 The *regulated* case, in which the entrepreneur does not enter the market (meaning here that she puts the *entire* firm up for sale, whatever the price) – for example, because insider trading is very severely penalized – is simple to present. Since the market is risk neutral, the equilibrium price is independent of the information, given by

$$p = E(\tilde{a}).$$

The market provides complete insurance to the entrepreneur and her *ex ante* utility is equal to $\overline{U} = -\exp[-\rho E(\tilde{a})]$, which (to simplify comparisons further on) we can write as

$$\overline{U} = -|U_0| \exp\left[-\frac{\rho^2}{2}\mathrm{var}(\tilde{a})\right]. \tag{7.13}$$

Note that the same price and utility level would obtain if the entrepreneur had no insider information, whatever the market structure, competitive or monopolistic, or if the information $\tilde{s}$ were not correlated with $\tilde{a}$.

3 Now consider the case in which the entrepreneur is permitted to be active on the stock exchange, where her behavior is perfectly competitive, and where the price is considered exogenous and entirely beyond her control. According to the previous results, the equilibrium price is given by

$$\tilde{p} = E(\tilde{a}|\gamma), \quad \tilde{\gamma} = E(\tilde{a}|s) - \rho\,\mathrm{var}(\tilde{a}|s)\tilde{n} \tag{7.14}$$

and the *ex ante* expectation is written as[15]

$$U = -|\overline{U}|\sqrt{\frac{\mathrm{var}(\tilde{a}|\tilde{s})}{\mathrm{var}(\tilde{a}|\tilde{\gamma})}} \exp\left\{-\frac{\rho^2}{2}\mathrm{var}[E(\tilde{a}|\tilde{\gamma})]\right\}. \qquad (7.15)$$

When the insider is not informed, $\mathrm{var}(\tilde{a}|\tilde{s}) = \mathrm{var}(\tilde{a})$, and the expected utility reduces to $\overline{U}$ from Eqn (7.13). In general, there are two channels over which information impacts on the entrepreneur's utility, corresponding to the two factors that multiply the reference utility, $\overline{U}$:

1 The first, positive, is the term under the square root. It would be the only term if we were looking at a case of *pure speculation* by an informed agent with no initial resources in these securities (e.g, the entrepreneur is a well-informed manager in the firm with no shares in his own name). This speculator's utility is increasing with the ratio $\mathrm{var}(\tilde{a}|\tilde{\gamma})/\mathrm{var}(\tilde{a}|\tilde{s})$. The more precise the insider's information is compared to that of the market, in other words, the greater his informational edge, the greater his *ex ante* utility. This ratio is smallest in the two extreme cases of the private information being either absent or perfect – in the latter case, the entrepreneur fully reveals his information by an exaggerated reaction to it.[16]

2 The second term in the exponential, $\mathrm{var}[E(\tilde{a}|\tilde{\gamma})]$, always diminishes utility. It is associated with the fact that the entrepreneur seeks to rid herself of some of the initial risk by shifting it onto the other market participants. It translates the detrimental impact of information on insurance: Only the share of the security that is uncorrelated with information transmitted to the market can be insured.

When is information profitable to the entrepreneur? According to what we saw above, this requires that two conditions be met:

1 The risks are not too great: The speculative information advantage is independent of the variance in the original risk, while the Hirshleifer effect becomes more damaging as the initial risk increases.

---

15 The calculations are given in the appendix. Recall that $\mathrm{var}[E(\tilde{a}|\tilde{\gamma})] = \mathrm{var}\,\tilde{a} - \mathrm{var}(\tilde{a}|\tilde{\gamma})$.
16 Questions arise regarding the assumption that the entrepreneur behaves competitively when she is very informed: Her demand will react so strongly to the signal that it will be fully transmitted to the market. This should lead her to account for this information leakage and adopt a more strategic behavior. See the analysis of Demange and Laroque (1994, 1995) in a monopolistic and competitive framework, respectively.

2 The information is not very precise since, otherwise, it is revealed to the public (the numerator and the denominator in the fraction tend toward zero), and the informational advantage is low.

Should insiders be barred from the market? This model allows us to frame the debate: In a situation in which the risks to be shared are fixed and exogenous, such as when the information is public, the only impact of insiders' actions is to change the allocation of risks between economic agents. It is of no intrinsic interest to the society, and can even work against the insiders by reducing the hedging services provided by the stock exchange. The value of any early information arises from the increase in resources and the greater return to investors it is liable to induce, as is briefly discussed next.

5 Formation of Expectations and Investments

So far we have assumed that uncertainty regarding the future is exogenous. This assumption is only plausible in a very small number of cases: The weather, to some extent changes in consumer tastes, styles, and the like. As in most of the examples that come to mind, the distribution of firms' revenues (at least in the medium and long term) are not *exogenous data*, independent of market participant's actions. This creates a fundamental link: Agents' current decisions, such as investments, depend on expected future states, which are in turn impacted by these current decisions. This is the framework in which the notion of rational expectations, which was formally presented above, was introduced by Muth (1961):

The underlying principle is that economic agents seek to make the best forecasts: *Agents are said to have rational expectations at time t if the subjective probability distribution that they assign to future variables, conditional on the available information, coincides with the actual probability distributions of these variables.*

When the uncertainty is on exogenous variables, this principle means that agents use all available information at time t to generate their forecast. We already used this property in previous analyses, starting on p. 172. If uncertainty is on variables that are partly endogenous, this concept is much less tractable. Future events depend on decisions taken today – thus on agents' expectations today, and there is a feedback loop. While the target we seek to forecast is fixed in the exogenous case, here it moves in tandem with how expectations are formed. Thus, there may be several rational expectations, also called self-fulfiling. This possibility is often evoked in macroeconomics: When investors are confident, they invest, thus stimulating demand and justifying their initial confidence; conversely, when they are wary, they run down stocks and depress demand, again justifying their expectations.

To illustrate these broad principles, consider a market for a good produced by numerous competing firms. They decide on their investments one period before bringing the good to market. This decision is a function of the attitudes toward risk of the producers, of the shape of the production function, and of the price $\tilde{p}_{t+1}$ they expect at time $t + 1$.

If k_t is the amount invested today, then the output at $t + 1$ will be $g(k_t)$. The producer's discounted profit, assuming that the interest rate is zero between t and $t + 1$, equals

$$R(k_t, \tilde{p}) = \tilde{p}g(k_t) - k_t.$$

This is random, affected by uncertainty on the price. The investment decision depends on the future price, $\tilde{p}_{t+1}$. Denoting the probability distribution on future prices by ψ_t, the entrepreneur will choose to invest so as to maximize expected utility:

$$E_{\psi_t} u[R(k, \tilde{p})] = \int_p u[R(k, p)]\psi_t(dp),$$

computed with the probability distribution ψ_t.

Aggregate output at time $t + 1$, Q_{t+1}, is determined by decisions made by producers at time t:

$$Q_{t+1} = F(\psi_t).$$

For example, if producers are risk neutral, each maximizes the mathematical expectation of his profit, which is equal to

$$(E_{\psi_t}\tilde{p})g(k_t) - k_t.$$

His decision, and by extension the function F, only depends on the expectation of the future price.

If producers are risk averse and maximize a mean–variance function, then F depends both on the expectation and on the variance of the price.

The price of the good at time $t+1$ is determined competitively by setting supply equal to demand. Assume that the demand at time $t + 1$ is a linear function of the current price and a stochastic element $\tilde{\varepsilon}_{t+1}$:

$$D_{t+1} = \alpha - \tilde{p}_{t+1} + \tilde{\varepsilon}_{t+1}.$$

Setting supply and demand equal, $Q_{t+1} = D_{t+1}$, yields the equilibrium price:

$$\tilde{p}_{t+1} = \alpha - F(\psi_t) + \tilde{\varepsilon}_{t+1}.$$

Definition 7.4 *The expectation ψ_t is rational if it corresponds to the distribution of $\tilde{p}_{t+1}$, conditional on the information known at time t. In other words, ψ_t is a rational expectation if, jointly with $\tilde{p}_{t+1}$, it solves the system:*

1 $\tilde{p}_{t+1} = \alpha - F(\psi_t) + \tilde{\varepsilon}_{t+1}$,
2 the distribution of $\tilde{p}_{t+1}$, conditional on the information known at t, is ψ_t. ■

Assume, for example, that $\tilde{\varepsilon}_{t+1}$ is a random variable with mean zero and independent of all that is known at time t, and that $F(\psi_t) = \beta E_{\psi_t}\tilde{p}$, with $0 < \beta < 1$. The equation for equilibrium can be rewritten as

$$\tilde{p}_{t+1} = \alpha - \beta E_{\psi_t}\tilde{p}_{t+1} + \tilde{\varepsilon}_{t+1}.$$

Using condition 2 from Definition 7.4, we can compute the expectation of $\tilde{p}_{t+1}$ at time t by taking the mathematical expectation of the equilibrium equation. This yields

$$E_{\psi_t}\tilde{p}_{t+1} = \alpha/(1+\beta)$$

$$\text{and } \tilde{p}_{t+1} = \frac{\alpha}{1+\beta} + \tilde{\varepsilon}_{t+1}.$$

Maintaining the same conditions as before, except for the specification of F, which we set equal to

$$F(\psi_t) = \beta E_{\psi_t}\tilde{p} - \gamma\, \text{var}_{\psi_t}\tilde{p},$$

we have,

$$\tilde{p}_{t+1} = \alpha - \beta E_{\psi_t}\tilde{p} + \gamma\, \text{var}\,\varepsilon + \tilde{\varepsilon}_{t+1},$$

whence

$$E\tilde{p} = [\alpha + \gamma\, \text{var}\,\varepsilon]/(1+\beta)$$

$$\text{and } \tilde{p}_{t+1} = \frac{\alpha + \gamma\, \text{var}\,\varepsilon}{1+\beta} + \tilde{\varepsilon}_{t+1}.$$

In the two foregoing examples, the rational expectation does not depend on current information: It is equal to the marginal distribution of the price. This is generally not the case – usually, we have information available at present that is useful for the forecast. To illustrate this point, let us return to the initial function F, but assume that now the random term has the form:

$$\tilde{\varepsilon}_{t+1} = \tilde{\eta}_t + \tilde{\eta}_{t+1},$$

where the random variables η are independent and identically distributed with mean zero. Also assume that η_t is observed at time t by all agents in the economy. The equilibrium then becomes

$$\tilde{p}_{t+1} = \alpha - \beta E_{\psi_t}(\tilde{p}_{t+1}) + \tilde{\varepsilon}_{t+1},$$

whence

$$E_{\psi_t}\tilde{p}_{t+1} = (\alpha + \eta_t)/(1 + \beta)$$

$$\text{and } \tilde{p}_{t+1} = \frac{\alpha + \eta_t}{1 + \beta} + \tilde{\eta}_{t+1}.$$

The distribution of the future price depends on current information.

How do agents *learn* these rational expectations? In the exogenous case, Chapter 3 studies Bayesian learning of a distribution on the basis of independent observations. The same procedure can be extended to variables that, while still exogenous, are not necessarily independent. However, in the *endogenous* case, the difficulties of learning are exacerbated. First, the endogenous reality changes. Since we are reasoning conditionally on the circumstances that currently prevail, we can only verify the accuracy of the expectations by comparing forecasts made under identical circumstances. To apply a Bayesian approach, we would, thus, need to have a large number of observations associated with each version of history. Furthermore, behavior would have to remain consistent throughout the period for the probability distribution to remain constant and to validate the application of the Bayesian formula.

BIBLIOGRAPHICAL NOTE

The economic theory of information arose during the past 30 years. There are a variety of concepts and a multitude of results. This chapter only provides a cursory overview. The book by Hirshleifer and Riley (1992) provides a more in-depth review. In his 1971 article, Hirshleifer was the first to emphasize the dual role played by information: Advance notice of a risky event that stands in the way of risk-sharing contracts being concluded, and a more thorough knowledge of the environment allowing for wiser investments. The No-Trade Theorem, in its most common formulation, was demonstrated by Milgrom and Stokey (1982). Models of financial markets in which information filters through prices often are extensions of the work of Grossman (1976), and Grossman and Stiglitz (1980). Finally, the Muth (1961) article was the first to introduce the notion of rational expectations equilibrium.

Demange, G. and G. Laroque (1994). "Information asymétrique et émission d'actifs," *Revue Économique*, **45**(3), 639–656.

Demange, G. and G. Laroque (1995). "Optimality of incomplete markets," *Journal of Economic Theory*, **65**, 218–232.

Grossman, S. (1976). "On the efficiency of competitive stock markets when traders have diverse information," *Journal of Finance*, **31**, 573–585.

Grossman, S. and J. Stiglitz (1980). "On the impossibility of informationally efficient markets," *American Economic Review*, **70**, 393–408.

Hirshleifer, J. (1971). "The private and social value of information and the reward to inventive activity," *American Economic Review*, **61**, 561–574.

Hirshleifer, J. and J.G. Riley (1992). *The analytics of uncertainty and information*, Cambridge University Press, Cambridge, UK.

Milgrom, P. and N. Stokey (1982). "Information, trade and common knowledge," *Journal of Economic Theory*, **26**, 17–27.

Muth, J. (1961). "Rational expectations and the theory of price movements," *Econometrica*, **29**(3), 315–335.

Exercises

7.1 *Consider an economy with a producer and a speculator*   Their tastes bear on their income at time 1. Everyone's utility is represented by a mean–variance function.

$$u(\tilde{c}) = E(\tilde{c}) - \frac{a}{2}\text{var}(\tilde{c}), \quad a > 0 \text{ for the producer, and}$$

$$v(\tilde{c}) = E(\tilde{c}) - \frac{b}{2}\text{var}(\tilde{c}), \quad b > 0 \text{ for the speculator.}$$

Output that is determined at $t = 0$ is only available at $t = 1$. The price of the good at $t = 1$ is stochastic and denoted by $\tilde{p}$. This uncertainty motivates the creation of a futures market at $t = 0$. The price on this market is denoted by q. The speculator initially owns no risky resources.

I   Assume that production is fixed at the level y. Thus, the producer's initial resource is equal to $y\tilde{p}$.

1 Compute each agent's demand on the forward market. Show that the producer's utility is given by

$$u(\tilde{c}) = u(y\tilde{p}) + \frac{a}{2}\text{var}(z\tilde{p}).$$

2 Derive the equilibrium price and allocation. Compute the producer's utility level.

3 Assume that, owing to advances in weather forecasting, agents have access to better information on p before the futures market is opened. This information is modeled by a signal $\tilde{s}$, such that $\text{var}(\tilde{p}|\tilde{s}) < \text{var}(\tilde{p})$. Show that this information is, in fact, harmful to agents. To do this, prove that the level of utility expected *ex ante* (before having received the information) is lower than what was found in 1 (no additional calculations are required). Can you explain this result? You could first examine the case in which the signal is perfectly informative, that is, $\tilde{\theta} = \tilde{p}$.

II   Assume from now on that the producer chooses the level of production. The cost of producing y is $c(y)$, where c is convex and increasing, and $c(0) = 0$. The interest rate is zero.

1 What is the level of production when there is no futures market?
2 If there is a futures market, the production level only depends on the price q on this market. Compute the equilibrium price and derive the production level from it. Show that it is greater than when there is no futures market.

7.2 Incomplete markets, investment, and information   Consider an economy with a single good. There are two periods, $t = 0, 1$, and, at time 1, two states of nature, $e = 1, 2$. We index values corresponding to time 0 with 0, and use $e, e = 1, 2$ to identify values contingent on state e at time 1.

There are two consumers in this economy, 1 and 2.

The initial resources of consumer 1 are given a priori: She has $\frac{3}{4}$ of a unit of the good at time 0 and, regardless of the state, one unit of the good at time 1: $\omega^1 = (\frac{3}{4}, 1, 1)$. The consumption flow of agent 1 is denoted by $c^1 = (c_0^1, c_1^1, c_2^1)$.

Her tastes are represented by a von Neumann Morgenstern utility function:

$$u^1(c^1) = c_0^1 + \pi c_1^1 + (1 - \pi)c_2^1,$$

where π designates the probability of the occurrence of state 1. To simplify the math, we assume that there are no constraints on the sign of agent 1's consumption.

Consumer 2 owns $\frac{5}{4}$ of the good initially and has no resources at time 1: $\omega^2 = (\frac{5}{4}, 0, 0)$. He has access to a technology for producing the good that yields stochastic output. After investing k units of the good at time 0, the output of the productive process during the following period is $4\sqrt{k}$ in state 2, and nothing in state 1.

Agent 2 does not wish to consume in the first period. His tastes are represented by

$$u^2(c^2) = \pi \log(c_1^2) + (1 - \pi) \log(c_2^2).$$

1 Determine the Pareto optima of this economy. Compute the associated system of contingent prices using good 0 as the numeraire.
2 There is only one security. Its total quantity is nil, and it allows risk-free lending and borrowing operations between agents. One unit of security provides an unconditional claim to one unit of the good at time 1.

   Define the economy's competitive equilibrium under these conditions. Without calculation, determine the price of the asset at time 0 in terms of good 0.

   Compute the equilibrium allocation for $\pi = \frac{1}{2}$. Is this a Pareto optimum?
3 After having invested k, the entrepreneur deems that his productive activity exposes him to undue risk. He decides to go public. He creates a corporation that he endows with his right to receive all the firm's profits at time 1. The shares of the corporation are negotiable on the exchange at time 0.

   Define and compute the competitive equilibrium. Compute the firm's value on the stock market.

   Show that, *if agent 2 correctly anticipates how the stock value of the firm will vary with the initial investment k,* he will select a level of investment yielding a Pareto optimum. Comment.
4 For agent 2 to choose the right level of investment in the institutional setting of the preceding question, he needs a lot of foresight.

   When the state of nature is *publicly* observed, one can very well imagine that some financial intermediary creates another security in parallel to the risk-free security of the second question, totaling zero in quantity and yielding one unit of the good when state 2 materializes – nothing otherwise.

Compute the equilibrium of this economy. Compare with the third question.

5 As in the fourth question, assume that the state of the economy is public, say linked to the business cycle. However, imagine that the government sets up a forecasting agency capable of predicting the state and announcing it before the markets open.

What is the new equilibrium? Are the forecasts beneficial? Compare with the equilibria from the second and fourth questions.

6 In fact, unlike what was assumed in the fourth and fifth questions, randomness affecting production is frequently only directly observable by individuals immediately involved in the productive activity. Drawing on the institutional framework of the third question, this situation can be represented by assuming that some technological progress allows the entrepreneur to exactly predict the future after the investment has been made. This information is private, only known to him. What do you think will happen?

Appendix

The entrepreneur's wealth, with s and p known, is

$$p + \frac{E(\tilde{a}|s) - p}{\rho_1 \operatorname{var}(\tilde{a}|s)}(\tilde{a} - p),$$

which, using $p = E(\tilde{a}|\gamma)$, gives

$$E(u|s, \gamma) = -\exp\left(-\rho\left\{E(\tilde{a}|\gamma) - \frac{[E(\tilde{a}|s) - E(\tilde{a}|\gamma)^2]}{2\rho \operatorname{var}(\tilde{a}|\tilde{s})}\right\}\right). \tag{7.16}$$

We need to take the expectation over s, γ. Now, $E(\tilde{a}|\tilde{s}) - E(\tilde{a}|\tilde{\gamma})$ is independent of γ. Indeed,

$$E(\tilde{a}|\tilde{s}) - E(\tilde{a}|\tilde{\gamma}) = E(\tilde{a}|\tilde{s}) - \tilde{a} + \tilde{a} - E(\tilde{a}|\tilde{\gamma}).$$

Thus, we can separately compute the expectation of the two terms of the exponential function in (7.16). On the one hand,

$$E\{\exp[-\rho\, E(\tilde{a}|\gamma)]\} = \exp\left\{-\rho E(\tilde{a}) + \frac{\rho^2}{2}\text{var}[E(\tilde{a}|\gamma)]\right\}$$

$$= |\overline{U}|\exp\left[\frac{\rho^2}{2}E(\tilde{a}|\gamma)\right].$$

For the other term, we use Rao's formula: If $\tilde{z}$ is normally distributed, then

$$E[\exp(-\tilde{z}^2)] = \sqrt{\frac{1}{1+2\,\text{var}\,\tilde{z}}}\,\exp\left\{-\frac{[E(\tilde{z})]^2}{1+2\,\text{var}\,\tilde{z}}\right\}.$$

This equation must be applied to

$$z = \frac{E(\tilde{a}|s) - E(\tilde{a}|\gamma)}{2\,\text{var}(\tilde{a}|\tilde{s})}.$$

We have $E\tilde{z} = 0$. Writing $\tilde{a} - E(\tilde{a}|\tilde{\gamma}) = [\tilde{a} - E(\tilde{a}|\tilde{s})] + [E(\tilde{a}|\tilde{s}) - E(\tilde{a}|\tilde{\gamma})]$ and using the fact that $\tilde{a} - E(\tilde{a}|\tilde{s})$ is uncorrelated with either $\tilde{s}$ or $\tilde{x}$, we get

$$\text{var}(\tilde{a}|\tilde{\gamma}) = \text{var}(\tilde{a}|\tilde{s}) + \text{var}[E(\tilde{a}|\tilde{s}) - E(\tilde{a}|\tilde{\gamma})],$$

which finally yields

$$E\left(\exp-\left\{\frac{[E(\tilde{a}|s) - E(\tilde{a}|\gamma)]^2}{2\,\text{var}(\tilde{a}|\tilde{s})}\right\}\right) = \sqrt{\frac{\text{var}(\tilde{a}|\tilde{s})}{\text{var}(\tilde{a}|\tilde{\gamma})}}.$$

Intertemporal valuation

8

The equilibrium models studied so far are static models – they determine securities prices at a reference time on the basis of exogenous predictions of the future revenues to which they provide a claim. They ignore a key fact: These revenues themselves depend on the securities' future prices. To account for this, an economy in which markets are opened during an infinite number of consecutive periods must be considered.

A first step can be made in this direction with the *representative agent* model that serves as a benchmark. The main objective of Sections 1 and 2 of this chapter is to present the implications of the model for the spot curve and security pricing, starting with the case of certain resources. The economy consists of a single agent who consumes the available resources at each point in time and in every state of nature. An (implicit) supporting price for *any* good or asset can be defined as the quantity of the numeraire the consumer is prepared to surrender at the margin in exchange for one unit of the good or security under consideration. This, in particular, yields the spot curve and links it to the degree of impatience, attitudes toward risk, and the evolution of resources. Also, the dynamics of the spot curve can be derived, as well as the relationship between the forward rates, say for execution in 1 year, and the spot curve that will prevail then. Thus, even though the representative agent hypothesis is simplistic, it yields some useful insights on the impact of risk on interest rates and their evolution. Moreover, these insights partially extend to an economy with many agents provided markets are complete.

The implications derived by the model have been tested. Section 4 discusses one of the empirical paradoxes of the valuation of securities, the *equity premium puzzle*. Section 5 concludes with an examination of assets with an infinite life span in connection with the phenomenon of *bubbles*.

1 The Representative Agent Model

1.1 The Economy

Consider an intertemporal economy with an infinite time horizon, in which time is discrete, $t = 0, \ldots, \infty$. There is a single consumer in this economy, whose life span is also infinite.

From the perspective of time 0, future consumption may be uncertain. It is described through a consumption plan, $\tilde{c} = (\tilde{c}_t)_{t=0,\ldots,\infty}$, where $\tilde{c}_t$ is the (possibly stochastic) forecasted level of consumption at time t.

The consumer's preferences are defined over these consumption plans. They are represented with a von Neumann Morgenstern utility function U, which is intertemporally additive, $U(c) = \sum_{t=0}^{\infty} \delta^t u(c_t)$, where u is an increasing, concave, and continuously differentiable function from $\mathbb{R}$ into $\mathbb{R}$. The *psychological discount factor*, δ, is positive and less than one, capturing the consumer's preference for the present. The *psychological discount rate, j*, is connected to δ by the following relationship:

$$\delta = \frac{1}{1+j}.$$

The utility level associated with $\tilde{c}$ is given by

$$EU[(\tilde{c})] = E_0 \left[\sum_{t=0}^{\infty} \delta^t u(c_t) \right],$$

where the mathematical expectation is conditional on the information available at time 0. Note that the consumer's tastes are invariant over time: At time t, preferences are represented with the same utility function as that given above, the only difference being that the mathematical expectation is taken conditional on the information available at time t, and not that available at time 0. The analysis can easily be extended to the case in which the intertemporal utility is the sum of utility levels that may vary with time, $E_0[\sum_{t=0}^{\infty} \delta^t u_t(c_t)]$.

The resources in the economy that the agent receives are given by $\tilde{\omega}_t, t = 0, \ldots$. They are exogenous and fixed. The good cannot be stored, nor invested or transferred from one period to the next. Thus, the only resource allocation that is feasible is $\tilde{c}_t = \tilde{\omega}_t$, for all t.

Before proceeding, let us recall several definitions.

1.2 The Spot Curve: A Review

Assume we are at time 0. Recall that the spot curve can be easily obtained from the prices of zero coupons (see Chapter 1). A zero coupon maturing at τ provides a claim on the delivery of one unit of the good at time τ, $\tau = 1, \ldots$.

The *interest rate*, $r(\tau)$, on a loan taken at time 0 and due at τ, is defined from the price of the zero coupon, $q(\tau)$, maturing at τ, by

$$\frac{1}{[1 + r(\tau)]^{\tau}} = q(\tau). \tag{8.1}$$

All rates are measured per unit of time, regardless of the (remaining) life span of the underlying security or loan.

The *spot curve* at time 0 is the curve $\tau \to r(\tau)$, for $\tau = 1, \ldots$, that compares the yields, per unit of time, of loans with different maturities.

Recall that the current forward interest rate is the interest rate fixed today on a loan to be made at some future date, t. As explained in Chapter 1, due to of arbitrage, the current forward price $q^t(\tau)$ of buying at date t a zero coupon maturing[1] at $\tau + t$ is equal to $q(\tau + t)/q(t)$.

Therefore, *the current forward interest rate $f^t(\tau)$ for zero-coupon loans executed at time t maturing τ periods later* at time $t + \tau$ is defined by

$$\frac{1}{[1 + f^t(\tau)]^{\tau}} = q^t(\tau) = \frac{q(\tau + t)}{q(t)}. \tag{8.2}$$

We shall consider the *forward rates* at time 0 for loans to be made all at the same date t but for various lengths of time: $\tau \to f^t(\tau)$.

Spot and forward rates are observable at present. Typically, the forward rates evolve over time. We denote the spot curve that will materialize at t, r_t: $\tau \to r_t(\tau)$ (with this notation, we have $r(\tau) = r_0(\tau) = f^0(\tau)$). Studies of rate dynamics focus specifically on the relationship between forward rates, $f^t(\tau)$, that are observable today and future rates $r_t(\tau)$ that will be realized at t. In other words, what information about the realization at time t of spot curve $r_t(\cdot)$ can we glean from current observations on the forward rates, $f^t(\cdot)$?

The representative agent model allows this type of question to be addressed once expectations on resources and their evolution have been specified.

---

1 As explained in Chapter 1, one should be careful to distinguish the maturity date of the forward contract, here t, from the maturity date of the bond, here $\tau + t$.

In Section 2, resources are sure (though not necessarily constant) and perfectly anticipated. Subsequently this unrealistic assumption is relaxed The analysis is conducted under *rational expectations*: Future events are drawn from a distribution that is consistent with the agent's expectations.

2   Risk-Free Aggregate Resources

2.1   The Interest Rate Curve and Its Evolution

In the representative agent model, calculating the prices of zero coupons and the associated rates is simple when resources are sure. This gives some interesting insight on the relationship between the rates and the fundamental characteristics of the economy.

Consider a consumer who can buy a zero coupon maturing at τ at a price $q(\tau)$. Given preferences $E_0[\sum_{t=0}^{\infty} \delta^t u(c_t)]$, he adjusts his portfolio to satisfy the marginal condition:

$$q(\tau)u'(c_0) = \delta^{\tau} E_0[u'(\tilde{c}_{\tau})].$$

In an economy with a single agent, consumption satisfies

$$\tilde{c}_{\tau} = \omega_{\tau}$$

at equilibrium. Thus, we obtain

$$q(\tau) = \frac{\delta^{\tau} u'(\omega_{\tau})}{u'(\omega_0)}. \tag{8.3}$$

In other words, the price of a unit of the good available at τ in terms of the good available today is equal to the marginal rate of substitution between these two periods.

The spot curve is, thus, entirely determined by the evolution of resources and preferences:

$$\frac{1 + r(\tau)}{1 + j} = \left[\frac{u'(\omega_0)}{u'(\omega_{\tau})}\right]^{1/\tau}. \tag{8.4}$$

It immediately follows that:

> when resources are expected to be constant over time, the rates are all equal to the consumer's psychological discount rate. Because the rates are constant for all maturities, the spot curve is said to be flat.
>
> When resources are sure but vary over time, we have

$$\omega_\tau > \omega_0 \iff r(\tau) > j.$$

This property follows from the consumer's declining marginal utility. For him to accept a lower level of consumption at time 0 than at time τ, the price of the good at time τ must be lower than the discount factor δ^τ, implying that the return is greater than the psychological discount rate.

Finally note that an increase in resources does not necessarily mean that the spot curve is increasing, as Example 8.1 illustrates.

Example 8.1 Let the function u be isoelastic:

$$u(c) = \frac{c^{1-\gamma}}{1-\gamma}, \quad \gamma > 0, \ \gamma \neq 1 \text{ or } u(c) = \ln c.$$

Then,

$$1 + r(\tau) = (1+j)\left(\frac{\omega_\tau}{\omega_0}\right)^{\gamma/\tau}.$$

For resources that increase at a constant rate g, $\omega_\tau = \omega_0 g^\tau$, the rate curve is flat with a rate equal to $(1+j)g^\gamma - 1$. ■

We now examine the forward prices and forward rates for contracts maturing at t and compare them with the spot prices and spot rates that will materialize at t. Plugging the equilibrium values for the price q from (8.3) into (8.2) gives the forward price and rate:

$$\frac{1}{[1+f^t(\tau)]^\tau} = q^t(\tau) = \frac{q(\tau+t)}{q(t)} = \frac{\delta^\tau u'(\omega_{t+\tau})}{u'(\omega_t)}. \tag{8.5}$$

The price at t of a zero coupon maturing at $t + \tau$ and the corresponding rate are given by the same expression as (8.3), but offset by t periods.

$$\frac{1}{[1+r_t(\tau)]^\tau} = q_t(\tau) = \frac{\delta^\tau u'(\omega_{t+\tau})}{u'(\omega_t)}. \tag{8.6}$$

Thus, the comparison between (8.5) and (8.6) immediately gives the following:

if there is no uncertainty regarding aggregate resources, the forward prices and forward rates for contracts to be executed at t coincide with the spot prices and forward rates that will materialize at t.

Finally, recall that the identity

$$\frac{1}{q(t)} = [1 + r(t)]^t = \frac{q(0)}{q(1)} \prod_{\tau=1}^{t-1} \frac{q(\tau)}{q(\tau+1)} = [1 + r(1)] \prod_{\tau=1}^{t-1} [1 + f^{\tau}(1)] \quad (8.7)$$

holds by definition of the forward rates. It links the current rate for maturity τ and the current 1-year forward rates for successive maturity dates.

In the case of no uncertainty, as we have just seen, forward rates for term t are equal to the spot rates that prevail at date t: $f^t(1) = r_t(1)$. Thus, the preceding equation can be written as

$$\frac{1}{q(t)} = [1 + r(t)]^t = [1 + r(1)][1 + r_1(1)] \cdots [1 + r_{t-1}(1)].$$

The rate for maturity τ is the geometric mean of the successive short-term rates. Thus, a long-term rate exceeding today's short-term rate implies that the latter will rise and, in fact, eventually assume values greater than that of the current long-term rate.

In a model with uncertainty, the above relationship between rates at different dates no longer holds. However, the identity (8.7), which uses forward rates observable today, may give similar qualitative indications.

2.2 The Valuation of Risky Assets

Even if resources are certain, securities may pay stochastic dividends. The same valuation principle applies. Uncertainty is modeled by the "tree model" using a finite number of states of nature (Chapter 2). The state, e_t in $\mathcal{E}_t$, that prevails at date t determines the dividends to be distributed. Let $\pi(e_t)$ be the probability, at time 0, that state e_t will materialize at time t. Clearly, the values of risky assets at time 0 depend crucially on the expected distribution of future states. Assume that expectations are *correct*: The agent has perfect knowledge of the distribution π.

As we saw in Chapter 2, a convenient procedure consists of evaluating *state prices*, since they allow existing assets with a finite life span to be valued by arbitrage.

An Arrow–Debreu, or contingent, asset – defined as a security that provides a claim to the good at time τ if state e_τ materializes – can be associated with each date τ and each event e_τ. Its price, $q(e_\tau)$, is determined in a manner analogous to that of zero coupons. Let this security be tradable. The representative agent's optimization yields the first-order condition:

$$q(e_\tau)u'(c_0) = \delta^\tau \pi(e_\tau)u'[c(e_\tau)].$$

At equilibrium we must have

$$c_0 = \omega_0 \quad \text{and} \quad c(e_\tau) = \omega_\tau.$$

This directly yields the state prices $q(e_\tau)$ in terms of the good available at time 0:

$$q(e_\tau) = \frac{\delta^\tau \pi(e_\tau)u'(\omega_\tau)}{u'(\omega_0)},$$

or, using the price of the zero coupon from (8.3),

$$q(e_\tau) = \pi(e_\tau)q(\tau).$$

In other words, the price contingent on a state at time τ equals the price of the zero coupon maturing at τ multiplied by the probability of that state. Consequently, here the risk-adjusted probability is identical to the objective probability. Of course, this is because there is no aggregate risk: The interest rate is determined by the (sure) marginal utilities of resources at the times in question, and under the von Neumann Morgenstern assumptions, the risk-adjusted probability coincides with the (subjective and objective) probability of the occurrence of the states. Using the definition of the interest rate, the preceding equality can be written as

$$q(e_\tau) = \frac{1}{[1 + r(\tau)]^\tau}\pi(e_\tau).$$

Now consider a security with a finite life span and paying stochastic dividends: The owner of one unit of this asset receives $d(e_\tau)$ at time τ if the state of nature e_τ materializes; dividends are nil beyond some time T (in Section 5 this assumption is abandoned). Using the principle of the absence of arbitrage opportunities, this security price at time 0, p_0, expressed in terms of the good today, follows from the state prices[2]:

$$p_0 = \sum_{t=1}^{T} \sum_{e_t \in \mathcal{E}_t} q(e_t) \mathrm{d}(e_t),$$

or

$$p_0 = \sum_{t=1}^{T} \frac{1}{[1 + r(t)]^t} \left[\sum_{e_t \in \mathcal{E}_t} \pi(e_t) \mathrm{d}(e_t) \right].$$

The probability of the occurrence of the states $\pi(e_t)$ is conditional on the information available at present. Analogously, at time τ, the price is a function of the realized state e_τ:

$$p(e_\tau) = \sum_{t=\tau+1}^{T} \frac{1}{[1 + r_\tau(t)]^{t-\tau}} \sum_{e_t \in \mathcal{E}_t} \pi(e_t | e_\tau) \mathrm{d}(e_t). \qquad (8.8)$$

The following theorem captures these results.

Theorem 8.1 *Assume that the total resources of the economy are risk-free and known.*

1 *The forward rates for t: $\tau \rightarrow f^t(\tau)$ coincide with the spot rates that will materialize at t.*
2 *The value of a security with a finite life span and paying stochastic dividends that are correctly anticipated is given by (8.8). It is called the fundamental value of the security and it equals the discounted sum, using the term structure of interest rates, of the expected dividends it will yield conditional on the available information.* ∎

---

2 A direct argument can also be used. The additional utility that this security contributes at the margin equals

$$\sum_{t=1}^{T} \delta^t u'(\omega_t) \sum_{e_t \in \mathcal{E}_t} \pi(e_t) \mathrm{d}(e_t).$$

Its price, p_0, expressed in today's good, is thus

$$p = \frac{1}{u'(\omega_0)} \sum_{t=1}^{T} \delta^t u'(\omega_t) \sum_{e_t \in \mathcal{E}_t} \pi(e_t) \mathrm{d}(e_t),$$

yielding the result we seek.

3 Risky Future Resources

Though it serves a pedagogical purpose, the assumption that resources are risk-free is clearly too restrictive. The previous analysis can easily be extended to the case in which resources follow a dynamic stochastic process, provided this process is known. As a result, a stochastic model of the evolution over time of the interest rate curve is obtained.[3] From here on, resources $\tilde{\omega}_t$ are random and measurable with respect to the state e_t: one can write $\tilde{\omega}_t = \omega(e_t)$.

3.1 The Interest Rate Curve

Zero coupons can be valued applying an argument analogous to the above. At equilibrium, the agent expects to consume at time τ:

$$\tilde{c}_\tau = \tilde{\omega}_\tau.$$

Asset prices must be such that there is no incentive to deviate from this consumption. A marginal increase in the unconditional consumption of the good at time τ, made possible by a zero coupon, increases future utility by $\delta^\tau E_0[u'(\tilde{\omega}_\tau)]$ while decreasing current utility by $q(\tau)u'(\omega_0)$. Thus,

$$q(\tau) = \frac{\delta^\tau E_0[u'(\tilde{\omega}_\tau)]}{u'(\omega_0)},$$

and, for the interest rate, using the psychological discount rate, i, defined by $\delta = 1/(1+i)$,

$$\frac{1+r(\tau)}{1+j} = \left\{ \frac{u'(\omega_0)}{E_0[u'(\tilde{\omega}_\tau)]} \right\}^{1/\tau}. \tag{8.9}$$

In order to examine the impact of uncertainty on the spot curve, let us refer to a situation with no uncertainty in which the resource at time τ equals $\overline{\omega}_\tau$. Now consider an alternative in which resources are stochastic, but with the same mathematical expectation as in the reference situation:

$$E_0(\tilde{\omega}_\tau) = \overline{\omega}_\tau.$$

---

3 We here apply a simplified version of the model proposed by Lucas (1978).

According to Eqn (8.9), the interest rate with respect to the sure reference situation[4]

- increases if marginal utility is concave;
- remains unaltered if utility is quadratic; and
- decreases if marginal utility is convex.

The impact of uncertainty on the interest rate curve thus depends on very specific features of agents' preferences. It is ambiguous even in the simplistic model of the representative agent. However, the third case is frequently deemed the most plausible. It captures what is called the *precautionary* effect: Faced with a higher future risk, the individual prefers to increase savings today and transfer wealth to the future. This leads to a decline in rates in order to balance the market.

One can also look at the links between the forward prices of zero coupons and their prices in the future. The forward price fixed at time 0 for contracts executed at t $q(\tau + t)/q(t)$ and the future price at t, $q_t(\tau)$, of a zero coupon maturing at $\tau + t$ are, respectively, given by

$$\frac{q(\tau + t)}{q(t)} = \delta^\tau \left\{ \frac{E_0[u'(\tilde{\omega}_{\tau+t})]}{E_0[u'(\tilde{\omega}_t)]} \right\} \quad \text{and} \quad q_t(\tau) = \delta^\tau \left\{ \frac{E_t[u'(\tilde{\omega}_{\tau+t})]}{u'(\omega_t)} \right\}.$$

Seen from time 0, the future price, $q_t(\tau)$, is stochastic: It depends partly on the realization of wealth, ω_t (through the denominator), and partly on information concerning future wealth that may change the conditional expectation in the numerator. *Unless one assumes risk neutrality, it is unlikely that the forward price will be an unbiased estimate of the price in the future.* In general, $E_0[q_t(\tau)]$ differs from the forward price $q(\tau + t)/q(t)$.

Now consider the evolution of the forward price. At intermediary periods until the maturity of the contract, $s = 1, \ldots, t - 1$, the forward price for contracts executed at t bearing on the zero coupon maturing at $\tau + t$ is

$$\frac{q_s(\tau + t - s)}{q_s(t - s)} = \delta^\tau \left\{ \frac{E_s[u'(\tilde{\omega}_{\tau+t})]}{E_s[u'(\tilde{\omega}_t)]} \right\}.$$

As an illustration, imagine the simple (and unrealistic) situation in which there is no news between 0 and $t - 1$ on the resources that will be available at date t and date $\tau + t$. Under this assumption, both expectations $E_s[u'(\tilde{\omega}_t)]$ and $E_s[u'(\tilde{\omega}_{\tau+t})]$ stay constant, equal to their values at date 0, respectively, $E_s[u'(\tilde{\omega}_t)]$

---

4 The interest rate in the case of uncertainty is greater than in the case of certainty if $E_0[u'(\tilde{\omega}_\tau)] < u'[E_0(\tilde{\omega}_\tau)]$, which obtains if u' is concave.

and $E_0[u'(\tilde{\omega}_{\tau+t})]$. Then the forward rates are constant through $s = 0, \ldots, t-1$. At date t, current resources are known, and the realized spot price of the zero coupon in general differs from the previous forward prices because $u'(\omega_t)$ differs from $E_0[u'(\tilde{\omega}_t)]$. Thus,

$$E_0[q_t(\tau)] = \delta^\tau E_0 \left\{ \frac{E_0[u'(\tilde{\omega}_{\tau+t})]}{u'(\omega_t)} \right\} = \delta^\tau E_0[u'(\tilde{\omega}_{\tau+t})]E_0 \left[\frac{1}{u'(\tilde{\omega}_t)} \right].$$

The inverse function $(1/x)$ is convex. Applying Jensen's inequality yields

$$\frac{1}{E_0[u'(\tilde{\omega}_t)]} \leq E_0 \left[\frac{1}{u'(\tilde{\omega}_t)} \right],$$

which implies

$$E_0(q_t(\tau)) \leq \frac{q(\tau+t)}{q(t)}.$$

Thus, the spot price will, on average, be below the forward price. This type of analysis is often conducted on the spot rate, as in the next example.[5]

---

5 An important question is whether there is a systematic bias between the forward rates with respect to the mathematical expectation of the spot rates that will materialize. Note, however, that the forward price and the corresponding forward rate cannot be simultaneously unbiased estimates of the spot price and the spot rate, respectively. Consider, for example, 1-year loans. The forward price is an unbiased estimate of the spot price if

$$\frac{q(1+t)}{q(t)} = E_0 q_t(1),$$

which in terms of rates is equivalent to

$$\frac{1}{1+f^t(1)} = E_0 \left[\frac{1}{1+r_t(1)} \right].$$

If the spot rate at t is random from the perspective of time 0, applying Jensen's inequality again to the strictly convex inverse function gives

$$E_0 \left[\frac{1}{1+r_t(1)} \right] > \frac{1}{1+[E_0 r_t(1)]}.$$

Therefore, the forward rate $f^t(1)$ is surely strictly less than the expectation of the spot rate. The same argument can be used for rates of various maturities.

3.2 Spot and Forward Curves: An Example

We revert to the situation in Example 8.1, where preferences are of the form:

$$\frac{1}{1-\gamma} E\left[\sum_{t=0}^{\infty} \delta^t (c_t)^{1-\gamma}\right],$$

with γ strictly positive and not equal to one.

The distribution of resources (i.e., national output) is assumed to be lognormal: The joint distribution of the $\log(\tilde{\omega}_t)_{t=1,\ldots,T}$ is normal for all T.

Taking logs in (8.9), we obtain

$$\log[1 + r(\tau)] = \log(1+j) - \frac{1}{\tau}[\log E_0(\tilde{\omega}_\tau^{-\gamma}) - \log(\omega_0^{-\gamma})]$$

Note that the distribution of $\tilde{\omega}_t^{-\gamma}$ is lognormal: $\log \tilde{\omega}_t^{-\gamma}$ is normal with expectation $-\gamma E(\log \omega_t)$ and variance $\gamma^2 \text{var}(\log \tilde{\omega}_t)$. The following relationship for a variable X that is lognormally distributed holds:

$$\log E(X) = E(\log X) + \frac{1}{2}\text{var}(\log X). \qquad (8.10)$$

From this, the expression for the interest rate of maturity τ follows:

$$\log[1 + r(\tau)] = \log(1+j) + \frac{\gamma}{\tau}\left\{E_0[\log(\tilde{\omega}_\tau/\omega_0)] - \frac{\gamma}{2}\text{var}_0(\log \tilde{\omega}_\tau)\right\}, \quad (8.11)$$

which only depends on the values of $E_0(\log \tilde{\omega}_\tau)$ and $\text{var}_0(\log \tilde{\omega}_\tau)$.

Owing to its dual role in the representative agent's preferences, the parameter γ has two effects on the interest rate curve.

As in the case with certainty, it measures the individual's degree of complementarity between consumption at different periods. More precisely, the elasticity of intertemporal substitution is equal to $1/\gamma$ (see Exercise 8.1). If the individual expects an increase in income, for instance, the equilibrium interest rate has to be larger than the psychological rate since at equilibrium borrowing has to be nil. The larger the value of γ, the larger the interest rate.

But γ also measures relative risk aversion at a given point in time – and so the rate depends on the future variance, $\text{var}_0(\log \tilde{\omega}_\tau)$. Here, rates are decreasing with this variance. This is the precautionary effect mentioned above, which is stronger larger the γ.

One can study the relationship between the forward rates of (contract) maturity 1 and the spot rates that will materialize in one period. According to (8.2),

we have

$$[1 + f^1(\tau)]^\tau = \frac{[1 + r(\tau + 1)]^{\tau+1}}{1 + r(1)},$$

which, using (8.11) yields

$$\log[1 + f^1(\tau)] = \log(1 + j)$$
$$+ \frac{\gamma}{\tau}\left\{E_0(\log \tilde{\omega}_{\tau+1} - \log \tilde{\omega}_1) - \frac{\gamma}{2}[\mathrm{var}_0(\log \tilde{\omega}_{\tau+1}) - \mathrm{var}_0(\log \tilde{\omega}_1)]\right\}.$$

The spot curve that will materialize at $t = 1$ is given by

$$\log[1 + r_1(\tau)] = \log(1 + j) + \frac{\gamma}{\tau}\left\{E_1[\log(\tilde{\omega}_{\tau+1}/\omega_1)] - \frac{\gamma}{2}\mathrm{var}_1(\log \tilde{\omega}_{\tau+1})\right\}.$$

Seen from time 0, it is random, depending on the information available at time 1, which clearly includes ω_1. To examine the difference between forward rates and the expectation of spot rates,[6] notice that

$$\log[1 + f^1(\tau)] - E_0\{\log[1 + r_1(\tau)]\}$$
$$= -\frac{\gamma^2}{2\tau}\left\{[\mathrm{var}_0(\log \tilde{\omega}_{\tau+1}) - \mathrm{var}_1(\log \tilde{\omega}_{\tau+1})] - \mathrm{var}_0(\log \tilde{\omega}_1)\right\}.$$

We once again find the two previously mentioned effects: The first term between the square brackets captures the impact of new information at time 1 on future resources, and the second the impact of realized wealth at time 1. There is no reason why this expression should be equal to zero.

Thus, the forward rate is in general a biased estimate of the spot rate. The sign of the bias depends on the precision of the information that will be available at the maturity of the contract. If, for example, this information is not of good quality (the variances of $\log \tilde{\omega}_{\tau+1}$ are nearly equal at time 0 and time 1), the bias will be positive. On average, the forward rate will be higher than the future rate.

Let us develop these results when resources follow a first-order autoregressive process:

$$\log \omega_t = g + \rho \log \omega_{t-1} + \varepsilon_t,$$

where g is a real number determining the long-term level of resources, ρ belongs to the interval $(-1, +1)$, and the ε_t are independent normal variables with mean zero and variance σ^2.

---

6 To be rigorous, we work with $\log(1 + r)$, and not r. Analogous results can be derived when one directly studies the rates.

A simple calculation yields

$$E_0(\log \omega_t) = g\frac{1 - \rho^t}{1 - \rho} + \rho^t \log(\omega_0)$$

$$\text{and } \text{var}_0(\log \omega_t) = \sigma^2 \frac{1 - \rho^{t+2}}{1 - \rho^2}.$$

If resources are independent and identically distributed, $\rho = 0$ and

$$\log[1 + f^1(\tau)] - E_0\{\log[1 + r_1(\tau)]\} = \frac{\gamma^2}{2\tau}\sigma^2.$$

The forward rate is consistently above the expectation of the rate that will materialize, and this bias declines with the maturity of the loan. For non-nil ρ,

$$\log[1 + f^1(\tau)] - E_0\{\log[1 + r_1(\tau)]\} = \frac{\gamma^2}{2\tau}\frac{\sigma^2}{1 - \rho^2}(1 - \rho^3 - \rho^{t+2} + \rho^{t+3}).$$

Changes to the shape of the spot curve are not so simple any more. For the usual, positive, values of ρ, the increase in rates for maturities that are near is less than for more remote ones. The expected future spot curve has a steeper slope than the current spot curve.

3.3 The Dynamics of Securities Prices

As previously, it is convenient to begin by computing the prices of Arrow–Debreu securities:

$$q(e_\tau) = \frac{\delta^\tau \pi(e_\tau)u'[\omega(e_\tau)]}{u'[\omega(e_0)]},$$

since the price of any other security with a finite life span can be calculated with the state prices:

$$p_0 = \sum_{t=1}^{T} \sum_{e_t \in \mathcal{E}_t} q(e_t)d(e_t).$$

This equality is often written in different ways, using the *risk-adjusted probability* or the *stochastic discount factor*, or by incorporating returns.

Let us begin with the first formulation. By definition, the sum of the state prices for time τ is equal to the price of a zero coupon for the same date:

$$\sum_{e_\tau \in \mathcal{E}_\tau} q(e_\tau) = q(\tau).$$

Dividing the state prices by the price of the zero coupon, we obtain a probability. More precisely, we can write

$$q(e_\tau) = \frac{\delta^\tau E_0[u'(\tilde{\omega}_\tau)]}{u'[\omega(e_0)]} \frac{\pi(e_\tau)u'[\omega(e_\tau)]}{E_0[u'(\tilde{\omega}_\tau)]} = \frac{1}{[1+r(\tau)]^\tau} \pi^*(e_\tau),$$

where

$$\pi^*(e_\tau) = \frac{\pi(e_\tau)u'[\omega(e_\tau)]}{E_0[u'(\tilde{\omega}_\tau)]}.$$

By construction, π^* is a probability measure. It is equal to the objective probability π if expectations on resources are certain or if the individual is risk neutral. The price of an Arrow–Debreu asset as a function of interest rates has exactly the same expression as in the previous section with the objective probability replaced by the risk-adjusted probability. It directly follows that

$$p_0 = \sum_{t=1}^{T} \frac{1}{[1+r(t)]^t} \left[\sum_{e_t \in \mathcal{E}_t} \pi^*(e_t)d(e_t) \right],$$

or,

the value of a risky asset is equal to the discounted sum, using the term structure of interest rates, of the mathematical expectation of the dividends it will yield, computed with the risk-adjusted probability.

These equations can also be written in terms of returns. Let $R_k(e_t, e_{t+1})$ represent the gross return of asset k at time t in state e_t. If the state at $t+1$ is e_{t+1}, then,

$$R_k(e_t, e_{t+1}) = \frac{p_k(e_{t+1}) + d(e_{t+1})}{p(e_t)}.$$

The fundamental price-setting relationship is thus

$$1 = E\left[\delta \frac{u'(\tilde{\omega}_{t+1})}{u'(\omega_t)} \tilde{R}_k \,\middle|\, e_t \right]. \tag{8.12}$$

Let $\tilde{\delta}_{t+1}$ be the *stochastic discount factor*[7] defined by

$$\tilde{\delta}_{t+1} = \delta\frac{u'(\tilde{\omega}_{t+1})}{u'(\omega_t)}.$$

According to (8.12), without risk on consumption, all securities should have the same expected return equal to the non-random quantity $1/\delta_{t+1}$, regardless of the risk of their payoffs. Thus, there should not be a risk premium. However, consumption varies over time – and these variations cannot be forecasted perfectly.

It is within this variation, and in the correlation between movements in consumption and asset returns, that the risk premium arises. To see this, rewrite (8.12)

$$1 = E_t(\tilde{\delta}_{t+1})E_t(\tilde{R}_k) + \mathrm{cov}_t(\tilde{\delta}_{t+1}, \tilde{R}_k).$$

Applying the formula to the risk-free asset (indexed $*$) and the stocks (security 1), and taking the difference, we find

$$E_t(\tilde{R}_1) - R_* = -\frac{\mathrm{cov}_t(\tilde{\delta}_{t+1}, \tilde{R}_1)}{E_t(\tilde{\delta}_{t+1})}.$$

The differences between the covariances of the returns and the stochastic discount rate create differences between the expected returns in the model. The correlation is essential: The expected return on a security whose return is uncorrelated with forecasted consumption, sometimes called a zero-β, is equal to the risk-free return R_*.

Example 8.2   Let us illustrate with the isoelastic utility function:

$$u(c) = \frac{c^{1-\gamma}}{1-\gamma}, \quad \gamma \ge 0.$$

Assume that all variables are lognormal. Taking the log of (8.12), and using again the formula (8.10) for lognormal variables, we obtain

$$0 = \log\delta + E(\log\tilde{R}_k) - \gamma E\left[\log\left(\frac{\tilde{c}_{t+1}}{c_t}\right)\right] + \frac{1}{2}\mathrm{var}\left[\log\tilde{R}_k - \gamma\log\left(\frac{\tilde{c}_{t+1}}{c_t}\right)\right].$$

7 This formulation is often used in econometric tests, where the "true," historical, probability is preferred.

Let σ_k represent the standard error of the log of security k return, σ_c the standard error of the growth rate of consumption, and σ_{kc}, the covariance of the log of k's return with the log of the growth rate of consumption. Then,

$$0 = \log \delta + E(\log \tilde{R}_k) - \gamma E \left[\log \left(\frac{\tilde{c}_{t+1}}{c_t} \right) \right] + \frac{1}{2}(\sigma_k^2 + \gamma^2 \sigma_c^2 - 2\gamma \sigma_{kc}). \quad (8.13)$$

Applying the formula to the risk-free asset (indexed $*$) and the stock (security 1), and taking the difference, gives

$$E(\log \tilde{R}_1) - \log R_* + \tfrac{1}{2}\sigma_1^2 = \gamma \sigma_{1c}, \quad (8.14)$$

which yields the risk premium:

$$E(\tilde{R}_1) - R_* = R_* \left(\exp(\gamma \sigma_{1c}) - 1 \right). \qquad \blacksquare$$

4 Empirical Verification

It is reasonable to seek to test empirically the foregoing equations. The real returns of bonds and shares are known over long periods. For example, the log of the annual return of the Standard and Poor's 500 index from 1889 to 1994 shows a mean of 6.0 percent, and a standard error of 16.7 percent. The same calculation applied to 6-month commercial debt instruments – the best approximation to the risk-free rate available for long periods – gives a mean of 1.8 percent. Is the 4.2 percent average premium on shares justified by the risks that they impose on stockholders? In the representative agent approach, the risk premium depends on the shape of the utility function and on the consumption process.

4.1 Isoelastic Utilities

The first empirical studies were conducted by Mehra and Prescott (1985) on US data. Their results, which were subsequently confirmed, led to what is known as the *equity premium puzzle*. They assumed an isoelastic utility function as in the previous examples, and sought to verify whether (8.13) and (8.14) are compatible with the orders of magnitude suggested by the statistics. We have already described the yields of stocks and bonds. It remains to specify the evolution of consumption.

In practice, one considers the purchases of nondurables and services.[8] For the United States, the mean of the log of the ratio c_{t+1}/c_t over the period 1889–1994 was 1.7 percent and the standard error was 3.3 percent. One can use the historical value of the standard error, under the assumption that intertemporal variability throughout the past century is equal to the conditional variance at any given date (bear in mind that we are really only looking at orders of magnitude: more precise calculations have revealed that the phenomenon persists when the evolution of the variance over time is accounted for). The left-hand side of (8.14), evaluated with the aforementioned data, yields a little over 6 percent (the risk-free rate, 1.8 percent, is barely greater than the mean of the variance of the securities' yields, $(0.167)^2/2$). Thus, the key term is the covariance between the rate of growth of consumption and the return on the stock exchange. A high correlation (agents consume more when the market is high) indicates that the stock exchange is poorly suited for providing investors with insurance to smooth shocks to their consumption profile: Investors demand a risk premium that increases with the correlation. Indeed, over the period, the correlation is high (0.49), resulting in a covariance of 0.27 percent. Nonetheless, it remains too low: Eqn (8.14) implies a coefficient γ greater than 20.

This value is highly implausible. Experiments that deal with risky choices tend to yield values for γ that are below 4 or 5. For such values of γ, an agent facing the observed market conditions would purchase high-return risky securities and sell sure assets.

There is a further problem related to the risk-free interest rate. Equation (8.13) applied to the risk-free rate allows us to estimate the psychological discount rate when the coefficient γ and the growth rate of consumption are known:

$$\log \delta = -\log R_0 + \gamma E\left[\log\left(\frac{c_{t+1}}{c_t}\right)\right] - \frac{\gamma^2 \sigma_c^2}{2}.$$

Since the mean rate of growth of consumption is approximately equal to the risk-free rate (1.7 or 1.8 percent), and the standard error of consumption is 3.3 percent (variance 0.001), we see that a reasonable value for γ, between 2 and 10, implies a psychological discount factor greater than 1, an unreasonable value. This is the *risk-free rate paradox*. Put another way, given the low interest rate, consumers

8 Purchases of durables fluctuate considerably with the business cycle, styles, and expected price rises. In all likelihood, the services that these goods provide to consumers, which enter into the utility function but are not directly observable by statisticians, evolve much more smoothly than the purchases.

with a discount factor less than 1 wish to incur debt and consume more today than tomorrow. Only when future consumption is very uncertain and/or when they are highly risk averse can the mean growth rate of their consumption be equal to the risk-free interest rate.

4.2   Beyond the Representative Agent

The preceding analysis requires many ancillary assumptions: the choice of the form of the utility function, lognormality of returns and consumption growth, as well as a representative agent. This raises the question of whether these assumptions lie at the root of the incompatibility between the theory and the observations, or whether the whole portfolio choice model must be scrapped.

Here, we draw on the approach in Hansen and Jagannathan (1991). The central idea is to retain the rationality of agents while assuming as little as possible regarding the unobservable, in particular, the stochastic discount factor. Given observations on securities yields, a range of admissible values for the mathematical expectation and the variance (or volatility) of the stochastic discount factor is derived.

Consider an investor operating on the markets for these assets. Applying the same reasoning as above, a marginal investment in security k leaves the investor's expected utility unchanged if

$$u'[\omega(e_t)] = \delta E\{u'[\omega(e_{t+1})][R_k(e_t, e_{t+1})|e_t]\}.$$

Note that this equality, derived above in the context of the representative agent economy (where consumption is, in fact, macroeconomic consumption), also applies to any individual market participant, provided purchases and sales of k are not constrained (in this case, aggregate values for consumption and utility are replaced with the corresponding quantities for individual agents).

Let us identify some forms for the stochastic discount factor that are compatible with the statistical observation on returns. Equation (8.12) can be written in terms of the expectations and covariance as follows:

$$1 = E(\tilde{R}_k)E(\tilde{\delta}) + \text{cov}(\tilde{R}_k, \tilde{\delta}).$$

Stacking up these equalities for all securities yields the following equation, in matrix notation:

$$1_K = E(\tilde{\delta})\, E(\tilde{R}) + \text{cov}(\tilde{R}, \tilde{\delta}). \tag{8.15}$$

From this, one can derive a lower bound for $\text{var}(\tilde{\delta})$ given a value of $E(\tilde{\delta})$. If $\tilde{\delta}$ is in the L^2-space of measurable random variables defined on the fundamental space, then $\tilde{\delta}$ can always be decomposed into its projection $x'\tilde{R}$ on the subspace generated by the securities' returns and an orthogonal element to that space. We have, surely: $\text{var}(\tilde{\delta}) \geq \text{var}(x'\tilde{R})$. If we denote by Γ the variance–covariance matrix of the returns, this inequality becomes

$$\text{var}(\tilde{\delta}) \geq x'\Gamma x,$$

and the first-order condition (8.15) is written as

$$1_K = E(\tilde{\delta})\, E(\tilde{R}) + \Gamma x.$$

Whence, taking x out of the first-order condition and substituting it into the inequality,

$$\text{var}(\tilde{\delta}) \geq x'\Gamma x = [1_K - E(\tilde{\delta})\, E(\tilde{R})]'\Gamma^{-1}[1_K - E(\tilde{\delta})\, E(\tilde{R})],$$

or,

$$\text{var}(\tilde{\delta}) \geq [E(\tilde{R}')\Gamma^{-1}E(\tilde{R})][E(\tilde{\delta})]^2$$
$$- 2[1_K'\Gamma^{-1}E(\tilde{R})]E(\tilde{\delta}) + [1_K'\Gamma^{-1}1_K]. \tag{8.16}$$

Inequality (8.16) identifies a lower bound on the volatility of the stochastic discount factor. When this inequality holds as a strict equality, the set of points $1/E(\tilde{\delta})$ as a function of $\sigma_{\tilde{\delta}}/E(\tilde{\delta})$ describes a hyperbola in the plan $(1/d, \sigma/d)$ (just as in the case of the mean–variance efficient portfolios of Section 2.2, Chapter 4). A stochastic discount factor is admissible when its representative point $[\sigma_{\tilde{\delta}}/E(\tilde{\delta}),\, 1/E(\tilde{\delta})]$ in the plan has a standard error that is greater than the minimum and is thus located to the right of the hyperbola.

The lower bound improves (i.e., becomes more binding) as the variety of securities under consideration increases. If a single security were to represent the entire market (security 1), the hyperbola would collapse into its two asymptotes and the inequality (8.16) would reduce to

$$\frac{\text{var}(\tilde{\delta})}{[E(\tilde{\delta})]^2} \geq \frac{[E(\tilde{R}_1) - 1/E(\tilde{\delta})]^2}{(\sigma_1)^2}.$$

If the expectation of the stochastic discount factor is equal to the reciprocal of the mathematical expectation of the return of the asset, then there is no bound on its volatility. Otherwise, there is a strictly positive lower bound to the discount factor's volatility or, more precisely, to the ratio of its standard error to its mathematical expectation, which increases with the distance between $1/E(\tilde{R}_1)$ and $E(\tilde{\delta})$ and decreases with σ_1.

When this computation is implemented for a representative set of financial assets, the problems of the previous section come up again. With an isoelastic utility function and data on fluctuations in consumption, Hansen and Jagannathan (1991) demonstrate that the stochastic discount factor does not satisfy the inequality given above.

These negative results have led to revise the model more drastically by introducing, for instance, credit constraints, non-expected utility. These extensions are out of the scope of this book.

5 Fundamental Value and Bubbles

Let us return to the case of sure aggregate resources, as in Section 2. The *fundamental value* of a risky security was derived for securities whose dividends are correctly anticipated and null after a finite number of periods. The observed value may deviate from the fundamental value if expectations are incorrect. A deviation may also occur when the asset's life span is not finite, even if expectations are assumed to be correct. In this case, the deviation is called a *bubble*.

To illustrate this vocabulary and simultaneously examine the dynamics of asset prices, it is enough to consider resources that are constant over time. Then the interest rate curve is flat and all rates, at all times, are equal to the psychological discount rate i (see Eqn 8.4). Consider an asset delivering a nonnegative dividend linked to the evolution of the state of nature e_t, possibly of infinite maturity. The owner of one unit of this asset receives $d(e_\tau)$ at time τ if the state of nature e_τ materializes. The additional utility that this security contributes up to time T at the margin equals

$$\sum_{t=1}^{T} \delta^t \sum_{e_t \in \mathcal{E}_t} \pi(e_t) d(e_t).$$

As T increases, the above expression does not decrease because dividends are nonnegative. Therefore, whenever bounded, the sum converges as T tends to ∞. Using $\delta = 1/(1+j)$, this means that the price in today's numeraire that the representative agent is ready to pay in exchange of the dividends served by one

unit of asset is equal to

$$P(e_0) = \sum_{t=1}^{\infty} \frac{1}{(1+j)^t} \sum_{e_t \in \mathcal{E}_t} \pi(e_t)d(e_t).$$

This is the expression of the fundamental value. Similarly, at time τ, if the state e_τ materializes, the price (after the dividend has been paid) will be

$$P(e_\tau) = \sum_{t=\tau+1}^{\infty} \frac{1}{(1+j)^{t-\tau}} \sum_{e_t \in \mathcal{E}_t} \pi(e_t|e_\tau)d(e_t). \tag{8.17}$$

We have assumed here that the owner of the asset keeps it forever. What happens if the asset can be traded on a market at all periods and the agent contemplates reselling the asset? Let p be the (state-dependent) price process. Correct expectations imply a fundamental property between two successive prices. Using the identity of the conditional probabilities for $\tau \geq 0$,

$$p(e_\tau) = \frac{1}{1+j} \sum_{e_{\tau+1} \in \mathcal{E}_{\tau+1}} \pi(e_{\tau+1}|e_\tau)[p(e_{\tau+1}) + d(e_{\tau+1})].$$

The price of the asset today equals the discounted value of the mathematical expectation of its resale price tomorrow, increased by the dividends. This property is directly inferred from the rationality of the agent's behavior, and is often assimilated to the notion of the *efficiency* of financial markets: Markets completely reflect all available information. Iterating this relation for a security with finite life span gives the fundamental value: once the asset is no longer in circulation, its price is null.

The argument is not valid for a security having an infinite life span. This is easy to see, for example, by considering an asset that does not yield any dividends regardless of the state of nature. This is a property of money. Its fundamental value is equal to zero. However, the equation:

$$p(e_\tau) = \frac{1}{(1+j)}E[p(e_{\tau+1})|e_\tau]$$

is solved by many series of prices. The (non-stochastic) solutions are given by

$$p(\tau) = (1+j)^\tau p(0),$$

for any nonnegative $p(0)$. A priori, all these solutions are acceptable. The null solution is the only one that, like the security and the resources, is stationary. Nonstationary solutions are called *bubbles*. The price of the security today is only justified by the fact that it is expected to increase at the rate i tomorrow, and so on into the future. This price rises exponentially until expectations collapse and . . . the bubble bursts!

The crucial point in this simple model that explains the bubble is that, in exchange markets, the current price of an asset is driven not only by its future dividend but also by its future price, which cannot be determined without ambiguity. This phenomena is at work in more complex situations, in which future prices are not common knowledge, owing to differential perceptions.

BIBLIOGRAPHICAL NOTE

The representative agent model was introduced by Lucas (1978) and provides the basis for many asset valuation models. Campbell (1986) contributed a useful extension.

We have focused our description on consistency relationships between the stochastic features of securities' returns and movements in consumption, working with returns rather than prices. The earliest empirical studies sought to test for equality of the price of a security with the discounted expectation of the future income it will provide its owner. Shiller (1981) rejected this property, called the *efficiency of markets*: For plausible discount rates, price variations appear too great compared with the variance in dividends. The literature subsequently turned its attention to the choice of discount rate, which led to the CCAPM and the stochastic discount factor, as described here. Mehra and Prescott identified and popularized the *equity premium puzzle* and Weil (1989), on the same dataset, shows the interest rate puzzle. Hansen and Jagannathan (1991) proposed a nonparametric test for the equity premium puzzle. Kocherlakota (1996) surveys subsequent attempts to solve these puzzles.

Campbell, J.Y. (1986). "Bond and stock returns in a simple exchange model," *Quarterly Journal of Economics*, **101**, 785–803.

Hansen, L. and R. Jagannathan (1991). "Restrictions on intertemporal rates of substitution implied by asset returns," *Journal of Political Economy*, **99**(2), 225–262.

Kocherlakota, N. (1996). "The equity premium: it's still a puzzle," *Journal of Economic Literature*, **XXIV**, 42–71.

Lucas, R.E. (1978). "Asset prices in an exchange economy," *Econometrica*, **46**(6), 1429–1435.

Mehra, R. and E.C. Prescott (1985). "The equity premium: a Puzzle," *Journal of Monetary Economics*, **15**, 145–151.

Shiller, R.J. (1981). "Do stock prices move too much to be justified by subsequent changes in dividends?" *American Economic Review*, 71, 421–436.

Weil, P. (1989). "The equity premium puzzle and the risk-free rate puzzle," *Journal of Monetary Economics*, 24(2), 401–421.

Exercises

8.1 *Recursive preferences*   The relative risk aversion coefficient and intertemporal elasticity of substitution are equal when the utility index is isoelastic. The following exercise introduces preferences that are almost as easy to handle, but that disentangle the two notions.

1 In a two dates model, consider a consumer with preferences over (c_1, c_2) represented by

$$\frac{1}{1-\gamma}[c_1^{1-\gamma} + \delta E(c_2^{1-\gamma})]$$

and facing the budget constraint

$$c_1 + qc_2 = \omega_1 + q\omega_2,$$

with $q = 1/(1 + r)$ (there is no uncertainty). q is the price of one unit of good available at date 2 in terms of good available at date 1. The intertemporal elasticity of substitution is defined as the relative variation in the consumption ratio c_2/c_1, caused by a change in this price:

$$e = -\frac{\partial(c_2/c_1)}{c_2/c_1} \frac{\partial(q)}{q}.$$

In other words, if the price increases by 1 percent, then the consumption ratio falls by e percent. Compute this elasticity. Compare it with the risk aversion.

2 Now assume that preferences are given by

$$\frac{1}{1-\gamma}[c_1^{1-\phi} + \delta E(c_2^{1-\gamma})^{(1-\phi)/(1-\gamma)}]$$

Answer the same questions again. Draw conclusions.

8.2 *Slope of the spot curve*   In a very simple model, we study how the slope of the spot curve is related to expectation on future rates and to the supply of bonds. At $t = 0$, consider two zero-coupon bonds:

1 a zero coupon with maturity 1 with price $1/(1 + r(1))$;
2 a zero coupon with a longer maturity, here 2, and costing $q(2)$ today. Let $\tilde{q}_1(1)$ represent its (random) price at time 1, as expected by the market. This expectation is assumed identical for all investors.

There are I investors at time $t = 0$. Investor i, $i = 1, \ldots, I$, has wealth ω^i and preferences over consumption at time 1. They are represented by a mean–variance function. Investor i seeks to maximize

$$E(\tilde{c}) - \frac{\rho^I}{2}\mathrm{var}(\tilde{c}),$$

subject to his budget constraint.

1 Compute the quantity of zero coupons demanded by investor i.

2 The government supplies the zero coupons as follows. The supply of zero coupons maturing at 2 is fixed at M while that for zero coupons maturing at 1 is adjusted so as to make the short-term rate, $r(1)$, equal to a given value r.
   (a) Derive the equilibrium price $q(2)$ as a function of the anticipated variance of $\tilde{q}_1(1)$ and the supply M.
   (b) Comment.

3 (a) Recall the relationship linking $q(2)$ to the rate $r(2)$ with maturity 2, and that linking the price $q_1(1)$ that will be realized at time 1 to the rate $r_1(1)$ of maturity 1 at time 1. Derive the equilibrium relationship between the rates.
   (b) Using the fact that the rates are small relative to 1, linearize the foregoing expression. Under what conditions is the "short-term" rate $r(1)$ greater than the "long-term" rate $r(2)$? Can the spot curve be increasing, decreasing?

Note: In this simple exercise, it is only the anticipation on the distribution of next price $\tilde{q}_1(1)$ that matters. This anticipation may be correct or not.

part 3

The Firm

In Part 2 of this book, the resources of the entire economy were wholly consumed when they became available. They could neither be stored nor reused for purposes of production. Aggregate savings were nil, and we were concerned with the *allocation* of exogenously given risky resources. This last part introduces physical investments so that production activities may alter the size of the available cake. Also, because the revenues to investments are typically uncertain, production decisions also affect risk profiles. Before addressing the problems stemming from risks, it is worth reviewing briefly the basics of investment decision making in a riskless economy.

There is no uncertainty in the economy, but the good available at time 0 may be invested to produce additional resources at time 1. Thus, even in the absence of financial markets, an agent can modify the time profile of her available resources. We begin with the case in which there is no financial market, and then examine the role of such a market in this set up.

Choice of investment without a financial market Consider an entrepreneur who contemplates making an investment. In the absence of financial markets, she needs to save to finance the investment – her consumption today and tomorrow are directly linked to the size of the investment.

Investment opportunities are described by a production function, f: An investment of k units of the good at time 0 yields $f(k)$ at time 1. The function f is assumed concave and marginal productivity, $f'(k)$, is decreasing.

Denote by (ω_0, ω_1) the entrepreneur's initial resources at the two dates. The set C of consumption profiles, (c_0, c_1), that can be realized in the absence of financial markets is given by

$$c_0 = \omega_0 - k, \quad c_1 = \omega_1 + f(k), \quad k \geq 0, \tag{P3.1}$$

With preferences represented by $U(c_0, c_1)$, the entrepreneur selects the investment level $k \geq 0$ that maximizes

$$U[\omega_0 - k, f(k) + \omega_1].$$

The necessary and sufficient first-order conditions are

$$\frac{U_0'(c_0, c_1)}{U_1'(c_0, c_1)} \geq f'(k) \text{ with equality when } k > 0. \tag{P3.2}$$

There is no investment if the marginal rate of substitution between current and future income, evaluated with consumption equal to the initial endowments, exceeds the marginal productivity of capital at the origin. Otherwise, the agent invests, by reducing current consumption in favor of future consumption, until the marginal rate of substitution equals the marginal productivity of the investment.

Instead of a single entrepreneur, consider a firm owned in equal shares by two investors, each contributing half of the investment and receiving half of the output. Investor $i, i = 1, 2$, wishes the total investment of the firm to be equal to $k^i \geq 0$, where k^i maximizes

$$U^i \left[\omega_0^i - \frac{k}{2}, \frac{f(k)}{2} + \omega_1^i \right].$$

The first-order condition is still given by Eqn (P3.2) (replacing U with U^i). Unless the preferences and/or endowments of the two individuals are identical, their preferred choices are unlikely to coincide. Individuals usually desire different investment levels, either because they differ in their impatience for consumption or they have different income profiles.

This can be illustrated graphically. Consider first a single investor. Figure P3.1 depicts the set C (in the (c_0, c_1), space) of realizable consumption profiles from which the investor must choose. The preferred profile is located at the tangency of the indifference curve and the set of possibilities – or, in the absence of a tangency point, at the corner Ω, where no investment occurs.

The same graph can be used when the two investors have identical endowments. It is sufficient to define C as the set $\{(c_0, c_1) = \omega_0 - k/2, f(k)/2 + \omega_1),$ $k \geq 0\}$. A priori, there is no reason why the two investor's indifference curves should be tangent at the same point.

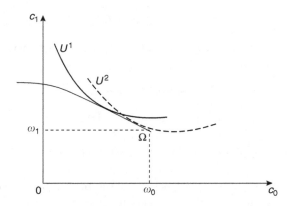

Figure P3.1   The entrepreneur.

Choice of investment with a financial market   A market for lending and borrowing allows these types of conflicts of interest between shareholders to be resolved.

Assume that the entrepreneur has access to a financial market where the risk-free interest rate is r. The profile of consumption possibilities is described by

$$c_0 = \omega_0 - k - z, \quad c_1 = \omega_1 + f(k) + z(1+r), \quad k \geq 0, \qquad (P3.3)$$

In the absence of any restriction on the sign of z, the foregoing equalities are *equivalent* to the intertemporal budget constraint:

$$c_0 + \frac{c_1}{1+r} = \omega_0 + \frac{\omega_1}{1+r} + \frac{f(k)}{1+r} - k, \quad k \geq 0. \qquad (P3.4)$$

A consumption profile is realizable if, and only if,

its discounted value equals the sum of the discounted values of the resources and production net of investment costs.

Consider as before an entrepreneur/investor who chooses the consumption profile, (c_0, c_1), and the level of investment k, under the constraint (P3.4). Since investment only comes into play in her discounted wealth, any investor, regardless of her income profile or utility function, invests the amount k^* that maximizes the *discounted value of net output* or *discounted profit*:

$$\frac{f(k)}{1+r} - k. \qquad (P3.5)$$

This expression is none other than profit from microeconomic theory, computed using prices discounted at time 0. The optimal investment decision is thus independent of, or separable from, the consumption decision (this result is known as the Fisher Separation Theorem). The investor's optimal choice is obtained by

1 setting investment k^* to maximize the discounted value of net output;
2 maximizing utility under the budget constraint (P3.4) associated with the optimal investment $k = k^*$.

When k^* is strictly positive, these two conditions yield the equilibrium:

$$\frac{U_0'(c_0, c_1)}{U_1'(c_0, c_1)} = 1 + r = f'(k^*). \qquad (P3.6)$$

A geometrical depiction of this result can be seen in Figure P3.2. Starting from any realizable point, M, the entrepreneur can borrow or lend to attain any consumption profile on the line having the slope $-(1 + r)$ and passing through that point. Letting M vary in C gives rise to the set of all attainable consumption

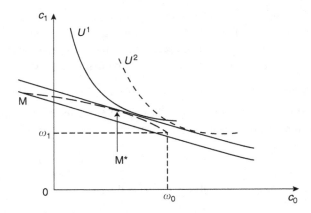

Figure P3.2 The financial market.

profiles. Thus, profiles located on the tangency to the set C and with slope $-(1+r)$ "dominate" all others. As a result, the entrepreneur selects a point on the tangency regardless of his preferences. All these points represent the same investment level as that associated with the point of tangency M^*.

If the firm is owned in equal shares by two investors, each of whom contributes half of the investment and receives half of the output, then each will obtain half of the net discounted value of production. *Thus, they are in agreement to maximize the discounted value of net output, regardless of their preferences.* Furthermore, each intervenes on the financial market to obtain the consumption profile that best suits her preference for the present and initial endowments. This result can be generalized to any number of investors. Summarizing, if a financial market operates without borrowing constraints, at equilibrium there is

1 equality between the marginal rates of substitution, the marginal productivity of investment, and the interest rate;
2 agreement between the different investors on the optimal level of production.

Financing of the firm and uncertainty According to the previous results, if the economy is riskless, the availability of a financial market without any frictions implies simple properties: The value of a firm is unambiguous; the owners of the firm agree on the goals to set for the manager (maximization of discounted profit) and there are no particular difficulties financing production by borrowing on the financial market.

Uncertainty undermines these properties in a fundamental way. The existence of a diversity of financing instruments further complicates the analysis. Chapter 9 presents a general accounting model of the financial flows within the firm, distinguishing between the contributions of stockholders and bondholders and introducing limited liability. The "value" and a "stock market valuation" of the firm can be defined in an uncertain environment just as under certainty, provided markets are complete. If markets are incomplete, these definitions are no longer valid. Under some conditions, however, the Modigliani–Miller theorem establishes a link between the value of all securities issued by the firm.

Chapter 10 examines the firms' financing practices and their interaction with investment choices. Even when markets are complete, conflicts of interest may arise between stockholders and bondholders when there is limited liability, and the investment level chosen by the stockholders may be suboptimal. Finally, we address situations involving asymmetric information between the entrepreneur and the financial backers, whether stockholder or banker. This leads us to discuss the effect of insider trading on the stock exchange and to examine credit rationing.

Corporate finance and risk　　9

Firms take risks. Any investment, hiring, or production decision is a bet on the future. Stakeholders in the firm share these risks in various ways: The labor contract specifies the amount of wage risk assumed by workers, regulations governing the collection of taxes and social security contributions determine the receipts of public creditors in the event of bankruptcy, and so on. This chapter examines a very stylized representation of the firm as a meeting place for financial backers and the entrepreneur/manager. makes two kinds of decisions: economic and financial. The former deal with investments, levels of output and employment, wages, sales price, and the like. These choices require capital. Financial decisions pertain to raising capital from various sources and the associated allocation of risk. We present these in a simplified accounting framework of the activities of the firm (Section 1). Many questions arise. Can the profit maximization criterion from microeconomics be adapted to account for randomness? What are the goals of a firm? Who sets them? Can we define its value, its stock market valuation? These seemingly simple questions in fact prove quite difficult. This chapter, for the most part, concentrates on financial aspects and treats economic decisions as fixed.

The fundamental concepts are first introduced in an intertemporal framework without uncertainty. Section 2 then shows that no conflict of interest arises between the various stockholders, or between stockholders and managers, and that the traditional concept of profit used in microeconomics is justified.

In the presence of uncertainty, these results only partly generalize. Section 3 specifies the conditions under which the value of the firm can be unambiguously defined exclusively on the basis of economic choices regardless of the financial structure. It discusses the Modigliani–Miller theorem, which is derived from the absence of arbitrage opportunities. As a result, the theorem only reflects a consistency in the structure of the prices of securities that firms issue. It should not be misinterpreted as determining all the securities prices. In particular, it is not useful to predict how a firm value would be modified by changes to economic decisions – except in the case of complete markets (or more generally under a spanning condition). This issue will be addressed in Chapter 10.

1   A Simple Accounting Representation

The financial backers of a firm share the *net cash proceeds* (NCPs) that are the aggregate result of economic choices. We examine the principles governing this distribution, which leads us to introduce the notions of firm value and stock market valuation.

1.1   Financial Backers

Three broad categories of financial backers can be distinguished.

1 *Stockholders* A firm issues stocks, usually in exchange for money (sometimes, however, in exchange for an in-kind contribution such as a patent, goodwill, etc.) to increase its equity. Stocks establish property rights on the firm: Their owners participate in the management of the firm by voting and receive dividends. Stockholders equity is the permanent resources of a firm. A stockholder has no claim for his initial contributions on the firm equity and must sell his stocks to a new investor if he wishes to divest from the firm. If this firm is listed on the stock exchange, that is where the sale will occur. Otherwise, a buyer must be found outside of the market, or OTC.
2 *Medium- and long-term lenders* These are usually banks and, to a lesser extent, individuals holding bonds issued by the firm.
3 *Short-term lenders* Intercompany credit is a way for firms to finance ongoing operations. Suppliers provide credit and typically require payment of their bills after 3 months, or at the end of the quarter. The firm may, itself, extend credit to its clients. Overall, in the entire economy, this is generally quite a small amount (it corresponds to "trade" in Table 9.1). This aspect of the firm's financial environment is ignored in this chapter as well as the next one.

A stylized balance sheet of the US nonfarm, nonfinancial firms is presented in Table 9.1. It aggregates the noncorporate and corporate sectors. Only the latter issues stocks, which may be traded on a market. The real estate assets of the

Table 9.1 Nonfarm, nonfinancial business balance sheet USA: amounts outstanding at the end of 2003 (in trillions of dollars)

	Assets	Liabilities
Total tangible assets	**15.8**	
Real estate	10.5	
Other tangible assets	5.3	
Total financial assets	**12.4**	**13.4**
Liquidities and credit market instruments	1.8	7.2
Trade	2.2	1.8
Miscellaneous	8.4	4.3
Net worth		**14.8**

Source: http://www.federalreserve.gov/releases/Z1/Current/

firms are approximately equal to the US GDP in 2003 (11 trillions dollars), while physical equipment and inventories amount to less than half a year of production. When one looks at financial instruments, total assets are not very different from total liabilities, both approximately equal to 1 year of production. Interfirm trade credit corresponds to 1.5–2.0 months of production. Net recourse to credit and bond issues contributes 5.4 trillions dollars to the financing of the firms' activities, but they hold in miscellaneous assets (equity and bonds of other firms directly held or through home pension funds) a net wealth of 3.9 trillions dollars. All considered in the aggregate, financial wealth is close to zero and tangible wealth is close to the net worth, 14.8 trillions dollars, of the firms. The data aggregate those from noncorporate and corporate firms. Of the net worth of 14.8 trillions dollars, the share of noncorporate firms was 4.8 trillions at the end of 2003. The corporate net worth, much more liquid, was 10 trillions, hence approximately equal to the total (farms included) market value of equities outstanding. This equality is not the rule: at the end of 1999, at the time of the stock market bubble, the accounting corporate net worth was equal to 8.2 trillions, while the market value of equities was 85 percent larger, at 15.2 trillions.

Unlike fixed-income government bonds, securities issued by firms (stocks and bonds) are risky, owing to uncertainties associated with productive activity. Bonds frequently contain a variety of clauses, allowing for such things as the conversion into stocks or reimbursement at a date chosen by the debtor. Moreover, even when they guarantee fixed revenues a priori, they always bear an element of *default*

Table 9.2 Stylized balance sheet variations

Variations in assets (or uses)	Variations in liabilities (or resources)
Variations in working capital	Revenues – operating costs
Investments	
Interest costs	Variations in indebtedness
Dividends	Variations in equity capital

risk: In the event of financial difficulties, the issuer may request rescheduling of the maturity, or even go bankrupt. By their very nature, incomes from stocks are risky, since they provide a claim on the firm's residual revenue once all other creditors have been paid. The total amount accruing to medium- and long-term financial backers is called the *NCPs*, which we now define.

1.2 The Net Cash Proceeds

We use a generic cash-flow table to represent the financial flows in the firm. Table 9.2 represents variations in the items over 1 year. The left-hand column gives the variation in assets (or uses) and the right-hand column that of liabilities (or resources).

Under resources, we find first resources generated by the year's activity, which we call *revenues — operating costs*, and then the net contributions by financial backers – variations in equity capital coming from new stock issues and retained earnings on the one hand and changes in indebtedness on the other hand. In corporate accounting, the former corresponds to total sales minus operating expenses (purchases, wages, etc.) and taxes. To clearly identify the relationship between the firm and its financial backers, we diverge from the usual accounting practice by excluding from the expenses interest and fees on loans.[1]

Under uses, we find investments, variations in working capital (increases in inventories and advances to clients linked to business development), and payments to creditors and stockholders. The accounting identity translates the fact that the

---

1 The (revenues — operating costs) is thus equal to the operating cash flow plus interest costs. Technically, it is adjusted for tax deductions on interest payments (these payments reduce the year's earnings and thus the associated taxes). Thus, for any firm that is subject to taxes on earnings, if the nominal interest rate is r and the tax rate τ, the interest cost per dollar borrowed is only $r(1 - \tau)$.

contribution to the year's resources from financial backers and from the proceeds of business are used to compensate the backers and for business development.

Economic decisions affect the revenues — operating costs, investments, and variations in working capital. For our purpose, it is enough to consider the aggregate result of these decisions, which we call the NCPs. They are defined as the (revenues — operating costs) minus all investment expenses and variations in working capital. The accounting identity yields

NCP = (dividends — variations in equity capital) + (interest costs — variation in indebtedness).

In other words, by construction: *The NCPs equal the financial backers' net revenues.*

2   Intertemporal Decisions without Uncertainty

Let us first examine financial practices when both revenues and the interest rates are riskless. In this risk-free environment, without loss of generality, one can assume that *debt is always repaid.*[2]

2.1   The Accounting Framework

Consider for the time being the following sequences, supposed known as of time 0:

1 The NCP, $y_t, t = 0, \ldots, T$, where T is the finite life span of the firm.
2 The interest rates, $r_t, t = 0, \ldots, T$, where r_t is the rate associated with lending or borrowing operations between t and $t+1$. Unlimited lending and borrowing is possible at these rates.

By assumption, these data are known from the start and do not change. In particular, we are exclusively interested in financial decisions that are assumed to

---

2 Strictly speaking, this assumption does not apply to corporations with limited liability, since stockholders cannot be forced to contribute to repaying the debt beyond their initial outlay. But there is no uncertainty, everything is known in advance, so that the debt holders know from the start what they will get in the end.

leave unchanged the sequence of NCPs, (y_t). We note

1. d_t the dividends received at t;
2. f_t the total equity at t, computed as the sum at historical dollar values of the shareholders' contributions and retained earnings up to time t;
3. l_t the total level of indebtedness at t. To focus our thoughts, let us assume that all loans incurred by the firm are short term: If l_t is the level of debt contracted at time t, then the firm must repay the principal, l_t, plus interest payments at time $t + 1$. By *arbitrage*, interest payments are equal to $r_t l_t$ since there is no default risk. The firm can take out another short-term loan, l_{t+1}, but not beyond the final date: $l_T = 0$.

In some cases, we shall distinguish between firms created at $t = 0$ and firms already set up. If the firm starts at date 0, it does not inherit any equity or debt. In this case, it is convenient to set $f_{-1} = l_{-1} = 0$. If it started before, it inherits equity, f_{-1}, and debt, l_{-1}.

At each date, the NCPs are distributed to the financial backers, in keeping with the accounting identity:

$$y_t = [d_t - (f_t - f_{t-1})] + [r_{t-1}l_{t-1} - (l_t - l_{t-1})]. \qquad (9.1)$$

Various measures of values, for the firm, the stocks, the debts, can easily be computed. The reason is that, in a riskless setup without arbitrage opportunities, the present value of any sure revenue flow is well defined (assuming the appropriate market for lending and borrowing as here). Recall, as first shown in Chapter 1, that the value at $t = 0$ of a revenue flow, $a_t, t = 0, \ldots, T$, is equal to

$$\sum_{t=0}^{T} q(t)a_t,$$

where the discount factors $q(t)$ are defined as

$$q(0) = 1 \quad \text{and} \quad q(t) = \frac{1}{1 + r_0} \times \frac{1}{1 + r_1} \times \cdots \times \frac{1}{1 + r_{t-1}}, \qquad t \geq 1.$$

The value of the firm and of the associated financial instruments are determined according to this principle.

2.2 Value of the Firm

The firm generates a revenue flow equal to y_t, $t = 0, \ldots, T$. This leads to defining the *value of the firm at time 0* as[3]:

$$V_0 = \sum_{t=0}^{T} q(t)y_t.$$

This value is the translation into our accounting framework of the *discounted profit* used in microeconomic theory. The NCPs, y_t, are the excess at time t of sales over purchases and other production-related expenditures during period t, measured in accounting units. The NCP at current prices are discounted by multiplying by $q(t)$.

How do financial backers appropriate this value? Let us multiply the accounting identity (9.1) for time t by $q(t)$ and sum from 0 to T. The term corresponding to debt, l_t, for t, $0 \leq t < T$, is equal to

$$[-q(t) + q(t+1)(1+r_t)]l_t,$$

which is null by definition of the discounting factors. Since $l_T = 0$, the terms associated with debt incurred as of time 0 cancel,[4] which gives

$$V_0 = \sum_{t=0}^{T} q(t)y_t = \sum_{t=0}^{T} q(t)[d_t - (f_t - f_{t-1})] + (1 + r_{-1})l_{-1}. \qquad (9.2)$$

This equation describes the distribution of the value of the firm among the two categories of financial backers – creditors and shareholders – and has important consequences. Indeed, since shareholders run the firm, various questions arise. In particular, can shareholders increase their wealth by requesting that the firm's financial officer adopt any particular debt management or dividend distribution practice? The financial officer may, for example, change the borrowing plan l_t into $\bar{l}_t$, and consequently modify the distribution of dividends according to (9.1), which becomes $\bar{d}_t$ instead of d_t. In this transformation, the purely financial operation leaves the sequence of NCPs, y_t, unchanged.

---

3 The value is computed at the beginning of the period before the realization of y_0. For consistency, the stock market valuation is defined before decisions pertaining to finances, the distribution of dividends, and increasing capital, have been made. This is an accounting convention: one could just as easily use the end of period.

4 If there is no final period, $T = \infty$, the same result holds provided the debt is growing more slowly than the interest rate, that is, if $\lim_{t \to \infty} q(t)l_t = 0$.

To understand the impact of such decisions and interpret Eqn (9.2), observe that

$$d_t - (f_t - f_{t-1})$$

corresponds to the net revenues received by the stockholders[5] at time t. Thus, the first term on the right-hand side of Eqn (9.2),

$$\sum_{t=0}^{T} q(t)[d_t - (f_t - f_{t-1})]$$

gives the discounted value of net revenues received by all stockholders, current and future. The second term, $(1 + r_{-1})l_{-1}$, is the initial *value of the debt*.[6] Thus, Eqn (9.2) yields a first expression of the famous Modigliani–Miller theorem:

> the value appropriated by current and future stockholders is equal to the value generated by the firm diminished by the value of the initial debt, independently of the future financial policy.

This implies that the financial officer cannot increase the discounted sum of net revenues paid out to the shareholders, which remains unchanged, independent of his actions, equal to $V_0 - (1 + r_{-1})l_{-1}$.

For a firm that starts at time 0, past indebtedness is nil. In this case, $l_{-1} = 0$, and one immediately gets

> the value generated by the firm as of its creation is entirely appropriated by the stockholders.

We have only considered short-term debts. The preceding analysis can easily be extended to cover debts with a longer term and varied repayment profiles. Basically, it suffices to observe that the aforementioned calculations demonstrate that the value, at time 0, of the flows generated by a debt contracted at time 0 or later is nil. To prove this point, consider a debt incurred at time 0 or later: It yields l_t at the time it is received and specifies the repayment schedule, including interest and capital, $a_\tau, \tau = t + 1, \ldots, T$. These payments are all known with certainty.

---

5 It may seem contrived to simultaneously distribute dividends and raise capital from stockholders, but such decisions, which happen in practice, affect differently new and "old" stockholders.
6 As we shall see, this terminology is particularly apt if the debt does not need to be fully repaid at time 0.

By arbitrage, the value of the loan at the time of issue equals the discounted values of the payments to which it gives rise:

$$l_t = \sum_{\tau=t+1}^{T} \frac{1}{1+r_t} \times \frac{1}{1+r_{t+1}} \times \cdots \times \frac{1}{1+r_{\tau-1}} a_\tau = \sum_{\tau=t+1}^{T} \frac{q(\tau)}{q(t)} a_\tau.$$

This implies that the total flows associated with the debt contracted *as of* time 0 have a discounted value of zero at time 0:

$$q_t l_t - \sum_{\tau=t+1}^{T} q_\tau a_\tau = 0.$$

Instead, the value of the flows associated with debts predating 0 is not nil: Their value is equal to the discounted value of the associated reimbursements. A calculation analogous to that in Section 2.1, with the value of the debts replacing $(1 + r_{-1})l_{-1}$, can then be performed.

So far we have discussed the distribution of the value of the firm between creditors and shareholders. More precisely, the previous analysis bears on the value accruing to *all* shareholders over the life span of the firm. When the structure of stock ownership remains stable, the value is of course received by the current stockholders. In particular, if the founders of the firm remain in place, they receive the value of the firm – each one's share prorated to her initial contribution. In a situation in which the ownership composition changes, such as when the stock is listed on the exchange, the accounting identity (9.2) reveals nothing concerning the distribution of this value amongst the various stockholders.

2.3 Stock Market Valuation

What happens if the firm is listed on the stock exchange, and the structure of the stock ownership changes?

Consider initially a firm that is not public. The value at time 0 of the firm to its shareholders is given by $S_0 = V_0 - (1 + r_{-1})l_{-1}$. One question is whether by listing the firm on the stock exchange and by possibly issuing some new shares, the current shareholders who appropriate this value, can gain more or can lose.

Let the firm be first listed at $t = 0$. Consider an announced sequence of dividends and variations in capital resulting from equity issues for instance. Provided that this sequence does not change the economic decisions and is feasible, meaning that (9.1) is satisfied at all dates, the arguments that lead to the derivation of Eqn (9.2) still apply and give:

$$V_0 - (1 + r_{-1})l_{-1} = \sum_{t=0}^{T} q(t)[d_t - (f_t - f_{t-1})].$$

This means that by arbitrage, at $t = 0$, the value of the claims over the firm by the shareholders of time 0, taken before the distribution of dividends at time 0 and incorporation of reserves and the possible emission of shares, is necessarily equal to S_0, independently of any future financial policy and variations in equity. This result is again driven by the arbitrage principle. Any future equity issue will be priced at its "fair" value, that is, the cash raised at the time of issue is equal to the discounted values of the payments to which it is associated. Viewed from date 0, the net value is nil. In other words,

> at any given date, the value of the firm minus the value of its debt is independent of any future change in the ownership. It is the value accruing to the *current* shareholders.

Let us now assume that the firm is quoted on the market at time 0. Since the number of shares may vary, it is convenient to distinguish the price of a share, denoted by p (or p_t if necessary), from the stock market valuation, that is, the total value of the stock, denoted by S.

The previous argument applies: by arbitrage, at $t = 0$, the market value of the stock, before the distribution of dividends at time 0, retained earnings and possible emission of shares, is necessarily equal to

$$S_0 = \sum_{t=0}^{T} q(t)[d_t - (f_t - f_{t-1})] = V_0 - (1 + r_{-1})l_{-1}.$$

That is, S_0 is the *stock market valuation*.

To better understand stock market valuation, and how it is affected by possible stock issues, let us examine an example. Initially, n shares are held by the public. The price of a share, p, satisfies

$$np = S_0.$$

Assume that the capital is increased at time 0: $\bar{n} - n$ shares are issued to the public (new stockholders are eligible alongside the incumbents) and the funds that are raised are equal to $\bar{f}_0 - f_0$. Thus, we have

$$(\bar{n} - n)\bar{p} = \bar{f}_0 - f_0,$$

where $\bar{p}$ is the share price after the issue.

If the increase in capital is purely a financial operation that does not affect the subsequent NCPs, y_t, the accounting identity (9.1) at time 0,

$$\bar{f}_0 - f_0 = \bar{d}_0 - d_0 - (\bar{l}_0 - l_0),$$

indicates that the injection of fresh capital can serve to reduce indebtedness, so that the new $\bar{l}_0$ is below the old l_0, or to boost the overall distribution of dividends, which will rise from d_0 to $\bar{d}_0$ or both.

At the following period, $(1 + r_0)\bar{l}_0$ has to be reimbursed instead of $(1 + r_0)l_0$, and assume to simplify that afterward the borrowing and dividend policy are unchanged ($\bar{l}_t = l_t$ starting at date 1, and $\bar{d}_t = d_t$ from date 2 onward). Thus, the distributed dividend at time 1 satisfies

$$0 = \bar{d}_1 - d_1 + (1 + r_0)(\bar{l}_0 - l_0).$$

Let $\bar{S}_0$ be the market valuation of the shareholders' claims on the firm after the stock issue. The variation satisfies

$$\bar{S}_0 - S_0 = (\bar{d}_0 - d_0) + \frac{1}{(1 + r)}(\bar{d}_1 - d_1)$$

which, from the above identities, is equal to $\bar{f}_0 - f_0$. Therefore, the market valuation has increased exactly by the cash raised in the stock issue. The total stock market valuation after the increase in capital $\bar{S}_0$ is equal to $\bar{n}\bar{p}$. Hence,

$$\bar{n}\bar{p} = np + (\bar{n} - n)\bar{p},$$

which implies that *the value of the share is unchanged*: $\bar{p} = p$.

If the injection of fresh capital had been used to reduce indebtedness, the total distributed dividends would not have changed ($\bar{d}_0 = d_0$), the per share dividend would have decreased with respect to the initial situation. Thus, initial shareholders would have received less at that period. This loss, However, would have been compensated later, by an increase of the dividend.

This confirms that, from the perspective of the firm's stockholders, the operation is neutral. Clearly, this result can be generalized to any future operation on capital and is, as always, based on arbitrage. At the time of the share issue, new stockholders have a perfect knowledge of future dividends and infer the *fair market price* from it.

2.4 Limited Liability

The value of the firm, V_0, is the discounted sum of future profits. The only difference with the stock market valuation comes from inherited debt, which must be honored in any event. This property provides the justification for the traditional microeconomic approach that retains profit maximization as the sole decision variable regardless of the structure of the stock ownership or the relationship between managers and owners. Let us now examine economic choices. Maximizing profit is equivalent to maximizing the stock market valuation – there is no conflict between the managerial perspective and the stockholder perspective. If the firm is indebted and cannot repay these debts, problems arise owing to limited liability. Consider the case in which no fresh capital is injected by the firm stockholders after time -1: $f_t = f_{-1}$ for all t. Under the principle of limited liability, the stockholders cannot be compelled to disburse any money in excess of their initial contributions. Dividends being positive or nil, Eqn (9.2) can only obtain if

$$V_0 \geq (1 + r_{-1})l_{-1}.$$

In our framework, with no uncertainty and fully informed creditors, this inequality must always be satisfied:

1 If V_0 is negative, creditors will not lend. Suppose that the firm can shut down costlessly: then the firm must stop its operations since it is no longer solvent.
2 If V_0 is positive and $V_0 < (1 + r_{-1})l_{-1}$, creditors should have lent less. Even if the firm pays no dividends to the stockholders, the revenues generated by its activity are insufficient to allow it to repay the loans it has incurred. It is bankrupt and the creditors will recuperate the value V_0, at most.

Since V_0 is the value of the discounted profit from microeconomic theory, the economic operation of the firm appears to be conditional on a positive discounted profit.

2.5 Comments on the Leverage Effect

The result that the financial structure is irrelevant to stockholders appears to contradict what financial analysts call the *leverage effect*. This is only an outward discrepancy: The leverage effect results from an *ex post* accounting illusion, and not from an *ex ante* property.

The argument underlying the leverage effect is as follows. First, the economic profitability of physical investments and the financial profitability of stocks are measured (see below for definitions of these two terms). Then, if the rate of economic profitability exceeds the interest rate, financial profitability increases with the level of indebtedness: Compensation to stockholders is supplemented by the difference (economic profitability − interest rate) per additional unit of debt.

In practice, accounting information on future revenues is not available. Also, financial analysis defines ratios on the current accounts – generating a sort of snapshot. Some ratios pertain to economic activity; others to financial decisions. To illustrate this, let us define two profitability ratios for a single period. The firm makes an initial investment, k_0, corresponding to negative NCPs financed by f_0 and l_0. This yields y_1, which is entirely distributed[7]:

$$k_0 = -y_0 = f_0 + l_0 \quad \text{and} \quad y_1 = d_1 + l_0(1 + r_0).$$

Economic profitability equals the resources generated per unit of capital, that is,

$$\rho_{eco} = \frac{y_1 - k_0}{k_0}.$$

Financial profitability equals revenues paid out to stockholders per unit of equity capital, after they have recovered their outlay, that is,

$$\rho_{fi} = \frac{d_1 - f_0}{f_0}.$$

The *debt–equity ratio* is given by $\alpha = l_0/f_0$. According to (9.1), $d_1 = y_1 - (1 + r_0)(k_0 - f_0)$, or,

$$\rho_{fi} = \rho_{eco} + \alpha(\rho_{eco} - r_0).$$

This relationship, which translates the leverage effect into algebra, indicates that, from the stockholders' perspective, if one is focused on financial profitability, then the optimal way to finance the firm would appear to be as follows: Finance exclusively from borrowing if the economic profitability exceeds the interest rate.

However, the analysis in terms of ratios is deceptive: It does not capture the initial value of the securities or the movements of funds associated with changes in indebtedness and stock issues (see Exercise 9.2). At time 0, before any financing

7 The NCPs include earnings and variations in investments, so in this case, the resale of the initial, possibly depreciated, investments is counted.

decision, the value of the firm equals

$$V_0 = \frac{y_1}{(1 + r_0)} - k_0.$$

This discounted amount is in the hands of the firm owners, regardless of how they acquired their interest – which could, for example, be through their know-how or the development of a new product, not necessarily by injecting financial capital.

The realization of this value, which is only a potential, is conditional on the financial management finding k_0 in funding at time 0. If they have available funds, do the stockholders have an interest in investing them in their firm, or would they be better off putting them into some other activity?

Let us do the accounts for an investment of f_0 financed by a stock issue, f_0, and a loan, l_0, with $k_0 = f_0 + l_0$. The stockholders' net revenues are $-f_0$ at time 0, and $d_1 = y_1 - (1 + r)l_0 = y_1 - (1 + r)k_0 + (1 + r)f_0$ at time 1. The discounted value of this flow equals V_0 and is independent of f_0: Stockholders are indifferent as to how the activity is financed – they only care whether the value of the firm, V_0, is positive. The illusion associated with the calculation of financial profitability is linked to the fact that, in the foregoing presentation, it has been forgotten that the stockholders (or others having the right or ability to appropriate the firm earnings) have the potential for profits *before* the financial decision is made. If financial markets are perfect, the financing method is irrelevant. Indeed, stockholders may actually borrow on their own account and then re-lend this money to the firm! This is one form of the Modigliani–Miller theorem, as explained later.

All of the reasoning in this section occurred in an environment of certainty, with no uncertainty on debt payments. Now we study whether the neutrality properties extend to situations in which the firm earnings and the securities it issues entail risk.

3 Financial Structure

To capture the uncertainty affecting the NCPs, it is convenient to use the tree structure introduced in Chapter 2. Let us denote by $y(e_t)$ the NCP at time t if state e_t occurs. As in the case without uncertainty, revenue flows can be compared using state prices, that exist provided there are no arbitrage opportunities. State prices, however, must be used with care when markets are incomplete. Thus, as usual, it is useful to distinguish the cases of complete and incomplete markets.

3.1 Complete Markets

Assume that markets are complete. Then there exists a unique system of state prices associated with an equilibrium. Let us denote by $q(e_t)$ the price to be paid today, at time 0, for one unit of money in state e_t. Every contingent income flow $y(e_t), t = 0, \ldots, T$, has a well-defined value equal to $\sum_{e \in \mathcal{E}} q(e_t)y(e_t)$ at time 0. Now the equations from the case without uncertainty apply, simply replacing the discount factors with the state prices.

Thus, the value of the firm at time τ, in state e_τ, is defined as the value of its future NCP discounted with state prices (computed at e_τ), or

$$V(e_\tau) = \sum_{e_t > e_\tau} \frac{q(e_t)}{q(e_\tau)} y(e_t).$$

Using the following facts:

1 $y(e_t)$ is the sum of net compensation to the financial backers,
2 the stock market valuation is the sum of the compensation to stockholders discounted by the state prices in e_τ,
3 the value of all flows generated by debt incurred from time τ onward discounted with the state prices in state e_τ is nil,

we immediately obtain

> if markets are complete, the value of the firm is defined as the value of its NCP discounted by the state prices. It is equal to the sum of its stock market valuation and the value of its current debt.

This statement is a simple version of the Modigliani–Miller theorem. To enhance the understanding of these basic principles, they are first applied to the case of an indebted firm that may default. Then a change in the capital structure is examined.

The Case of an Indebted Firm

Consider at time 0, a firm that will stop its activities at time 1. Investments have been made and financed. They will yield nonnegative revenues ($y(e)$) at time 1. The firm has incurred a debt whose face value is m. Thus, the firm repays m unless it declares bankruptcy. If m is too high, then revenues may not suffice to ensure reimbursement: $y(e_1) < m$ for some states at time 1. Under limited liability, stockholders are under no obligation to inject further capital to honor this debt. Thus, revenues associated with this debt are equal to $\min[y(e), m]$. They vary with the state that will materialize: they are risky.[8] The discounted value of the repayments is equal at time 0 to:

$$\sum_{e \in \mathcal{E}} q(e) \min[y(e), m].$$

This is known by the market, so that the value of the debt l_0 must be equal to this discounted value:

$$l_0 = \sum_{e \in \mathcal{E}} q(e) \min[y(e), m]. \tag{9.3}$$

Now consider shares. The revenue of the stockholders equals the firm's income minus repayments to bond holders, provided this quantity is positive. Thus, stockholders receive

$$\max[y(e) - m, 0]. \tag{9.4}$$

If this is correctly anticipated, the stock market valuation at time 0 equals

$$\sum_{e} q(e) \max[0, y(e) - m].$$

It is easy to check that the Modigliani–Miller theorem obtains. The relationship

$$y(e) = \max[y(e) - m, 0] + \min[y(e), m],$$

which holds in all states, implies

$$\sum_{e} q(e) y(e) = \sum_{e} q(e) \max[y(e) - m, 0] + \sum_{e} q(e) \min[y(e), m].$$

The value of the firm is equal to the sum of its stock market valuation and of the value of its debt.

Remark 9.1 In this very simple model with only one form of debt (a zero coupon), Eqn (9.4) reveals that owning stock is analogous to buying a *call option on the firm final revenues*, the strike price of which is equal to the reimbursement of the debt. This remark underlies a number of models for valuing risky debt. Under some assumptions on the evolution of the firm's revenues, the stocks are valued

---

8 Instruments, known as *credit derivatives*, have been developed to make it possible to trade this default risk.

as an option on these revenues using options valuation techniques. The value of the debt is then computed as the difference between the value of the firm and the value of the stocks.

Remark 9.2 At time 0, formula (9.3) prices the *whole* debt that matures at time 1, be it issued at time 0 or before. In realistic situations, a firm has many different outstanding debts that were issued at different dates. Arguing as above, the value of a given bond issued by the firm is affected by other outstanding debts (if any), since the latter affect the possibility of bankruptcy. But it also depends on the priority rules, which specify how the various bond holders are reimbursed in case of bankruptcy.

Stock Issues and Debt Repurchase

According to the Modigliani–Miller theorem, the total value of the various securities issued by the firm is not affected by a change in financing policies. *However, the distribution of this value among the firm's various financial backers generally is.* The following example aims to illustrate this last point, which has considerable practical importance.

Consider a firm having incurred a debt before time 0, which, for simplicity, consists of m units of zero-coupon bonds maturing at time 1 and paying out one unit of money each. We compare two situations:

1 No new debt is issued at time 0. A unit of the bond is traded at the price q_ℓ

$$q_\ell = \sum_{e \in \mathcal{E}} q(e) \min \left[\frac{y(e)}{m}, 1 \right],$$

so that the total debt value is mq_ℓ and the price of the n shares in circulation is

$$np = \sum_{e \in \mathcal{E}_1} q(e)\{y(e) - \min[y(e), m]\}.$$

2 New capital is raised at time 0: $\bar{n} - n$ shares are issued to the public (new stockholders are eligible alongside the incumbents) for an amount $\bar{f}_0 - f_0$. Thus, we have

$$(\bar{n} - n)\bar{p} = \bar{f}_0 - f_0,$$

where $\bar{p}$ is the new share price. The increase in capital is a purely financial operation serving to reduce the debt load, that is, to buy back zero coupons – it does not affect the NCPs at time 1. Assume that the firm buys back $m - \bar{m}$ zero coupons. Since dividends are unaffected, the accounting equality at time 0 is

$$(\bar{n} - n)\bar{p} = (m - \bar{m})\bar{q}_\ell, \tag{9.5}$$

where $\bar{q}_\ell$ is the new bond price satisfying

$$\bar{q}_\ell = \sum_{e \in \mathcal{E}} q(e) \min \left[\frac{y(e)}{\bar{m}}, 1 \right].$$

If, in the reference situation, the firm does not fully reimburse its debt in all states of nature (i.e., $m > y(e)$ for at least one state), then buying back part of the debt increases the value of the bonds, $\bar{q}_\ell > q_\ell$, since fewer bond creditors will remain to share the residual assets in the event of bankruptcy. As the value of the firm remains unchanged, we have

$$\bar{n}\bar{p} + \bar{m}\bar{q}_\ell = np + mq_\ell.$$

Using (9.5), we find that $p > \bar{p}$, so that the stock price decreases.

Thus, financing practices are the key to how the firm's assets are divided among the financial backers. If there is a risk of bankruptcy, an increase in capital for purposes of buying back the debt essentially raids the incumbent stockholders to benefit bond holders. Similarly, stock buyback operations financed by debt issues benefit stockholders. It should be noted that laws are not always very precise in terms of what financial policies a firm may adopt, and vary widely between countries. Stock buyback operations, for instance, are widely practiced in the United States but closely controlled in some European countries. As a result, the degree of protection of bond holders (or also minority stockholders) vary as well across countries. The preceding example illustrates a principle that extends to numerous other situations (see Exercise 9.2).

3.2 Incomplete Markets

The case of complete markets is quite particular, and it is unrealistic to assume that contingent markets exist for every random event that a firm is likely to encounter. What happens when markets are incomplete?

First, in the absence of arbitrage opportunities, there is always a system of state prices with which one can value the contingent flow of revenues. However, one must be careful: This valuation is only meaningful if the revenues at stake can be replicated by a portfolio of market securities (the spanning condition studied in Part 2). Otherwise, the fact that the state prices are indeterminate translates into indeterminate valuations.

The value of a security is the market's estimate of the flow of dividends to which it provides a claim. This is a general principle. In particular, if a bond is risky, its market value will account for that risk. Consider a firm whose shares and bonds are listed on the exchange. For all securities we observe a market price that represents the firm's payments – in the form of dividends, interest, or reimbursements – to its financial backers. Let us compare the market value of all shares, bonds, and other debts for two firms having made the same economic decisions but with differing financial structures.

Theorem 9.1 Modigliani–Miller theorem *Let there be two firms that are listed on the stock exchange. Assume that their NCPs are identical for all states of nature and that their debts are tradable on financial markets. Then, the sum of the values of the shares and debts issued by the former equals the sum of the values of the shares and debts issued by the latter, regardless of their respective financial structures.* ∎

Proof of Theorem 9.1 Let $(y(e_t))$ be the two firms' NCP. Owing to the absence of arbitrage opportunities, there exists at least one vector of state prices, $(q(e_t))$, such that the price of any asset at time 0 equals the value of its contingent revenues discounted by these state prices. *For all states*, the revenues distributed by firm 1 to its financial backers is $y(e_t)$, which is also the sum of revenues paid out by firm 2. Furthermore, by assumption, these revenues can be replicated with securities exchanged on the market. This directly gives that the values of both firms are equal to $\sum_{e_t} q(e_t) y(e_t)$. ∎

Theorem 9.1 applies in particular to the case in which a firm is very indebted and the revenue it pays to its bond creditors is risky. However, if bond creditors demand liquidation of the firm, *whenever this liquidation bears a cost*, then the firm no longer generates the same revenues since it is burdened by the cost of the bankruptcy: The theorem no longer applies.

What is the difference with complete markets? Assume that firm 2 changes its financial structure and issues a security that cannot be replicated by existing assets. A priori, the state prices and market valuations are modified to reflect the new opportunities for exchange (the value of the firm, which is the sum of the asset values, is different). However, the Modigliani–Miller theorem tells us that we continue to have equality between the (modified) value of firm 1 and the sum (similarly modified) of the values of the securities issued by 2. If markets were complete, these values would remain unchanged. Indeed, the stock market valuation is invariant with the financial structure of 2 when the issued securities are generated by existing assets (this is again the *spanning* condition).

3.3 Some Limitations

Many analysts are skeptical of the Modigliani–Miller theorem and maintain that a firm value is affected by its debt–equity ratio.[9] More precisely, the value might be a function of the debt–equity ratio: Increasing first and then falling (a bell-shaped curve) – implying the existence of an optimal debt–equity ratio.

Taxation may explain divergences from the idealized framework of the theorem. Interest charges diminish the firm's taxable profit. Thus, it is preferable for stockholders to lend to the firm and receive interest payments rather than to contribute their own funds and receive taxable dividends. There are many other distortions in the tax system that undermine the Modigliani–Miller theorem and can come into play in financial decision making. Thus, capital gains on securities values are taxed less than dividends. This can induce firms to buy back their own stocks on the market so as to drive up the price rather than pay out dividends, regardless of the damage to bond holders we previously observed.

BIBLIOGRAPHICAL NOTE

There are many textbooks that describe the methods of corporate finance. Two of the most frequently quoted are Brealey and Myers (1992) and Copeland et al. (1991).

The seminal article by Modigliani and Miller (1958) is recommended. The contributions of Drèze (1974) and Stiglitz (1969) specify the scope of its applicability. Models for the valuation of risky debt that are based on stocks as options on the firm value were introduced by Merton (1974). They are currently the focus of a great deal of work in the literature on "credit risk."

Brealey, R. and S. Myers (1992). *Principles of corporate finance*, McGraw-Hill, New York.
Copeland, T., T. Koller, and J. Murrin (1991). *Valuation : measuring and managing the value of companies*, John Wiley, New York.

9 This contradicts the theorem. Note, however, that changing the debt level can, through general equilibrium effects, modify the *span* of the revenues attainable with the financial assets, by changing the risk of bankruptcy, for example.

Drèze, J. (1974). "Investment under private ownership: optimality, equilibrium and stability," In J. Drèze, ed., *Allocation under uncertainty*, McMillan, London.

Merton, R. (1974). "On the pricing of corporate debt: the risk structure of interest rates," *Journal of Finance*, **29**, 449–470.

Modigliani F. and M.H. Miller (1958). "The cost of capital, corporation finance and the theory of investment," *American Economic Review*, **48**, 261–297.

Stiglitz, J. (1969). "A reexamination of the Modigliani–Miller theorem," *American Economic Review*, **59**, 784–793.

Exercises

9.1 *Bankruptcy and financial structure*   We use the simplest possible situation to illustrate that default on debt repayment has no impact on a firm's value provided it is correctly anticipated and there is no cost to bankruptcy. For this, consider in a model with two dates a firm with revenue y at time 1 and a debt with face value denoted by d.

1 Assume that the firm revenue is sure. If r is the interest rate, compute the value of the debt (l_0) and the stocks (p_0) at time 0. Verify that, even if $d > y$, the value of the firm equals the sum of its stock market valuation and the value of its debt, that is,

$$\frac{y}{1+r} = p_0 + l_0.$$

2 Assume that markets are complete and generalize to the case with uncertainty.
3 Now we no longer assume complete markets. Let there be two firms, a and b, with identical revenues. Firm a is debt-free, while firm b is indebted to the point of being unable to consistently make its debt payments at face value. There is no penalty when it fails to make these payments in full. Verify that the stock market valuation of a equals the sum of the stock market valuation and the value of the debt of b.

9.2 *Financing the firm and the interests of existing financial backers*   The purpose of this exercise is to demonstrate with a simple example that the financing practice of the firm managers, which has no impact on the overall value of the firm according to the Modigliani–Miller theorem, provides an advantage to one or the other of the categories of incumbent financial backers.

Consider an economy with two states of nature, $e = b$ or $e = h$, and complete markets. Today's state prices are $\frac{4}{5}$ and $\frac{1}{5}$, respectively. There is a firm whose economic activity yields \$1M if $e = b$ and \$2M if $e = h$. It is financed by 1,000 bonds with a face value of \$1,100, and there are 1,000 shares held by the public.

1 Compute the interest rate in this economy. At what price will the firm's bonds and shares trade?

2 The financial officer decides to issue an additional 1,000 bonds at the same face value of $1,100. How much fresh capital is injected into the firm? What are the prices of the bonds and shares after this operation? What do the original financial backers think of this initiative?

3 Revert to the original situation: Now answer the same question in the event of a share issue.

Financing investments and limited liability 10

Investment decisions are frequently compromises between diverse parties within a firm. The management team, stockholders, and long-term lending institutions may all pursue differing goals, a priori. These differences can be traced to a number of factors: This chapter analyzes the role of incomplete markets, asymmetric information, and limited liability.

Section 1 first examines the circumstances under which the goals of all stockholders are aligned. This is the case if markets are complete. There is no conflict between the various stockholders, who all agree to maximize the stock market valuation which, by definition, is the sum of future dividends discounted with the state prices. However, the lenders to the firm, whose objective is to maximize the value of the debt that they hold, may disagree with stockholders' decisions. Owing to limited liability, new investments by a firm that is in debt and in danger of bankruptcy may increase the probability of default, thereby reducing the value of the standing debt. If markets are incomplete, a further problem arises: There is no longer unanimity among the stockholders (except under a "spanning" condition).

In order to go further, we limit our exposition to single-proprietorships with well-defined goals. The objective is to deal with the financing methods of a small firm and the problems of information that are inextricably linked to them, as well as their interaction with the investment.

A major decision for an entrepreneur is whether to let its firm go public. Being listed on the stock exchange implies complying with strict rules on the dissemination of information. It increases the risk that managers will lose control of the firm with the arrival of outside stockholders. Also, it is likely that the entrepreneur is in possession of information on the firm's prospects prior to the potential buyers of its shares: An IPO may be marred by inside information and the associated adverse selection cost. Section 3 examines the trade-offs faced by an entrepreneur, drawing on the CARA-normal model from Chapter 7. We underscore the damaging impact the insider information has on trades and risk sharing. In order to mitigate these difficulties, stock exchanges have implemented rules governing both the publication of accounts and participation in the markets by corporate insiders (insider trading). We explain why, from a long-term perspective, entrepreneurs who are better informed than the public may well benefit from these types of limitations.

For whatever reason, linked to a loss of control or to information, many firms (especially the smallest) do not seek financing on the stock exchange, but rather opt for bank credit. Section 3 concludes with a look at the market for bank credit. Particular attention is paid to the role of limited liability in distorting the incentives of an entrepreneur.

1   The Choice Criteria for Investments

According to the classical microeconomic theory of perfect competition, maximizing *profit* is the appropriate goal of the firm (the resulting equilibrium is Pareto optimal). Under uncertainty, however, the definition of profit is not self-evident. A simple one-period model in which uncertainty is represented by an exogenous set of states of nature is useful to illustrate the problems that arise. Not surprisingly, it is useful to distinguish between complete and incomplete markets.

1.1   Complete Markets

When markets are complete, the system of state prices associated with equilibrium is unique and allows any contingent revenue flow to be valued. In particular, the value of the firm and the stock market valuation can be unambiguously defined. Since shareholders decide on investment, the main question is how they choose it. Do they agree on the decisions to be made, and if the answer is positive, do they maximize the firm's value?

To address these questions, we consider the following simplified framework. There are two dates. At date 0, a firm is facing new investment opportunities on which it has to decide. At date 1, the firm stops its activities, and distributes all the returns to investments, past or present. These returns are affected by the state of nature that materializes. If the firm is not a start up, it inherits at date 0 for date 1 some debt obligations as well as revenues attributable to past investments.[1] The initial situation of the firm is characterized by

1. the expected revenue at $t = 1, y_1(e)$ if state e materializes, attributable to past investments;
2. the noncontingent payment, m, that the firm is committed to make at time $t = 1$ from previous debt contracts;
3. the investment opportunities that the firm is facing at date 0; they are represented by the revenues they generate: $y(k, e)$ at date 1 if state e materializes when k was invested at time $t = 0$.

Recall that, building on Chapter 9, *thanks to complete markets*, the value of the firm is well defined for any level of k: It is the sum of the revenues from real activities in each state discounted by the state prices[2] $(q(e))$. If k is the level of investment, the value of the firm is

$$V_0(k) = \sum_e q(e)[y_1(e) + y(k, e)] - k.$$

This value is independent of the way the firm finances its investment: Maximizing the value of the firm is a well-defined criteria. Since y_1 comes from the past and cannot be changed, the criteria reduces to $\sum_e q(e)[y(k, e)] - k$, which is the standard profit of classical microeconomic theory.

Why is this criteria interesting? Recall that the value is entirely distributed to the financial backers of the firms. As a result, maximizing the value of the firm amounts to maximize the overall revenues to those who have a claim on the firm's activities, be it shareholders or bondholders. Thus,

> from the perspective of all financial backers, an optimal investment is the one that maximizes the value of the firm.

Note that the bondholders are those who are entitled to the claim of m. We shall refer to this debt as the "senior" debt, so as to distinguish it from the new debt that may be issued.

---

1 There may be payments and revenues during period 0, related to past or current activities: We place ourselves after all these transfers have been carried out.
2 This implicitly assumes that the firm is small so that the activities of the firm, that is, here the chosen level k, do not affect the state prices. This assumption makes sense only if the states are macroeconomic states. We shall come back to this point.

The Stockholders' Perspective

The shareholders have to decide on the investment level and its financing. Formally:

1 At date 0, they choose k, and how it is financed from equity, f, and new "junior" debt, l, under the budget constraint $k = f + l$. Assuming that the debt is issued at par, let us denote by r_ℓ the interest rate applying to this debt. This means that the lenders are entitled to a claim of $(1 + r_\ell)l$ at date 1. This rate is determined later on.
2 At date 1 owing to limited liability, the dividend distributed in state e to shareholders is equal to

$$d(e) = \max[\, y(k, e) - (1 + r_\ell)l - m, 0].\qquad(10.1)$$

Thus, once k, f, and l have been decided, the overall value accruing to the shareholders is

$$\sum_e q(e)d(e) - f,$$

where $d(e)$ is given by (10.1) and $f + l = k$.

Note that $\sum_e q(e)d(e)$ is the stock market valuation once investments have been made. Therefore,

> from the perspective of the stockholders, an optimal decision – investment and financing – is one that maximizes the stock market valuation net of contributions.

It is important to note that stockholders are unanimous in maximizing this criteria. To see this, consider a particular stockholder owning z shares and whose nonfinancial incomes are ω_0 and $\omega_1(e)$. If markets are complete, we know that the budget constraints he is facing at times 0 and 1 combine into a single intertemporal budget constraint. More precisely, by trading on the market, he can generate any consumption profile that satisfies the intertemporal budget constraint:

$$c_0 + \sum_e q(e)c_1(e) = \omega_0 - zf + \sum_e q(e)[\omega_1(e) + zd(e)].\qquad(10.2)$$

Thus, the decision of the firm only affects the stockholder through the intertemporal budget constraint, that is, through the stock market valuation net of contributions, $\sum_e q(e)d(e) - f$.

It follows immediately that all stockholders, regardless of their wealth or attitude vis-à-vis risk, are always in agreement. They deem an investment profitable (unprofitable) if it generates a positive (negative) variation in contingent revenues, as evaluated using state prices – *stockholders all agree to maximize the stock market valuation net of contributions.*

Clearly, this result holds because, owing to the completeness of markets, stockholders are able to transform their financial income (dividends) in any contingent income stream of their choice.

The Stockholders' Choice

When an investment opportunity arises, one may wonder whether the stockholders' decision is influenced by the financial structure inherited from the past – the preexisting level of debt in this case. By assumption, earlier debt repayment commitments have all been honored and only the future schedule needs to be considered. Is the investment choice influenced by the inherited debt? First, as a benchmark, consider a debt-free firm, to simplify, a start-up.

Start-Up

For a start-up, the previous model simplifies by taking past decisions, m and $(y_1(e))$ to be nil. The value of the firm if k is chosen is

$$V_0(k) = \sum_e q(e)y(k, e) - k.$$

Since there is no senior debt, we know that the founders of the firm have title to this value whatever the financing policy. In other words, the stock market valuation net of contributions associated to a level k is equal to $V_0(k)$, independent of its financing. Thus, shareholders will choose the investment that maximizes the value of the firm. To better understand the difference with the case of an indebted firm, let us repeat the argument that shows the independence of the financial policy.

Let k be financed by f and l. If r_ℓ is the nominal interest rate on the debt, creditors are entitled to $\min[y(k, e), (1 + r_\ell)l]$ if state e materializes. Thus, by arbitrage, the nominal interest rate must be set so as to satisfy

$$l = \sum_e q(e) \min[y(k, e), (1 + r_\ell)l].$$

Note that this incorporates the possibility of default. Recall that $\sum_e q(e) \times (1+r) = 1$, where r is the risk-free market rate. Thus, r_ℓ is equal to the risk-free market rate only if the debt is not risky, and is otherwise higher. As for the dividend, it is given in state e by

$$d(e) = y(k, e) - \min[\, y(k, e), (1 + r_\ell)l\,].$$

It follows that the value accruing to the founders is

$$\sum_e q(e)d(e) = \sum_e q(e)y(k, e) - l.$$

The equality $k = f + l$ and the definition of V_0 give

$$\sum_e q(e)d(e) - f = V_0(k),$$

the desired result.

Therefore, the investment choice is unaffected by the financial structure of the firm. Note that the argument relies on the valuation of the debt by arbitrage. In particular, it is essential that the creditors perfectly foresee the possibility of default. Otherwise, the stockholders could exploit this ignorance and benefit from issuing a large debt. In practice, the notation given by rating agencies to the debt issues of large firms helps the market to assess the risk of default. Also, creditors like banks use various "rating" techniques to evaluate the risk.

The analysis extends to a horizon of several periods, provided everything is planned *ex ante* for any contingency: The financial operations are neutral from the point of view of the shareholders because the value of the firm accrues entirely to them.

Indebted Firm

Does this result hold for an existing firm inheriting a debt, which is due at time 1, when it faces a new investment opportunity? Recall that the value of the firm, when it intends to invest k, is

$$V_0(k) = \sum_e q(e)[\, y_1(e) + y(k, e)\,] - k.$$

To simplify, consider the case where all the investment is either self-financed, or financed by the shareholders (no new debt is issued).[3] Then the value of the existing debt is equal to

$$\sum_e q(e) \min[\, y_1(e) + y(k, e), m].$$

Therefore, the stock market value is equal to

$$V_0(k) - \sum_e q(e) \min[\, y_1(e) + y(k, e), m].$$

As a consequence,

> if the firm is indebted, the investment that maximizes the value of the firm is not necessarily the same as the one that maximizes the stock market value.

If the initial debt is risky, and the new investment allows reimbursements to increase, the value of the existing debt increases. For example, assume that for some states $y_1(e) < m$ and $y(k, e)$ is positive. In this case, and unlike in the case of a start-up, the value of the investment is not entirely appropriated by the stockholders. Some of it accrues to the bondholders.

In the other direction, the stockholders can appropriate more than the value created by the new investment. If, for example, the initial debt is risk-free while the risky project creates a danger of bankruptcy, the value of the debt is likely to fall. The argument extends to a horizon of several periods. More precisely, the investment choice is affected by the inherited debt that is due when the revenues associated with the new investment (if it is undertaken) become available.

Conﬂicts of Interest between Bondholders and Stockholders

The previous analysis has direct implications for the choice of investment.

Let us simplify the preceding example even further and assume that the opportunity for investment is characterized by a fixed value, k, and a risk-free

3 To analyze the impact of an issue of new debt, one needs to specify the priority rules of old and new debts in case of default. When all types of debts are equally treated (there is no priority), issuing new debt typically dilutes the value of the old one and benefits the shareholders, all other, things equal (see Exercise 9.2). In any case, the stock market value and the shareholders' preferred investment are related to the financial policy of the firm.

revenue, $y(k)$. The stockholders choose to invest if

$$\sum_e q(e) \max[\, y(e) + y(k) - m] - k \geq \sum_e q(e) \max[\, y(e) - m, 0].$$

When there is no risk of default, this amounts to investing whenever

$$\left[\sum_e q(e)\right] y(k) - k \geq 0,$$

that is, if the project is *profitable*. In the presence of risky debt, this project could be detrimental to stockholders. There is a conflict of interest between stockholders and bondholders. This conflict of interest may account for the focus bondholders, frequently banks, place on the debt–equity ratio (an emphasis that the Modigliani–Miller theorem fails to explain), and possibly make it desirable for them to exercise some control. In the absence of a guard rail, the interests of bond creditors may be harmed and the market for loans dry up.

This allows us to stress one of the limits of the Modigliani–Miller theorem. It shows that the financial structure does not impact on the value of the firm, *provided that all investment decisions are fixed, today and in the future*. But the financial structure may have a differential impact on the various financial backers who, as a result, may disagree on the decisions to make. For instance, the stockholders of two firms that are identical in terms of their productive activities, but differ in their indebtedness, will not have the same interests.

Indeed, risky debt may impede a stock issue designed to finance a profitable investment. This is called the *debt overhang effect*. This problem, identified by Myers (1977), can be laid at the feet of limited liability, which relates to the legal structure of the firm. It may cause socially desirable investments to be abandoned. We shall see below that it also gives rise to other types of dysfunction.

1.2 Incomplete Markets

The situation changes when markets are incomplete. Let us begin with the study of an individual entrepreneur, indexed with i. Her preferences determine the marginal utility of risky income received in the various states of nature, and consequently the marginal willingness to pay today for a unit of money in state e_t, $q^i(e_t)$. We must not only label this marginal willingness with the letter q, like a price, but must also index it with i since, in the absence of complete markets, it is likely to vary from one agent to the next. It is now trivial to ascertain that, if the entrepreneur wishes to hire a manager to run her firm, it is optimal for her to instruct the manager to maximize the quantity $\sum_{e_t} q^i(e_t)d(e_t) - f$. Two firms with the same technical characteristics, but whose sole owners have different attitudes toward risk or different resources, will generally opt for different production programs.[4]

And what if we are dealing with a firm with several shareholders? For a firm listed on the stock exchange, as seen earlier, once the decisions have been made and their results correctly valued by the market, all stockholders agree on the market valuation. They also all agree on the value of physical or financial decisions that modify the flow of dividends from the status quo in any direction spanned by existing securities. However, they tend to disagree on changes to future revenues that cannot be replicated on the market. To see this more clearly, let $\mathcal{A}$ be the vector subspace of $\mathbb{R}^{\mathcal{E}}$ of revenues that can be generated with a portfolio of existing securities and $\mathcal{A}_\perp$ its complement. Markets are incomplete if $\mathcal{A}_\perp$ is not reduced to the null vector.

The vector of contingent revenues of the firm can be decomposed on these two subspaces:

$$y(k, e) = y_{\mathrm{proj}}(k, e) + y_\perp(k, e).$$

First, consider an unlisted firm whose stocks are not tradable. If it chooses an investment level k, $y_{\mathrm{proj}}(k, e)$ can be evaluated by replication. If all investment payoffs are *spanned* by the existing securities, that is, if $y_\perp(k, e)$ is nil whatever k, the same analysis as in complete markets holds. In particular, stockholders all agree on which investment level to choose. The next section provides an example in which this spanning condition holds. The market tells us nothing regarding the value of $y_\perp(k, e)$. In the absence of agreement on this value among the owners, the choice of investment becomes a possible source of conflict.

If the firm is listed, the situation is better, though not fundamentally different. The stock issued by the firm yields $y(k^*, e) - (1+r)k^*$ for an observed investment level k^* (assuming it does not default). In this case, $y_\perp(k^*, e)$ equals zero and the market provides a value for the firm. However, it provides no information on how to evaluate alternative investments whose returns are not spanned by existing securities: If $y_\perp(k, e)$ differs from zero for investment k, stockholders may disagree on whether changing k^* to k is worthwhile.

---

4 This can occur for the same reason in a risk-free environment when there is not market for borrowing and lending, as seen in the introduction to Part 3.

Thus, there is no unambiguous goal for the firm manager when the stockholders are not unanimous on the new direction.[5] These hurdles to defining the goals of the firm when markets are incomplete, which are both theoretical and practical, are vital to decisions on physical investments.

1.3 Multiplicative Risk

As just seen, even when markets are incomplete, an investment choice criterion can be defined on which all stockholders agree under the spanning condition. Consider the following situation. The risk of a firm is said to be *multiplicative* if there is a vector $(p_g(e))$ for which

$$y(k, e) = p_g(e)g(k) \quad \forall k, \forall e.$$

Thus, choosing the investment level determines the scale at which revenue $(p_g(e))$ is obtained. This occurs, for instance, if the firm output, $g(k)$, is unaffected by uncertainty and risk only impacts the future selling price of the good, $p_g(e)$ in state e.[6] Assume that there is a risk-free asset.

In the absence of default, dividends take the form:

$$\tilde{d} = g(k)\tilde{p} - (1 + r_\ell)l,$$

which is a linear combination of the vector $\tilde{p} = [p(e)]_{e=1,...,E}$ and of the constant vector. Consequently, the space of contingent revenues generated by the securities issued by the firm is fixed independent of its (non-nil) level of investment: The spanning condition holds. Let $p_{0,g}$ be the market value at time $t = 0$ of the random revenue[7] $\tilde{p}_g$. The value of the firm is now given by

$$V(k) = p_{0,g}g(k) - k.$$

---

5 When there are $i = 1, \ldots, I$ stockholders whose marginal propensity to pay is q^i, and each of whose share in the firm is z^i, it has been suggested in the theoretical literature that the manager maximizes profit using a state price equal to $\sum_{i=1}^{I} z^i q^i$. However, this notion has no practical relevance.

6 This also applies when there is no uncertainty on prices, but production levels retain the same proportion in the different states of nature regardless of the investment. The choice of the firm is the scale of production.

7

$$p_{0,g} = \frac{E\{v'^i[c^i(e)]p_g(e)\}}{u'^i[c^i(0)]} \quad \forall i.$$

This is the price that consumers are prepared to pay at the margin for the income $\tilde{p}_g$.

If the firm takes this price as given and maximizes its own value, one has

$$p_{0,g}g'(k) = 1,$$

at equilibrium. $1/g'(k)$ is interpreted as the marginal quantity of good k that must be forfeited at $t = 0$ to increase the scale of production. If there is no debt overhang, then maximizing the value of the firm suits the stockholders.

2 Investments, Equity Financing, and Insider Information

Section 1 has underscored the importance of the assumption of complete markets. This raises the question of whether this assumption is plausible, especially in the context of investments. Uncertainty over revenues has many sources: Some are macroeconomic, for example, dealing with the prices of supplies or exchange rates, while others are microeconomic and may involve sector-specific issues or the behavior of agents within the firm: Managers, workers, and the like. While the assumption of complete markets may be acceptable when the only uncertainty bears on a macroeconomic shock, it makes no sense when applied to idiosyncratic risks. The individual, idiosyncratic, component of risk inherently plays a very large role in small firms. Not only are these risks not spanned by the market, but the financial backers also may lack information to evaluate them. The remainder of this chapter provides an overview of the problems that arise and emphasize the asymmetry of the information between the entrepreneur and her financial backers. The entrepreneur is better informed than the financiers on the risk associated with her firm, but has every interest in painting a rosy picture and thus it lacks credibility. This predicament arises in the case of both stock market funding, the subject of this section, and on the credit market, which is examined in Section 3.

We use the CARA-normal framework that is quite restrictive but allows equilibria to be explicitly solved when information is asymmetric. More specifically, an individual entrepreneur, who is better informed than the public, weighs the benefits and disadvantages of going public, as in the model developed in Section 4 of Chapter 7. However, while the size of the firm was treated as given in that case, here we are interested in the impact of the financial decision on the realized level of physical investment.

The entrepreneur is the sole proprietor of the firm and is contemplating offering it for sale on the stock exchange. The revenues that the firm will generate from an initial investment of k equal $\tilde{p}_g g(k)$, where $\tilde{p}_g$ is normally distributed. The entrepreneur maximizes the utility of her future wealth, given a risk aversion coefficient of ρ:

$$-E[\exp(-\rho \tilde{W})].$$

The market for loans is assumed to function well. To simplify, the risk-free rate is zero. We avoid the problems associated with limited liability by supposing that *the entrepreneur always honors the incurred debt repayment obligations*. Each of the three institutional contexts of Section 4 of Chapter 7 is examined in turn and we compare the level of investment and the entrepreneur's welfare in each case.

1 In the *absence of a stock exchange*,[8] the entrepreneur assumes all the risks associated with her activity. The income she receives from her investment is

$$\tilde{W} = \tilde{p}_g g(k) - k.$$

Maximizing expected utility is equivalent to maximizing

$$g(k)E(\tilde{p}_g) - \frac{\rho}{2} g(k)^2 \mathrm{var}(\tilde{p}_g) - k,$$

yielding the first-order condition:

$$g'(k)[E(\tilde{p}_g) - \rho g(k)\mathrm{var}(\tilde{p}_g)] = 1.$$

When the production function g is increasing and concave, any solution to the first-order condition is a local maximum (one only needs to check that the second derivative is negative). This condition can also be written as

$$E(\tilde{p}_g) - \rho g(k)\mathrm{var}(\tilde{p}_g) = \frac{1}{g'(k)},$$

indicating that the marginal cost is set equal to the expected price minus a risk premium. The concavity of g also implies that, ceteris paribus, the higher the variance of the price, the lower the level of investment: *Risk leads the entrepreneur to invest less*.

2 *The firm is listed on a stock exchange*. Furthermore, the entrepreneur has no insider information. To keep the math tractable, assume that the market is risk

---

8 This is of course an extreme assumption. The argument goes through provided $\tilde{p}_g$ is uncorrelated with the dividends of the tradable securities.

neutral. The market provides full insurance to the entrepreneur. In the absence of information, the price of the firm is

$$p = E(\tilde{p}_g)g(k) - k.$$

Since the entrepreneur can hedge her risks without cost, it is optimal for her to sell the firm *in toto*[9] and to choose the level of production so as to maximize $E(\tilde{p})g(k) - k$.

The level of investment is thus given by the first-order condition:

$$g'(k)E(\tilde{p}_g) = 1.$$

Marginal cost is equated to the mathematical expectation of the sales price. The allocation of risk that the stock exchange makes possible allows for a higher level of investment. It is easy to show that the entrepreneur's level of utility increases relative to the previous situation. However, this is a partial equilibrium result, which is only valid if the firm is small relative to the overall market. If not, the increase in production could change the product sales price and, by the law of supply and demand, reduce $\tilde{p}_g$. It is thus possible that the benefit could be reduced, and even change sign (see Exercise 10.2).

3 As in case 2, the firm is listed on the stock exchange but the entrepreneur possesses information on the firm profitability in advance of the market, as is more realistic. The physical investment decision is made *before* knowledge of this information. Information is modeled by an advance signal $\tilde{s}$ on the realization of the product sales price. If the stock is tradable on a competitive stock exchange, the fact that the entrepreneur may trade on the basis of this advanced information affects the exchanges and the resulting prices.

To study this more precisely, it is convenient to assume, as in Chapter 7, that some traders, "noise traders," intervene on the stock market. Their demand is equal to $\tilde{n}$. Let $(\tilde{p}_g, \tilde{s}, \tilde{n})$ be normally distributed. At the rational expectations equilibrium, the entrepreneur's information is only partially revealed by prices: The price of the firm sold on the stock exchange[10] is a function of γ, a "noisy" version of the entrepreneur's expectations $E[\tilde{p}_g|s]$. More precisely, the stock value $\tilde{p}$ derived from a physical investment decision k is given by

$$\tilde{p} = E[\tilde{p}_g g(k) - k|\gamma], \quad \tilde{\gamma} = E(\tilde{p}_g|s) - \rho \, \text{var}(\tilde{p}_g|s)\tilde{n}, \tag{10.3}$$

9 Indeed, if she opts to sell a share z different from 1 of her income, $(1 - z)[\tilde{p}_g g(k) - k] + zp$, it has the same expectation as p but is more risky.
10 See Chapter 7 and its appendix, taking $\tilde{a} = \tilde{p}_g g(k) - k$.

and the entrepreneur's *ex ante* expected profit is

$$U = -\sqrt{\frac{\operatorname{var}(\tilde{p}_g|\tilde{s})}{\operatorname{var}(\tilde{p}_g|\tilde{\gamma})}}$$

$$\times \exp\left(-\left\{\rho[g(k)E\tilde{p}_g - k] - \frac{\rho^2 g(k)^2}{2}\operatorname{var}[E(\tilde{p}_g|\tilde{\gamma})]\right\}\right). \qquad (10.4)$$

The same terms as in Section 4.3 in Chapter 7 reflect the impact of information on the entrepreneur's profit: A speculative, beneficial effect of information (the term under the square root), and a harmful one represented by the last factor, reflecting the reduced ability of the market to provide insurance when information is asymmetric. This is through this latter term that new investment is affected by insider information. The optimal level of investment satisfies the first-order condition:

$$g'(k)\{E(\tilde{p}_g) - \rho g(k)\operatorname{var}[E(\tilde{p}_g|\tilde{\gamma})]\} = 1.$$

For purposes of our comparison with the previous cases, it is useful to decompose the variance of prices:

$$\operatorname{var}(\tilde{p}_g) = \operatorname{var}[E(\tilde{p}_g|\tilde{\gamma})] + \operatorname{var}(\tilde{p}_g|\tilde{\gamma}).$$

Compared with the case in which there is no stock exchange, investment is greater, as is the entrepreneur's utility. However, it is lower than when there is a stock exchange and no insider information. There is a risk premium equal to $\rho g(k)\operatorname{var}[E(\tilde{p}_g|\tilde{\gamma})]$ that captures the detrimental impact of information on insurance: Only the part of the security payoff that is uncorrelated with information transmitted to the market can be insured, and $\operatorname{var}(\tilde{p}_g|\tilde{\gamma})$ is assumed by the entrepreneur.

This negative impact on investment of trades based on inside information underlies the regulation of insider trading. It motivates an institutional structure that reduces to the greatest possible extent the entrepreneur's ability to use her insider information on the market. If the entrepreneur is forbidden to trade, the market provides full insurance and investment is maximized (as in case 2).

But this is only part of the story: Here information is the villain, since its only role is to give an advantage to one of the market participants. This is because physical investment is decided before the signal is available. These results may be reversed if the information is known *before* the decision on physical investments is made. Then one may invest a great deal when prices are high and little when prospects are less advantageous. Formally, let $U(k, \tilde{p}_g; \tilde{s})$ be the entrepreneur's *interim* expected utility before opening of the stock exchange when she has invested k in the firm. The insider information she has received is given by the random variable $\tilde{s}$ and her (personal) price expectation is the random variable $\tilde{p}_g$. As we saw in Chapter 7, if physical investment can be decided after the signal is known, two effects come into play: The entrepreneur bears a risk related to fluctuations in the stock exchange, but can eventually increase output to benefit from higher prices, at least if production is sufficiently flexible.

3 The Market for Credit

The stock exchange is only accessible to firms that are large enough to assume the costs of the demanding procedures governing the dissemination of information on their prospects and investment projects. In the case of a small firm, or a firm engaged in an activity that requires confidentiality (research, easily copied innovations, etc.), financing can consist of bank credit. The bank may access to the firm secrets for which it is bound to maintain confidentiality.

Sharing information, even when this is possible, only addresses part of the problem: The market is fundamentally incomplete and contingent contracts on all states of nature cannot be defined. Then, the risk of bankruptcy is liable to undermine the functioning of the market for credit. The presentation below builds on the model of Stiglitz and Weiss (1981).

Consider a small firm that wishes to undertake an investment that requires external financing. The entrepreneur is better informed than potential lenders on the quality of the project. Insider information and incentives (moral hazard) can coexist with credit rationing at equilibrium.

3.1 The Market without Dysfunction

For purposes of comparison, as a benchmark, let us start by examining a credit market without dysfunction, in which distortions due to limited liability and information-related problems are absent.

In the sequel, the focus is on the demand side of the market, the demand for loans. Therefore, supply is described as simply as possible. Banks collect deposits that they lend to investors. The cost to banks of collecting a level of deposits s is $C(s)$, where the function C is strictly increasing and strictly convex. This function is assumed to be exogenously given: The compensation to deposits is fixed and independent of the conditions of bank credit. This is a simplifying assumption (which roughly holds when regulation forbids deposits to be remunerated).

To simplify further, assume that a single type of contract can be signed between the parties: This contract specifies that, for a nominal market interest rate of r_ℓ, a credit of one dollar obligates the borrower to repay the lender $(1 + r_\ell)$ dollars at time 1. The question is to determine the level of the rate r_ℓ and the amount of the loan.

When there is no default, the bank supply of risk-free loans at the rate r_ℓ maximizes its profit:

$$r_\ell s - C(s).$$

Since C is strictly convex, the supply $s(r_\ell)$ is unique and characterized by the first-order condition $r_{\ell l} = C'[s(r_\ell)]$ (we are abstracting from corner solutions). It follows that supply, s, is increasing with the rate. The associated profit, $\pi^b(r_\ell)$, is the maximum profit that the bank can earn at rate r_ℓ when it lends $s(r_\ell)$. It is worth noting that this profit, π^b, is increasing[11] in r_ℓ. We denote by S the banks' aggregate supply.

For now, we simply assume that the entrepreneur's demand for loans is given by a function $K(r_\ell)$. The shape of this demand will be examined in the following section.[12]

In a competitive framework, a rate r_E is an equilibrium if the total supply of credit at that rate equals the demand: $S(r_E) = K(r_E)$. This is the traditional definition when all agents, especially banks, treat prices as given.

To justify this definition, let us examine the case of a bank that seeks to deviate from equilibrium by proposing an interest rate r_ℓ that differs from r_E. If it charges a rate that is higher than r_E, another bank will take its place and it will lose all of its clients (here the assumption of perfect competition – that is, with many agents that are small relative to the market – comes into play: This would not be the case with a monopoly). The only feasible deviation is to *lower* the rate. Here, this is not a profitable strategy for the bank, *since profit is an increasing function of the rate*. Below, we shall encounter conditions under which profit is not increasing with

11 When C is strictly convex, the optimum, $s(r_\ell)$, is unique and differentiable with respect to r_ℓ. Since $\pi^b(r_\ell) = r_\ell s(r_\ell) - C[s(r_\ell)]$, differentiating with respect to r_ℓ and using the first-order condition yields $\pi^{b\prime}(r_\ell) = s(r_\ell)$, which is strictly positive.
12 Under the usual assumptions, this demand is decreasing in rate, but this is immaterial to our reasoning.

rates, and in which we need to call on another description of the functioning of the market than that given by competitive equilibrium.

3.2 Default Risk

So far we have assumed that there is no default on repayment. This may be plausible when the debt load is sufficiently small relative to the firm revenues, but it is unrealistic for a start-up. Even in the case of an unincorporated sole-proprietorship, in which the entrepreneur's liability is unlimited in principle, the bank is unable to recover more than the owner's personal possessions. It is useful to examine the market when loans allotted by the banks are risky owing to bankruptcy. We first examine the demand for loans, then the supply, and finally equilibrium.

The entrepreneur chooses a level of investment, k, that generates a stochastic revenue, $y(k, e)$ if state e materializes. Inaction is possible: $y(0, e) = 0$. The number of states is finite. Marginal productivity is assumed to be decreasing: The function y is strictly concave in k. We study the demand for loans and the default risk when the entire investment is borrowed. The entrepreneur is assumed risk neutral.

Under unlimited liability, she maximizes:

$$P(k, r_\ell) = E[\, y(k, e) - (1 + r_\ell)k].$$

Under limited liability, if revenues are insufficient to repay the debt, default occurs and the lender only recovers $y(k, e)$. The entrepreneur then chooses an investment that maximizes:

$$P_\ell(k, r_\ell) = E\{\max[\, y(k, e) - (1 + r_\ell)k, 0]\}.$$

Also it is convenient to assume that y is continuous and differentiable with respect to k.

Proposition 10.1 *Let $K(r_\ell)$ and $K_\ell(r_\ell)$ be the demand for loans of companies with unlimited and limited liability, respectively. Under the usual assumption of decreasing marginal productivity, K is decreasing and $K_\ell(r_\ell) \geq K(r_\ell)$ for all r_ℓ. In other words, ceteris paribus, limited liability increases the demand for funds relative to unlimited liability.* ∎

Consequently, entrepreneurs are more prepared to invest if they only bear a limited liability. This result, which is quite intuitive, is attributable to the fact that they are "off the hook" when the firm becomes insolvent.

Proof of Proposition 10.1   The aforementioned assumptions imply that $y(k, e)/k$ is decreasing and always above marginal revenue:

$$\frac{y(k, e)}{k} > y'_k(k, e) \quad \forall k > 0, \, e. \tag{10.5}$$

Note that owing to the decline in average revenue, the set of states in which there is bankruptcy can only become larger as the level of investment increases.

We show that optimal investments satisfy the first-order condition (which, owing to discontinuities, is no trivial result under limited liability). The result then follows from comparing marginal profits with and without limited liability.

First-order conditions   In the case of unlimited liability, the expected profit is concave, and the derivative

$$P'_k(k, r_\ell) = E[\, y'_k(k, e) - (1 + r_\ell)],$$

is strictly decreasing in k. Investment demand, $K(r_\ell)$, is characterized by the equality $P'_k = 0$.

In the case of limited liability, $\max[\, y(k, e) - (1 + r_\ell)k, 0]$ is not necessarily concave. The expected profit has a derivative equal to

$$P'_{\ell,k}(k, r_\ell) = E\{[(y'_k(k, e) - (1 + r_\ell)]\mathbf{1}_{\{e|y(k,e)-(1+r_\ell)k>0\}}\},$$

at all points k such that $y(k, e) - (1 + r_\ell)k$ differs from zero in all states.

Elsewhere, at an investment level for which revenue just covers the debt payment in some state, profit is not differentiable. We prove that the derivative features upward discontinuities, so that such an investment level is surely not optimal. To see this, consider an investment value, say k^*, for which profit is just equal to zero in a state e^*: $y(k^*, e) = (1 + r_\ell)k^*$. When k increases above k^*, the set of states in which there is bankruptcy becomes larger, including e^*. Furthermore, thanks to (10.5), marginal productivity $y'_k(k^*, e^*)$ is below $1 + r_\ell$: This state no longer contributes to the entrepreneur's revenue. The difference between the right and the left derivatives is thus positive, equal to $- [\, y'_k(k^*, e^*) - (1 + r_\ell)]$ multiplied by the probability $\pi(e^*)$.[13] Thus, the demand for loans, $K_\ell(r_\ell)$, satisfies

13 When there is a continuum of states, say e is real-valued with an absolutely continuous density with respect to the Lebesgue measure, and the derivative of $y(k, e)$ with respect to e is always strictly positive, the reasoning is simpler. The profit is in fact everywhere continuously differentiable.

the condition:

$$P'_{\ell,k}(k, r_\ell) = 0.$$

Comparison of marginal profits From the perspective of the entrepreneur, the marginal profit of an investment equals the mathematical expectation of the difference between its marginal revenue and the interest rate, computed either over all states (when there is unlimited liability) or over those states in which the firm does not go bankrupt (when there is limited liability). This means that the marginal profit is greater under limited liability:

$$P'_k(k, r_\ell) \le P'_{\ell,k}(k, r_\ell),$$

with strict inequality in the case of positive probability of bankruptcy. Indeed, in a state e where there is default, $y(k, e) - (1 + r_\ell)k \le 0$, implying $y'_k(k, e) < (1 + r_\ell)$ because of (10.5). In other words, in a state in which there is bankruptcy, marginal revenue is surely below the interest rate. It is, thus, sufficient to compare the expression for marginal profits to derive the desire inequality: $P'_k(k, r_\ell) \le P'_{\ell,k}(k, r_\ell)$.

Comparison of investments Applying the preceding inequality to $k = K_\ell(r_\ell)$,

$$P'_k[K_\ell(r_\ell), r_\ell] \le P'_{\ell,k}[K_\ell(r_\ell), r_\ell] = 0.$$

Thus, $K_\ell(r_\ell) \ge K(r_\ell)$ because P'_k is decreasing.

The fact that investment demand K decreases with r_ℓ is a direct consequence of the fact that P'_k is decreasing in r_ℓ. ∎

Consequently, a first effect of limited liability is to increase the demand for loans. If we assume that banks and entrepreneurs have access to the same information on the future yields of investments, a second effect is a reduced supply: Banks anticipate the default risk and consequently cut supply. More precisely, a bank expects the payoff:

$$E[\min(y(k, e), k(1 + r_\ell))].$$

Thus, from the perspective of the lending bank, the yield of a loan granted at the nominal rate r_ℓ is $\rho(r_\ell)$, given by

$$\rho(r_\ell) = E\left[\min\left[\frac{y(k, e)}{k} - 1, r_\ell\right]\right]. \tag{10.6}$$

It is below r_ℓ when default exists. Furthermore, when the rate varies, the *quality* of repayment can also vary owing to the reaction of entrepreneurs. In this context, it is legitimate to assume that banks account for the reaction of borrowers: This leads us to define the banks' supply when they anticipate that the mean expected profitability of loans at r_ℓ equals $\rho(r_\ell)$. Furthermore, if banks are risk neutral, they only care about the expectation of the yield, the *reduced form* ρ. A bank's supply at rate r_ℓ, $s_\ell(r_\ell)$, depends on expected profitability. It maximizes

$$\max_s \rho(r_\ell)s - C(s).$$

As before, capital letters indicate aggregate values.

Proposition 10.2 *Let $S(r_\ell)$ and $S_\ell(r_\ell)$ be the banks' supply of loans to unlimited and limited liability companies, respectively. We have*

$$S_\ell(r_\ell) \leq S(r_\ell).$$

While the maximum supply, S, and profit, π^b, are increasing with r_ℓ, supply S_ℓ and profit π^b_ℓ are not necessarily increasing: Their derivative with respect to r_ℓ has the same sign as the derivative of ρ with respect to r_ℓ. ∎

The proof is straightforward. We have already seen these properties in the case of unlimited liability – where banks bear no default risk. The case of limited liability follows directly, since $S_\ell(r_\ell)$ is given by $S[\rho(r_\ell)]$ and the maximum expected profit, π^b_ℓ, is $\pi^b[\rho(r_\ell)]$. Since S and π^b are increasing functions, supply and profit vary with r_ℓ in the same direction as ρ. Moreover, we have $S_\ell(r_\ell) \leq S(r_\ell)$, since $\rho(r_\ell) \leq r_\ell$.

3.3 Equilibrium

The previous analysis leads us to define an equilibrium when banks form correct expectations about the default risk: They anticipate that the expected profitability of loans at r_ℓ equals $\rho(r_\ell)$.

When expected profitability $\rho(r_\ell)$ is increasing with r_ℓ, the expected profit π^b_ℓ is also increasing in r_ℓ according to Proposition 10.2. Thus, the competitive equilibrium as defined above in the case with no bankruptcy is meaningful.

The equilibrium rate is that at which demand, K_ℓ, and supply, S_ℓ, are equal.[14] Comparing this equilibrium with those under unlimited liability, the higher demand and lower supply both drive up the equilibrium rate. This is in keeping with current observations: Rates paid by start-ups are higher than those granted to well-established firms that feature little risk and have a reputation to maintain.

We shall see below that expected profitability may be a decreasing function of the interest rate – at least locally. In this event, one needs to specify what notion of equilibrium to retain. The *reduced form*, ρ, is useful for this purpose. To simplify the presentation,[15] assume that the function ρ is first increasing for $r_\ell \leq r_\ell^*$, and decreasing afterward (by construction, $\rho(r_\ell) \leq r_\ell$). Also, assume that the rate r_ℓ^*, which maximizes the expected profitability of loans, is below the rate r_ℓ^c that establishes equilibrium between supply and demand. The argument below suggests that the equilibrium is established at r_ℓ^* and corresponds to a rationing of credit: Demand is not fully met. The argument is the following one.

A bank's supply, $s_\ell(r_\ell)$, is increasing up to r_ℓ^* and then decreasing, and profit maximization corresponds to the maximum expected profit, at r_ℓ^*. Assume that the rate offered by the other banks is r_ℓ^c. If $r_\ell^c > r_\ell^*$, the bank can lower its rate and lend an amount equal to its supply (the demand that will materialize will certainly exceed supply), and thus increase profits. The rate r_ℓ^c is not a stable equilibrium. This argument is valid as long as the proposed rate exceeds r_ℓ^*. Conversely, any rate below r_ℓ^* is not an equilibrium since profits are locally increasing, as in the standard case. Thus, the equilibrium is established at r_ℓ^*, where the supply of credit, $S_\ell(r_\ell^*)$, is below $K_\ell(r_\ell^*)$: Borrowers are rationed.

Example 10.1 Consider the case of an isoelastic production function with uncertainty on the sales price: $y(k, e) = p(e)\sqrt{k}$. Assume that the price $p(e)$ can take two values, $p_1 > p_2$, with probability π and $(1 - \pi)$. Default occurs in state 2 if $p_2 < (1 + r_\ell)\sqrt{k}$. In the absence of bankruptcy, investment is equal to

$$K(r_\ell) = \left[\frac{E(p)}{2(1 + r_\ell)} \right]^2,$$

---

14 Since demand is not necessarily continuous, one may wonder whether such an equilibrium exists. In fact, since discontinuities are upward, its existence is ensured provided the demand for funds is below supply for sufficiently high rates. However, there may be several equilibria.

15 The same logic can be applied when the function is piecewise increasing with downward discontinuities, provided that supply intersects demand after the point of discontinuity at a value of ρ below the previous maximum.

which gives an *ex ante* profit for the firm equal to

$$P(r_\ell) = \frac{1}{4}\left[\frac{[E(p)]^2}{1+r_\ell}\right].$$

At this level of investment, there will not be any bankruptcy provided $p_2 \geq E(p)/2$. Under this condition, the preceding calculations are valid.

On the other hand, if the entrepreneur expects to go bankrupt when the price is p_2, the level of the investment, computed so as to maximize earnings in state 1, is

$$K_1(r_\ell) = \left[\frac{p_1}{2(1+r_\ell)}\right]^2,$$

which, under the assumption that revenue in state 2 is nil, yields a profit (in mathematical expectation) of

$$P_1(r_\ell) = \frac{\pi}{4}\left[\frac{p_1^2}{1+r_\ell}\right].$$

There will indeed be a bankruptcy in state 2 if $p_2 \leq p_1/2$.

Assume $p_1/2 \geq p_2 \geq E(p/2)$. Investments K and K_1 both satisfy the first-order condition and correspond to local profit maximization. To determine the optimal investment, it suffices to compare the values of the associated profits, respectively, $[E(p)]^2$ and πp_1^2. We here encounter the intuitive result that, if the probability of state 1 is sufficiently high, it is optimal to choose the high level of investment $K_\ell(r_\ell) = K_1(r_\ell)$ and go bankrupt if the price turns out to be low.

In this example, the entrepreneur chooses whether to go bankrupt regardless of the rate r_ℓ. Thus, $\rho(r_\ell)$ is never decreasing: It is equal either to r_ℓ (if $[E(p)]^2$ is larger than πp_1^2), or to

$$\pi r_\ell + (1-\pi)\left[\frac{p_2}{\sqrt{K_1(r_\ell)}} - 1\right],$$

with $K_1(r_\ell)$ decreasing. Therefore, the equilibrium entails no rationing. This property extends to the case of any Cobb–Douglas production function with multiplicative risk. An examination of the expression for ρ given by (10.6) reveals that it must usually be increasing in r_ℓ under our hypotheses. This might induce the reader to wonder whether an equilibrium with rationing is not simply a theoretical curiosity. However, by broadening the framework somewhat, we shall provide examples of rationing. ∎

Example 10.2 This example is identical to Example 10.1, except that production is subject to a fixed cost, F. If the fixed cost is not too high relative to the interest rate, the demand for funds continues to be given by $K(r_\ell)$ and profit is simply $P(r_\ell) - F$. If this expression is negative, the firm produces no output – the demand for funds reduces to zero.

Similarly, in the event of bankruptcy when the price is p_2, the level of investment is $K_1(r_\ell)$ if $P_1(r_\ell) - \pi F \geq 0$ and nil otherwise. Everything is as if the fixed cost was partly paid by the bank, with probability $(1 - \pi)$. The fixed cost reinforces the incentive to declare bankruptcy. Indeed, the entrepreneur chooses to declare bankruptcy when $P_1(r_\ell) - \pi F > P(r_\ell) - F$, which is more likely to occur if F is large. With the specification retained above, this inequality is equivalent to $4(1 + r_\ell)(1 - \pi)F > [E(p)]^2 - \pi p_1^2$, which always holds for r_ℓ sufficiently large (for a null fixed cost, we fall back on the previous condition in which default is occurs only if $0 > E(p)]^2 - \pi p_1^2$, regardless of r_ℓ).

Consider, for example, the values $F = 0.1$, $p_1 = 2$, $p_2 = 1$, and $\pi = \frac{1}{2}$.

According to the previous calculations, the optimal choice for the entrepreneur is $K(r_\ell)$ for $r_\ell < 0.25$ and $K_1(r_\ell)$ for $r_\ell \geq 0.25$.

Therefore, the investment, which would be equal to $K(r_\ell)$ (a decreasing function of the interest rate) in the absence of limited liability, increases with the risk of bankruptcy. Even though the firm is solvent in both states of nature, if it invests $K(r_\ell)$ and the rate is 25 percent, it decides to set up a bigger stock of capital, $K_1(r_\ell)$, putting it into bankruptcy in state 2: The loss is partly borne by the bank, while the profits, which are greater in state 1, are appropriated exclusively by the firm. The yield to the loan, from the point of view of the bank, is $\rho(r_\ell) = r_\ell$ for $r_\ell < 0.25$ and, for $r_\ell \geq 0.25$,

$$\rho(r_\ell) = \frac{1}{2}r_\ell + \frac{1}{2}\left[\frac{p_2\sqrt{K_1(r_\ell)} - F}{K_1(r_\ell)} - 1\right],$$

that is,

$$\rho(r_\ell) = 0.9r_\ell - 0.05 - 0.05r_\ell^2.$$

When the interest rate crosses the value of $r_\ell^* = 0.25$, there is an upward discontinuity in the demand for loans and a downward discontinuity in the expected yield to banks.

If banks correctly anticipate entrepreneurs' reactions, it is in their interest to propose a rate that is just below r_ℓ^* to curb the number of defaults. Note that if the level of investment was observed by the bank, it could condition its supply of loans on the value of the investment: Rationing would not occur. ∎

Example 10.3 The entrepreneur has a choice between two investments, a or b. Both cost K and they, respectively, yield $R_a K$ and $R_b K$ if successful and 0 if not. The probabilities of success are p_a and p_b. Assume

$$R_a > R_b, \quad p_a < p_b,$$

so that project a is more risky than project b. The entrepreneur is risk neutral and must borrow the funds K. The realization of the project, R, is observable and liability is limited: Repayment is given by $\min[RK, (1 + r_\ell)K]$.

Let us determine the entrepreneur's choice when the nominal interest rate is r_ℓ. If she chooses project ℓ, her expected profit is

$$[R_\ell - (1 + r_\ell)]K p_\ell, \quad \text{if } R_\ell \geq (1 + r_\ell),$$

and 0 otherwise. We easily see that she will choose

- the least risky project, b, if

$$r_\ell < r^* = \frac{p_b R_b - p_a R_a}{p_b - p_a} - 1;$$

- project a if $r^* < r_\ell < \bar{r} = R_a - 1$;
- neither project if $r_\ell > \bar{r} = R_a - 1$.

For the intermediate value, r^*, the entrepreneur is indifferent between the two projects. The expected compensation per unit borrowed at r_ℓ, if project i is chosen is, $r_\ell p_i$. It follows that

$$\rho(r_\ell) = \begin{cases} r_\ell p_b, & \text{if } r_\ell < r^*, \\ r_\ell p_a, & \text{if } r^* < r_\ell < \bar{r}. \end{cases}$$

The function $\rho(r_\ell)$ has a maximum at r^*, followed by a downward discontinuity. When the rate varies, the *quality* of the repayment also varies endogenously.

The same type of phenomenon may occur if there are a priori differences between entrepreneurs, with some projects more risky than others. A high interest rate may dissuade some entrepreneurs from borrowing, even if their projects are as (or more) profitable but less risky, while limited liability may encourage others with more risky projects to borrow. Offering a lower rate will attract a higher quality of entrepreneur. With the same notation as above, assume that entrepreneurs choose an a-type project in proportion α and a b-type project in proportion $(1 - \alpha)$. Each entrepreneur knows the characteristics of her project that are unobservable to the banks.

It is easy to verify that, if $r_\ell < R_b$, all entrepreneurs demand financing, while only those with type a projects do if $R_b < r_\ell < R_a$. Thus, we have

$$\rho(r_\ell) = \begin{cases} r_\ell[\alpha p_a + (1 - \alpha)p_b], & \text{if } r_\ell < R_b, \\ r_\ell p_a, & \text{if } R_b < r_\ell < R_a, \end{cases}$$

and, since $p_a < p_b$, the expected yield has a maximum at R_b, followed by a downward discontinuity.

Private information that is too important generates dysfunctions, or even causes potentially profitable exchanges to be abandoned. We again encounter a phenomenon that we analyzed while looking at trading on a stock exchange. This justifies and explains the establishment of mechanisms and institutions that make exchanges possible, costly though they be.[16] Rating agencies, like Standard and Poor's and Moody's, provide information on the market for bonds issued by firms, which may be risky because of the danger of default. Their ratings seek to reflect the health of firms and to account for the seniority of each loan type. Such services are only of use to the largest issuers, owing to their cost. There is no comparable service for small firms that may lead to credit rationing. ∎

BIBLIOGRAPHICAL NOTE

This chapter deals with a variety of subjects that are still under development, making anything more than a summary quite impossible.

The relationships between different types of financial backers are developed in the theory of *corporate governance*. The difficulties associated with defining stockholders' *goals* when markets are incomplete and with potential conflicts between incumbent and new stockholders are probably best described by Drèze. (Other than the article quoted in Chapter 9, you might also consult the 1987 collection of articles.) Myers (1977) and Myers and Majluf (1984) examined conflicts between financial backers, first under symmetric information (as in Section 2) and then under asymmetric information. These key articles explain why debt, and more generally the financial structure, may influence investment decisions. Ekern and Wilson (1974) showed that if the technologies of a firm satisfy the spanning condition, shareholders are unanimous about the value of investment. The multiplicative risk condition was introduced by Diamond (1967) in an article on the role of the stock market.

---

16 Akerlof's (1970) article was the first to formalize this problem, drawing on the market for used cars.

Hirshleifer (1917) was the first to demonstrate the damaging effect on risky exchanges of the *premature* release of information. Though the argument is relatively simple when the information is public, it is less straightforward when it is private. Then it must be determined how this information affects trades. Rational expectations equilibrium is a way to do so. Akerlof (1970) was the first to formally examine a market in the presence of asymmetric information (e.g., the market for used cars) and, in particular, to demonstrate that such asymmetries may make trades impossible. Many models have been developed since then, such as the one by Stiglitz and Weiss (1981) for the credit market. They particularly focus on identifying mechanisms and institutions that allow the distortions caused by asymmetries to be reduced.

Akerlof, G. (1970). "The market for lemons: qualitative uncertainty and the market mechanism," *Quarterly Journal of Economics*, **84**, 488–500.

Diamond, P.A. (1967). "The role of a stock market in a general equilibrium model with technological uncertainty," *American Economic Review*, **57**, 759–776.

Drèze, J. (1987). *Essays on economic decisions under uncertainty*, Cambridge University Press, Cambridge, USA.

Ekern, S. and R. Wilson (1974). "On the theory of the firm in an economy with incomplete markets," *The Bell Journal of Economics and Management Science*, **5**, 171–180.

Hirshleifer, J. (1971). "The private and social value of information and the reward to inventive activity," *American Economic Review*, **61**, 561–574.

Myers, S. (1977). "Determinants of corporate borrowing," *Journal of Financial Economics*, **5**, 147–175.

Myers, S. and N.S. Majluf (1984). "Corporate financing and investment decisions when firms have information that investors do not have," *Journal of Financial Economics*, **13**, 187–221.

Stiglitz, J. and A. Weiss (1981). "Credit rationing in markets with imperfect information," *American Economic Review*, **71**, 393–410.

Exercises

10.1 *Financial structure and managers' incentives*   Deviations from perfect competition are a way around the Modigliani–Miller theorem to make the financial structure of a firm have an impact on its value. We here consider information-related problems that arise when some participants have insider information. The model has two periods and the market is risk neutral.

1 Two types of firms exist on the stock market, *a* and *b*. They are indistinguishable a priori, but their sure revenues at time 1 are, respectively, given by y_a and y_b,

where $y_a > y_b$. The proportion of type a (respectively b) firms is π (respectively $1 - \pi$). Investors cannot identify the firm type. We denote the value of the securities (debt plus stocks) issued by these firms V_a and V_b.

(a) Firms are indistinguishable if they adopt the same financial structure (same financing ratio). What is the value of their assets (debt plus stocks) in this case?

(b) Assume that firms a and b adopt different financial structures, and that this is known to investors. What is the value of assets issued by a and b? We now assume that the compensation to firms' managers is an increasing function of the firm value. Show that the managers of firm b have an interest in modifying its structure. Show that then $V_a = V_b$.

2 Now assume that the firms are administered by managers who know the type of their firm, but do not have the right to intervene on the market. If m is the face value of the firm's debt, the manager is compensated according to the following schedule:

$$f(m) = \begin{cases} (1+r)\gamma_0 V + \gamma_1 y, & \text{if } y > m, \\ (1+r)\gamma_0 V + \gamma_1 (y - c), & \text{if } y < m, \end{cases} \tag{10.7}$$

where V is the value at time 0 of securities issued, γ_0 and γ_1 are parameters that do not depend on the firm, and c is a strictly positive number.

(a) Interpret the compensation schedule.

(b) Let m_a and m_b be the face values of the debts of a and b. If $d_a \neq d_b$, what are the values of V_a and V_b? Under what conditions do no managers have an incentive to modify the structures of their firms? Comment.

10.2 Forward markets and investment What is the impact of a forward market on producers' decisions and profits? This exercise uses the example of I farmers facing risk on the sales price of their harvest. The aim of the exercise is to compute their outputs and profits in the absence (part I), and presence (part II), of forward markets, and then compare the two situations. Market participants (farmers and speculators) are assumed sufficiently numerous to ensure competitive behavior. They can borrow or lend on the credit market at an interest rate of zero.

I Without a forward market

1 Consider a typical farmer deciding how much to produce, y, at time 0. The output will be available and sold at time 1 at a stochastic price expressed in

dollars, $\tilde{p}$. Compute the farmer's supply knowing that

(a) his utility is represented by a mean–variance function of wealth $\tilde{c}$ at time 1 ($\rho \geq 0$):

$$U(\tilde{c}) = E(\tilde{c}) - \frac{\rho}{2}\text{var}(\tilde{c});$$

(b) the cost of producing y, paid at time 1, equals y^2;

(c) the farmer's expectation on the mean and variance of $\tilde{p}$ are p^e and v^e, respectively. We denote the supply by $y(p^e, v^e)$.

2 The price at time 1 is determined by the equation:

$$\tilde{p} = D - \beta Y + \tilde{\eta}, \tag{10.8}$$

where Y is total supply, D is a positive parameter, and $\tilde{\eta}$ is a random variable with expectation zero and variance v.

(a) Price $\bar{p}$ is said to be an equilibrium if

$$\bar{p} = D - \beta I y(\bar{p}, v).$$

Comment on this definition.

(b) Compute the equilibrium price. Derive the farmers' equilibrium productions and utilities.

(c) Examine the variations in the farmers' utility levels at equilibrium as a function of v. Comment on this result.

II   With a forward market

A forward market is opened at time 0. In addition to the farmers, J "speculators" participate. The price on the forward market is denoted q.

1 The typical speculator's initial wealth, w_s, is risk-free and her utility is represented by a mean–variance criterion:

$$U(\tilde{c}) = E(\tilde{c}) - \frac{\rho_s}{2}\text{var}(\tilde{c}).$$

Compute her demand, z, on the forward market as a function of q and the expected mean and variance of the price, (p^e, v^e).

2 The farmer simultaneously chooses his output and his position on the forward market. Choose as variables the level of output y and the part of the output that is not covered x ($y - x$ thus is the amount sold on the forward market). Show that his production decision only depends on q. Compute x as a function of q and the expected mean and variance of the price (p^e, v^e).

3 We continue to assume that the price $\tilde{p}$ is given by (10.8).

(a) In your opinion, when does a pair $(q, \bar{p})$ represent equilibrium prices?

(b) From now on assume that there are enough speculators for b/J to be negligible. Compute the equilibrium prices, outputs, and the farmers' utility levels.

(c) Under what conditions is the introduction of the forward market beneficial to farmers? Explain your results.

Index